Chesnutt and Realism

STUDIES IN AMERICAN LITERARY REALISM AND NATURALISM

Chesnutt and Realism

A Study of the Novels

Ryan Simmons

THE UNIVERSITY OF ALABAMA PRESS
Tuscaloosa

Typeface: Minion

∞
The paper on which this book is printed meets the minimum requirements of American National Standard for Information Sciences-Permanence of Paper for Printed Library Materials, ANSI Z39.48–1984.

Library of Congress Cataloging-in-Publication Data

Simmons, Ryan, 1969–
Chesnutt and realism : a study of the novels / Ryan Simmons.
p. cm. — (Studies in American literary realism and naturalism)
Includes bibliographical references (p. 187) and index.
ISBN-13: 978-0-8173-1520-7 (alk. paper)
ISBN-10: 0-8173-1520-9
1. Chesnutt, Charles Waddell, 1858–1932.—Criticism and interpretation. 2. African Americans in literature. 3. Realism in literature. 4. Race relations in literature. 5. National characteristics, American, in literature. I. Title. II. Series.
PS1292.C6Z86 2006
813′.4—dc22

2006002258

Contents

Acknowledgments

This project would not have gotten off the ground without the generous support of the School of Humanities, Arts, and Social Sciences at Utah Valley State College, which provided a reduced teaching load for research and writing during four semesters as well as a summer research grant that facilitated my research at the Chesnutt Collection of Fisk University. I would especially like to thank the School's dean, William Cobb, for his support and encouragement.

Reading Chesnutt's unpublished manuscripts in the Special Collections office of the John Hope and Aurelia E. Franklin Library at Fisk was a career highlight and ended up shaping my understanding of Chesnutt's novels in important ways. The kind assistance of Special Collections director Beth Madison Howse was particularly welcome. I'd also like to thank Chesnutt's descendant and literary executor, John C. Slade, for permission to use these materials.

Special thanks go to the staff at The University of Alabama Press and to the editorial board for the series Studies in American Literary Realism and Naturalism and its editor, Gary Scharnhorst. Their efficiency and attentiveness have made the process of getting this book into print almost shockingly humane and pleasant. I also wish to thank the anonymous reviewers of the originally submitted manuscript, whose adept and generous comments led to a stronger end result, as well as Lady Vowell Smith.

My colleagues at Utah Valley State College deserve recognition, including

Dorice Galbraith, Jen Wahlquist, and especially those who read portions of the manuscript, John Goshert and (most of all) Jans Wager. I am grateful for the time they spent helping me articulate and sharpen my ideas; any weaknesses that remain are mine.

Shelli B. Fowler first introduced me to Chesnutt's work and also serves as an inspiration for her determination and courage; for both of these reasons, I thank her.

My daughters, Claire and Isabel, put up with many hours spent on this book that could have been spent instead playing with them. I hope I can make it up to them.

Finally, I owe (as always) a great debt of gratitude and love to my confidant, best reader, and partner for life, Barb Simmons. This book is dedicated to her.

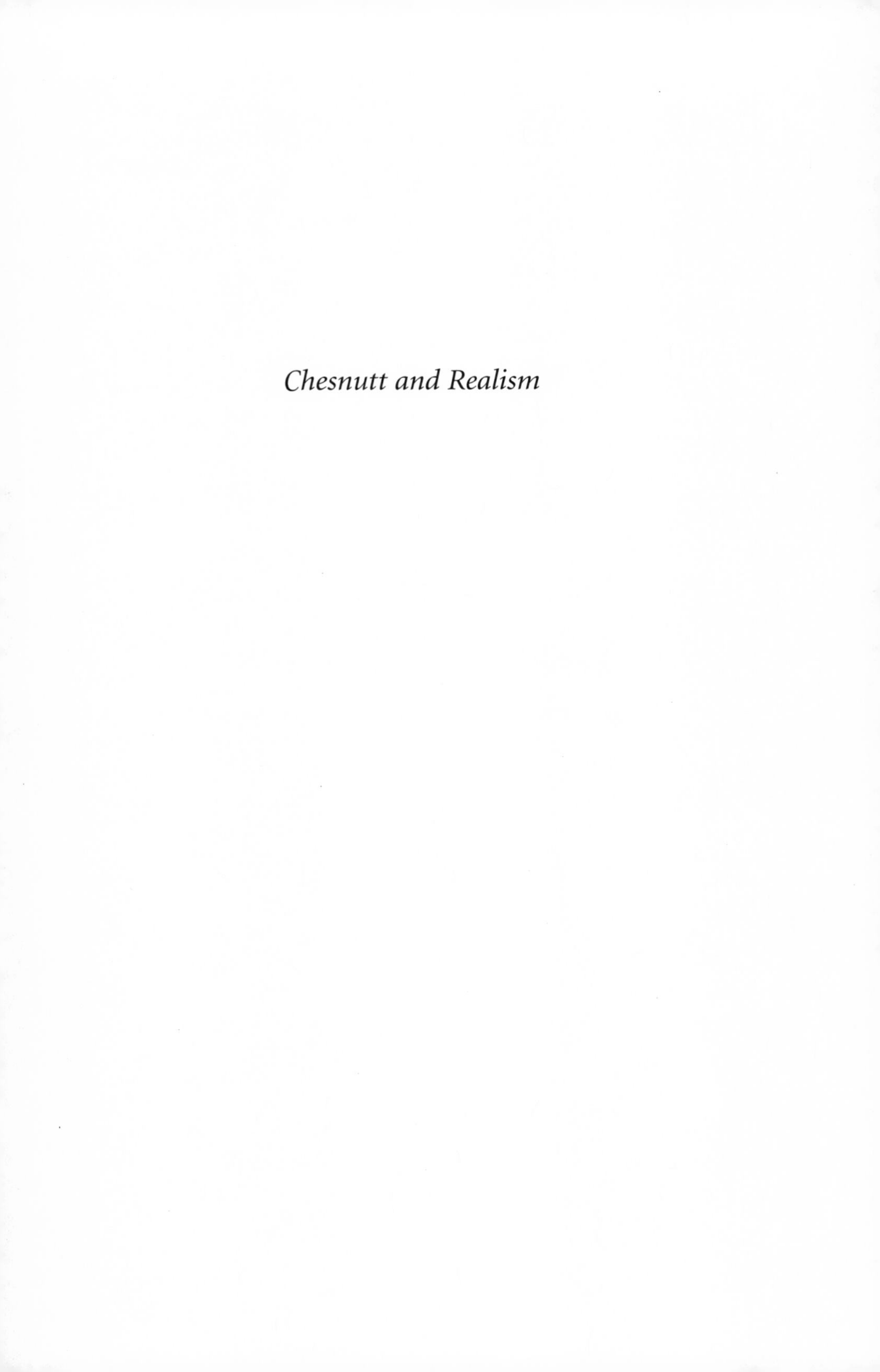

Chesnutt and Realism

Introduction

Of Race and Realism

In this book I propose to initiate a new line of discussion about the cultural work done by American literary realism, and about the pressures and possibilities surrounding racial discourse in this nation, by examining the novels of an author whose career neatly matches the period traditionally associated with American realism. Charles W. Chesnutt's career as a published writer of fiction ran from 1885, when his first short stories appeared, to 1930, when a final story appeared in *The Crisis.* His career publishing novels was much shorter, from 1900 to 1905, although several of the novels he wrote were rejected by publishers before and after that period. During these years, he lived in Cleveland but traveled in both the Northeast and the deep South, including his former home of North Carolina, where he researched the events that inspired *The Marrow of Tradition.* The geography of Chesnutt's life and career offers a compelling metaphor for his position as a writer: as someone who is both Northern and Southern, and as a person of mixed race, Chesnutt attempts—and, in my view, largely achieves—an equilibrium, crafting narratives on the basis of an insider's insight and an outsider's objectivity, an auspicious blend for a practitioner of realism. His narrators tend to have a canny, slippery quality, simultaneously adopting and skewering the particular perspectives they may seem to hold. Like writers who followed him—including monumental African American authors of the twentieth century such as Hurston, Ellison, and Morrison—Chesnutt recognized reality to be *problematic,* always contested, and undertook risky experiments to put forward a statement about reality that would help pin it down but would also be capable of shaping it. These experiments are best explained in relation to American literary realism.

While Chesnutt has often been characterized as a writer in the realist tradition, neither the critics who attempt to read him into this tradition nor those who try to read him out of it have always served his achievements well. In the former camp, the danger is that his fiction will be seen as merely imitative, an application of the doctrines of William Dean Howells and others to new territories, especially those concerning race. In this book I argue that the opposite view is more correct: Chesnutt was aware of and used realist ideals and techniques but also was himself a substantial contributor to those ideals and techniques. He not only applied realism to new topics but redirected and sharpened what realism was and could be. The second view—that Chesnutt does not qualify as a realist at all—has proved no more useful in gauging Chesnutt's methods and career. The problem, actually, is similar to that exemplified by many in the pro-realist camp. If the question becomes "does Chesnutt meet the standards set up by Howells and other canonical white writers for realism?" then (regardless of whether one's answer is yes or no) the effect is almost inevitably to make Chesnutt appear a minor figure, mimicking—with greater or lesser degrees of success—the techniques of his more important peers. Instead, Chesnutt ought to be considered a major contributor to the realist movement, both for his challenge to white audiences to consider realistically the nature of American race relations and for his career-long narrative experiment to determine how an entrenched majority might be compelled to see the social world more accurately and completely.

Though Chesnutt was acutely aware of the limitations faced by African Americans during his lifetime in attempting to shape social reality, his career is defined by its insistence in chafing against these restrictions. It was fundamental to him to expand the possibilities of what could be said, and therefore what could be known and done, always while working with (and within) available historical materials. And this work, the work of a realist author, was performed in constant awareness of the material effects that textual representations had upon the lives of African Americans. As he wrote in 1889, early in his literary career, "[t]o a white man [the 'Negro problem'] may be a question of personal prejudice, a question of political expediency, a question of conscience, a question of abstract justice, a question of wise statesmanship—any one, in fact, of a hundred questions. But to the man of Negro blood it is . . . the question of life itself" (*Essays and Speeches* 57–58). His novels are meant to lead to political and moral analysis of racial issues, but more importantly to an understanding of such issues that must not be merely abstract.

As practiced by Chesnutt, realism's purpose is not to document histories but to disassemble and re-create readers' methods for understanding these histories, all with the intent of changing not only what readers know, but also how they know it and how they are capable of responding to it. "Realism has in mind to see beyond forms traditionally recognized as aesthetically permissible," writes Katherine Kearns in her powerful reinterpretation of British and American realism's cultural work, *Nineteenth-Century Literary Realism: Through the Looking Glass* (1996). "But realism wants more than merely this un-costuming. . . . Realism would at once divest artistic vision of its habit of prettiness and give to art the right to paint and to write about that which is not pretty, *and* it would implicate one so thoroughly in this realness as to bring one to more genuine and immediate feeling" (3–4). If, Chesnutt seems to believe, readers understood racism in anything like the way he understood it, they could not help but act toward its eradication; and his novels are designed to instill an understanding of racism that is both fuller and more personal, less abstract and more real.

For Chesnutt, a workable mode of realism needed to allow for common reference between a writer and various readers, but must not rest too heavily on the exclusion of inconvenient voices. His writings, and in particular his novels, tend toward expansiveness, toward the incorporation of as many voices as the reader may be capable of responding to, rather than exclusiveness. This expansiveness is accomplished by means of a narrative approach that virtually never privileges one voice or another, however counterintuitive that assessment might initially appear even to a careful reader of his works. Much critical attention has gone into sorting out whose voice is favored and whose is flattened or subsumed. A key example is the debate concerning the respective positions of the accommodating African American doctor, William Miller, and the black revolutionary, Josh Green, in *The Marrow of Tradition.* This portion of the critical debate surrounding Chesnutt's novel is a dubious use of resources; the significant point is not whose voice is favored but that *it is not clear* whose voice is favored.[1] A number of critics, in noting this very point, find in it evidence of Chesnutt's evasiveness when it comes to the political questions with which his novels seem to be engaged. That is, given a seeming choice between a political message and an aesthetically acceptable demurral from political commentary, Chesnutt would appear to select the latter. However, a central point of this study will be that Chesnutt did not face such a choice—that he found ways for his aesthetics and his politics to line up quite strongly.[2]

Though no simple definition of realism seems possible, some statements are useful toward an understanding of the work it does. For example, some degree of fidelity to facts—both as recorded and as perceived—seems minimally to be required. Nineteenth-century writer and critic Hamlin Garland defined realism as "the truthful statement of an individual impression corrected by reference to the fact" (152). Flights of fancy, while not strictly excluded, are subject to suspicion; while imagination is not only allowable but essential to the work of a realist, it is employed as a means of understanding, not of escape. As Chesnutt wrote in 1908, "fiction to my mind ought to be, if not founded on fact, at least within the limits of probability" (*Exemplary* 38).

By no means, on the other hand, is Chesnutt's realism limited to verisimilitude. In the late nineteenth and early twentieth centuries, the realist movement was more experimental than it may appear from today's vantage point. As recent scholars such as Amy Kaplan have articulated, the realists of this period responded to their growing attentiveness to an old problem: that reality was not stable but shifty, disturbingly plastic and subject to manipulation. Writes Kaplan, realists "often assume a world which lacks solidity, and the weightiness of descriptive detail—one of the most common characteristics of the realist text—often appears in inverse proportion to a sense of insubstantiality, as though description could pin down the objects of an unfamiliar world to make it real" (9). Thus, according to Kaplan, realist authors are not marked by their attempts merely to document the world as it appears to them, but are much more deeply involved in constructing it: "The realists do not naturalize the social world to make it seem immutable and organic, but, like contemporary social reformers, they engage in an enormous act of construction to organize, re-form, and control the social world. This act of construction makes the social world at once mechanical and improvised, locked in place and tentative" (10). Chesnutt, from the beginning to the end of his writing career, may be seen working through the tensions implied by Kaplan's statement: the world is "locked in place and tentative," seemingly a given but also, as a construction of humans' perceptions and attitudes, at least theoretically capable of undergoing dramatic alteration at any moment.

In describing Chesnutt's contribution to realism, I emphasize in particular two tenets: the recognition that "reality" is contested and ultimately a matter of language and of perspective, and the observation that how language and perspective are employed—in particular, the ability of an individual to understand a variety of perspectives and to accept the social responsibilities such an understanding implies—determines one's moral agency. As practiced by Chesnutt, realism demands a deep awareness that "reality" is both negotiated and rooted in discourse, and it requires an experimental attempt to reorient readers' reception of language in order to do its work. In a trenchant comment, William L.

Andrews cites Chesnutt for helping to initiate in African American letters a "revisionistic attitude toward prevailing notions of the real, and [an] emphasis on reality as a function of consciousness mediated through language" ("Slavery" 7). In two of Chesnutt's earliest long works, the "passing" narratives *Mandy Oxendine* and *The House Behind the Cedars,* we see him exploring the possibilities and limits of language in depicting reality as he may have known and experienced it. In the earlier work, rejected for publication, Chesnutt ambitiously (and with mixed results) attempts what today might be called a deconstructive text, disorienting the reader through an odd, implausible series of events, apparently in hopes of forcing readers to think new thoughts about the realities—and absurdities—of racialized life. Rather than dwelling in frustration on the failure of this approach, however, Chesnutt completed an outwardly more normalized, less experimental novel, *The House Behind the Cedars,* that attempts similar work but also is capable of being read within the recognized tradition of the "tragic mulatta" tale. For closer readers, *The House Behind the Cedars* begins to unravel the perverse logic of the "tragic mulatta" genre, and of the segregated realities the genre represents. It begins to do the work of disassembling our knowledge of the "real" world, opening the way for a more challenging implication of the reader in *The Marrow of Tradition.*

Realism, then, is defined in opposition to "escapism," calling on its readers to shift perspective so that they acknowledge, understand, and respond to the world's realities rather than averting their eyes. Chesnutt's works, especially *The Marrow of Tradition,* are sometimes regarded as too manipulative to be realistic, but they are written on the assumption that reality properly portrayed and rightly understood must compel action. They are designed to produce a sense of things, as the narrator of *The Marrow of Tradition* remarks, "in their correct proportions and relations" (321)—a formulation Chesnutt used more than once, and which he apparently borrowed from Howells[3]—and any representation of reality that does not produce such an understanding cannot, Chesnutt suggests, rightly call itself realism.

Realism, according to this view, implicitly demands change, even revolution. Critics generally acknowledge the tendency of realist works to invite social reform. Writes Alfred Habegger, "[r]ealism minus the potentially effective human will is no longer realism" (111). Habegger describes realism as a "middle position" between sentimental romance, in which "the daydream was able to triumph over harsh social necessity," and Joycean modernism, in which "the world triumphs over the daydream in such a way that the most the daydreamer can possibly achieve is a moment of insight into his folly and the world's darkness" (111). *The Colonel's Dream* comes to mind as a novel which veers between these two positions: its readers continue to debate whether it is an idealistic appeal to the power of dreaming or a deterministic argument that dreams will always be squashed by social and political realities. In fact, it is both. In this novel, Chesnutt finds no use in narrow reforms such as Colonel French attempts, but does hint at something he cannot quite bring himself to say directly: that a material change in the reality of American life is possible, but only outside the confines of Western rationality and capitalism.

The Colonel's Dream is the fullest extension of an argument which permeates Chesnutt's novels, that understanding reality rightly *requires* action; passivity betrays a (perhaps willful, but nearly always misguided) misunderstanding of the world, particularly the underestimating of one's connectedness to others. Recognizing the connections between outwardly very disparate lives is necessary for more than idealistic reasons; condescension or pity is never adequate. Self-interest demands an understanding that racism ultimately helps virtually no one, Chesnutt consistently insists. Characters such as John and Rena Walden, Phil and Olivia Carteret, and Colonel Henry French face not just moral but material and physical peril because they make the fundamental mistake of separating their lives from the African American "other." The argument is not a simplistic appeal to common humanity; it approaches a Marxist analysis that finds people's isolation to be a form of false consciousness, the product of an economic system that ultimately benefits very few among those who prop it up. Though Chesnutt may seem, particularly in *The Colonel's Dream,* to advance a classical economic appeal to rational self-interest, his underlying message is that capitalist thought has rendered people largely incapable of assessing and working toward their real self-interest.

Although Chesnutt achieved many of the effects I am associating with realism in his short fiction, this project focuses on his novels, in which the effects are realized most completely. The truths Chesnutt speaks in his novels are complex ones that cannot be summarized in a few words or evoked with a handy reference his readers would immediately acknowledge. They are the truths of the novel: ideas and events that, while available to readers as part of a shared frame of reference, a common world, necessarily take hundreds of pages of prose to achieve in full. By complicating the world that, Chesnutt knew, his readers were taking for granted, he attempts to compel them to widen their perspective and acknowledge the real stakes involved in the ongoing process of making reality. As I show in chapter 3, complexity was not an end in itself for Chesnutt. In *The Marrow of Tradition,* in many ways the most complete realization of his aims as an author, Chesnutt questions the end result of the constant complicating of reality and demonstrates that such an approach may not always serve African Americans' political interests. Even so, the effects of the novel could not have been achieved as well in another genre. As Chesnutt attempts to develop several intense, clarifying moments at which the truth about racism is clearly visible, he prepares his readers for those moments through a precise, methodical approach. The effects of the novel's ending, for example, might be equally striking emotionally but would not *mean* as much had Chesnutt failed to prepare his readers in the three hundred previous pages to understand them more fully. In reading Chesnutt as a realist, I do not wish to discount the pyrotechnics of scenes such as the last chapter of *The Marrow of Tradition*, since such scenes are central to his vision and part of his realist approach, but I also hope to show that such dramatic moments are not cheap effects but the payoff of a carefully controlled depiction of reality.

In both Chesnutt's day and ours, a reconsideration of what "realism" can mean is needed, in part, to counteract the exclusively white canon of American literary realism that has somehow persisted for over a century. As Kearns writes, "it is only in the act of claiming a reality that one has a 'reality'" (23), and in neglecting to consider nonwhite authors' contributions to realism, their claims to reality at the turn of the twentieth century, critics contribute to the historical erasure of African American experiences and perspectives. Few critics who theorize realism also contend with race, and vice versa. Although there are important exceptions to this rule—by Kenneth W. Warren, Augusta Rohrbach, Cathy Boeckmann, and others—in none of these is the literary production of an African American writer considered for more than a chapter. This is mentioned not to disparage these critics' work, but to point out that important work remains to be done, for each of the critics mentioned above makes a significant contribution to studies in American literary realism, and does so by considering the presence of race in realist texts.

Warren, for example, in *Black and White Strangers: Race and American Literary Realism* (1993) broke important new ground by interrogating the claim, made in various forms by nineteenth-century critics such as Albion Tourgée and twentieth-century ones including Leslie Fiedler, Robert Bone, and Henry Louis Gates, Jr., that the methods of realism are inadequate to the job of articulating the realities of race. While appropriately reluctant to endorse the "emancipatory powers of realism" confidently advocated by many realist authors (9), Warren attempts to articulate how an understanding of realism might help readers sort through the roots of twentieth-century racial discourse. Conscious that to historicize realist texts is to recognize just how limited literature's ability to resist power, to be genuinely subversive, really is, Warren is not quite ready to accept that literature is incapable of meaningful resistance. To do so would be equally ahistorical to the realists' own assertions that they could reform the world through writing: "[L]inking too hastily resistance and the extension of power can obscure the nuances of the historical and cultural work that fictions perform" (8). Although realists' methods of characterization "helped, paradoxically, to define social distinctions between the majority of black and white Americans as 'real' and ineffaceable" (15), in their capacity to underscore the hidden, frequently racialized politics of the ordinary moments of everyday life, to suggest "how thoroughly political such moments had become" (42), they offer a crucial, if politically contorted, analysis.

Warren explains that his point is not to alter but to understand what realism was and is, "not to construct a racially integrated literary utopia but to highlight the intellectual and cultural anxieties that have made separatism and discrimination in a variety of forms seem viable solutions to the social problems of a supposedly democratic society" (*Strangers* 10). His analysis, he states, "is not meant to be comprehensive but suggestive, an indication of the possibilities that an attention to race may hold for further studies of American literature" (12). Warren's defense of the particular writers he examines closely—Henry James is the central figure of his narrative of realism—is exactly right: "[W]orks that can reveal to us the way that race has shaped and is shaping our history need not be about race" (16). Yet his work leaves uncontested, for the most part, the vexed question of what realism is, which is in part the question of who the realists were.

This question is complicated in important ways in perhaps the strongest critical study of race in American literary realism to date, Augusta Rohrbach's *Truth Stranger than Fiction: Race, Realism, and the U.S. Literary Marketplace* (2002). Locating the roots of realism several decades earlier than traditional critics do, Rohrbach traces its development from the abolitionist movement: since the realists were "united by an ethos rather than a literary aesthetic," their common interest in reform is the strongest attribute they share (xiv). Thus, the slave narratives and the writings of abolitionist William Lloyd Garrison are more central to American literary realism than is usually acknowledged. At its heart, according to Rohrbach, canonical American realism is "humanitarian realism":[4] it is identified not by particular formal features but by "a set of social values" and a determination not only to document events but (in the words of abolitionist James Birney, quoted by Rohrbach) "to affect the public mind—to rouse into healthful activity that conscience of this nation, stupefied, torpid, almost dead, in relation to Human Rights" (xiv-xv). This statement describes well the challenge Chesnutt presented to himself and his audience, and Rohrbach's book, though she does not deal with Chesnutt's writings specifically, is instructive in illustrating that his efforts fall within the cultural experiment known as American realism.

Though Chesnutt receives little mention in Warren's and Rohrbach's analyses, a few recent critical works have begun to describe his involvement in realist discourse.[5] The most relevant of these to my present purposes, Cathy Boeckmann's *A Question of Character: Scientific Racism and the Genres of American Fiction, 1892–1912* (2000), examines Chesnutt's capacity to work within the prescriptions and prohibitions he faced to open up a space for a strong representation of at least one mixed-race character, Rena Walden. Nevertheless, Boeckmann argues, *The House Behind the Cedars* ultimately seems unable to break out of generic and cultural expectations: "[T]he failure of Rena and Tryon's romance clearly demonstrates the strong grip of racial thinking and prohibitions" (167). In her view, the "meta-level discussion of the relationships between constructed notions of race and literary conventions" is the real contribution of the novel (139), paving the way for a yet more promising, first-person approach to a mixed-race character, Johnson's *The Autobiography of an Ex-Colored Man.*

As Boeckmann persuasively reads them, literary texts—especially those concerning mixed-race people—helped prop up notions of scientific racism during the realist period. Since the existence of people of mixed race made it more difficult for scientific racism to depend on "statistics and measurements of visible characteristics" (14), literary texts—including those by white supremacist writers like Thomas Dixon but also, in Boeckmann's view, works by Twain, Howells, and Chesnutt—suggested ways of categorizing people racially based on the more fluid notion of "character," a concept that "clearly straddles the conceptual worlds of science and literature" (15). Even as realism attempted to probe beneath the superficially available world into its complexities, those complexities were rendered fodder for figures like Hippolyte-Adolphe Taine, who "argued that fiction provides access to the essence of racial groups" (15). By mining observable data for insight into character, realists often unwittingly paved a path for the essentialist notions of Taine, who saw literature as a pathway to the "*real* subject of history," the "inner" man for whom physical characterizations are no more than a symbol (57). Realist literature's tendency toward depth of characterization enabled scientific racism to overcome a key problem: the notion of character is the basis for scientific racism, but "character can be imitated," making it harder to use "as a solid basis for racial policy" (44). If, however, as Taine suggests, literature reveals character more reliably than its author is aware of or able to control, then the need to look beneath the skin into the "inner" man can be converted into a potential argument, not a liability, for scientific racism.

Apparently, for Taine and his cohorts, literature reveals the character not only of its author but also of its subjects, at least if the writer is perceptive enough and faithful enough to external reality to be a good realist. Stephen Crane, for example, is described in a 1900 account as having "a certain 'phrenological' talent in that he is able to discern character in his own representations"

(49). Though Boeckmann makes little of the point, this would seem to be an important maneuver for the scientific racists because few texts by black or mixed-race authors were considered "literature"; damning evidence of African Americans' supposed inferiority could be extrapolated exclusively from the products of white authors' minds, as willfully interpreted from a racist standpoint. Thus, the ability of black writers to represent themselves realistically—and, equally important, their ability to be read appropriately—would seem to be key.

Neither Boeckmann nor any of the other critics discussed here, however, demonstrate more than passing interest in the absence of nonwhite writers from previous criticism about realism. From Chesnutt's perspective, such an absence signals a troubling problem that is both political and aesthetic in nature. While white authors, in his view, certainly could portray the lives of African Americans and the truths of the "color line" with accuracy and sensitivity (and had done so in several notable instances), the fullest achievement of this work must lie with an African American author. He recognized that the ability to portray the life of a culture, and to have that portrayal be accepted as truthful by the literary establishment, was a critical factor in that culture's prospects for self-determination.[6] On this grounds, and on the grounds of realism—which claimed that the truthful portrayal of life must not be inhibited by artistic convention—Chesnutt argued that the lives and perspectives of African Americans must ultimately be recorded, centrally if not exclusively, by African Americans.

From the moment he contemplated a literary career, Chesnutt committed himself to representing the lives of Southern blacks from a realistic, informed perspective. In an 1880 journal entry, he considered the financial success of Tourgée's novel *A Fool's Errand,* which Chesnutt noted was popular in part for its ability to tap into "something romantic, to the Northern mind, about the southern negro" (*Journals* 125). Contemplates Chesnutt, "if Judge Tourgee [sic], with his necessarily limited intercourse with colored people, and with his limited stay in the South, can write such interesting descriptions, such vivid pictures of Southern life and character as to make himself rich and famous, why could not a colored man, who has lived among colored people all his life; who is familiar with their habits, their ruling passions, their prejudices; their whole moral and social condition; . . . write a far better book about the South than Judge Tourgee or Mrs. Stowe has written?" (125). Not only is this work potentially lucrative, writes Chesnutt, it is socially significant in its capacity to amend whites' errant views about African Americans. Those in the remote North have romanticized Southern blacks, he writes, while Southern whites—unwilling to adapt to new circumstances after the abolition of slavery—retain a skewed, overly negative perspective on African Americans, who to a large degree remain their servants and employees (125–27). In response, he declares, "I intend to record my impressions of men and things, and such incidents or conversations which take place within my knowledge, with a view to future use in literary work. I shall not record stale negro minstrel jokes or worn out newspaper squibs on the 'man and brother.' I shall leave the realm of fiction, where most of this stuff is manufactured, and come down to hard facts" (126). He does not seem literally to mean that he will avoid writing fiction, but that his future "literary work" will abandon the obviously false portrayals that permeate published and unpublished discourse about race and replace them with more authentic depictions of African American life as he has seen and experienced it. In other words, Chesnutt announces at the inception of his literary career that he will pursue a realist aesthetic. Very quickly, he would come to appreciate the difficulty of attracting a substantial readership for this work (in 1880 he seemed to believe that he would easily find a receptive audience), and during the next half-century he would continually refine and calibrate his literary methods. But throughout this period his goal remained constant: to depict the highly racialized American social landscape objectively but from an insider's perspective, as an African American realist author.

Near the end of his life, in accepting the Spingarn Medal of the NAACP, Chesnutt retrospectively described his career in terms similar to those with which he had anticipated it nearly fifty years earlier: "I observed, as soon as I was capable of intelligent observation, that the Negro in fiction had become standardized, and that there were very few kinds of Negroes. [He goes on to list various common stereotypes: the 'bad Negro,' the 'good Negro who loved old "Massa,"' 'the good old Uncle and Mammy types,' the 'modern "white man's nigger,"' the 'wastrel' and the 'minstrel.'] When I began to write serious books, after the usual apprenticeship aspiring authors must go through, I thought I saw the literary and artistic value of different types of Negroes than these" (*Essays and Speeches* 513). In both the 1880 journal entry and the 1928 acceptance speech, Chesnutt allows that the stereotypes might prove true in some instances, but do not represent the majority of African Americans. In the latter speech, he says, "I did n't write my stories as Negro propaganda—propaganda is apt to be deadly to art—but I used the better types, confident that the truth would prove the most valuable propaganda" (513–14).

The remaining problem, as Chesnutt saw very early in his career as a writer, was that "the truth" might not be accessible to readers who had been trained, in a discursive environment permeated by racist attitudes, not to see it as it was. The problem, in fact, was similar to the one Howells and other champions of realism had articulated: convention was blinding readers to the truth. In "The Negro in Books," a 1916 speech for the "National Buy-a-Book Campaign in the

Interest of Negro Literature," Chesnutt explains, "[t]he literature of a country or of an age . . . is considered, and as a rule is, a fair reflection of the social conditions of that age or country. But conventions, in literature, as in religion, in politics, and in social usage, sometimes persist long past the point where they correctly mirror the time. This is particularly true where they are confused by prejudice" (*Essays and Speeches* 430). He goes on to list ways in which recent American writings on race have been marred by racist attitudes and assumptions, including the improper use of dialect, and then mentions several white American writers who have successfully depicted black lives in literature, such as Harriet Beecher Stowe, George Washington Cable, Tourgée, and Howells—the influence of each of whom upon Chesnutt has been thoroughly documented. As important as these writers' contributions have been, Chesnutt states, literary convention still seems strictly limited by a small number of conventions for writing about racial topics (434). Despite individual efforts by sympathetic whites, the opening-up of racial discourse and the freeing of racial topics from confining literary conventions can come about, he argues, only when two things happen: African Americans must begin buying books so that a freer and more truthful depiction of race can find a viable audience (437), and they must also become, more frequently, the authors of these books: "Who knows the Negro best, in his home, in his church, in school, in his work, in his play, in all the manifold phases of his life? . . . Other things being equal, the life of a people is best recorded by those who have shared their sorrows and sufferings and disappointments, their hopes, their successes, their joys[.] . . . It stands to reason that an author thus equipped, which could only be a colored author, given equal ability and skill to portray character, would portray it more truthfully than an equally competent man without his special advantages" (438).[7]

The question, as Chesnutt sets it up, is one not of racial authenticity—a concept he disparaged as a tool of white supremacists[8]—but of insight. Logically, he believed, only African Americans could truthfully represent the perspective of African Americans, and the absence of that perspective undermined the idea of realism. Of course, Chesnutt's own perspective as a black writer was no doubt limited by his detachment from all but the most culturally privileged of African Americans and his decision to live and work almost exclusively within white society. While he imagined his career as one that would replace African American "types" in literature with more nuanced depictions of the "best" colored people—and in fact he often succeeded in this mission—his writings seem more important today for their creative troubling of racial categories and their acute analysis of the tangled, pernicious, and confoundingly durable conventions of race in American society. Before he or any other African American writer could succeed at replacing stereotypical versions of reality with truthful accounts, the primarily white book-buying audience would have to be trained to read through new eyes.

As Dean McWilliams points out, until an African American readership was capable of sustaining black authors, Chesnutt believed that "[w]hites must be persuaded to enter the black world, morally and spiritually, to see the black condition from inside. This spiritual metamorphosis of whites is essential. Until it happens, whites will never understand blacks, and they will never allow blacks to enter white-dominated society as equals" (224). Chesnutt's own status as someone uncomfortably stuck between two worlds, the black and the white, is closely connected to his pursuit of realism, which requires (as he foresaw in 1880) inside knowledge of the lives and minds of both blacks and whites, as well as a degree of detachment from both.

Even white writers as fair-minded and liberal as Howells could not be said to look at racial issues from any but a firmly white perspective. The novella *An Imperative Duty,* Howells's most extensive fictional rumination on race, is replete with inclusive narrative references to a community defined by its mutual Anglo-Saxon heritage—an "us" (138)—in contrast to the surrounding populations of Irish and African Americans, for whom the narrator uses the pronouns "them" and "their" (140). The novella's liberalism on race issues is its capacity to regard Rhoda Aldgate, who is one-sixteenth African American, as rightly a member of the white community and not the black—part of "us," not "them." Howells was a racial liberal for his time, but he recognized that neither he nor the majority of his readers could successfully interpret racial codes from any but a white perspective. Because Rhoda Aldgate has, until adulthood, known herself as white, the prospect of "going away to find my mother's people" (229) is in the end unthinkable to her. On the other hand, because Rena Walden in *The House Behind the Cedars* has always known herself as black, separating herself from her "mother's people" is, if not quite unthinkable, at least disastrous in its consequences.[9] The point to be taken here is that realism necessarily depends on perspective; although both Howells and Chesnutt considered racial distinctions to be in some sense artificial, they understood themselves to be writing from within a historical moment and a cultural position in ways that their fiction would inevitably reflect. It is understandable, therefore, that Howells was quick to celebrate Chesnutt's emergence as the arrival of an African American realist, someone who could both achieve objective detachment and take advantage of the "special opportunities for knowing" provided by his access to the black community ("Chesnutt's Stories" 52).

According to Joseph R. McElrath, Jr., Howells's attitude metamorphosed into disappointment as Chesnutt abandoned realism in favor of "literary invective" ("Howells and Race" 257). Perhaps the scholar who has most substantively considered Chesnutt in the context of literary realism, McElrath explains from his perspective (as the title of his 2000 article states) "Why Charles W. Chesnutt Is Not a Realist." Chesnutt, asserts McElrath, should not be termed a realist because rather than creating fiction that was "true to nature" in the Howellsian sense, he consistently chose to structure imaginary, even fanciful, embodiments of some political ideal, in doing so willfully manipulating his readers ("Why" 96). Argues McElrath, for the term "realist" to have meaning it must not be applied to any author who happens to write about real things, for what author does not? "[T]he fact that a writer gives fictional treatment to real-world problems . . . does not mean that he or she is a Realist" (93). The crucial question is a formal one, and McElrath contends that "Chesnutt's aesthetic dramatically antedated" that of established realists, having more in common with that of romanticists like Stowe or Rebecca Harding Davis than with that of Howells or Henry James (93). Yet the underlying assumptions of such a classifying method bear scrutiny: defining realists as those whose writings look like those already accepted in the "pantheon" of realism (91) easily becomes circular if not girded by more substantial considerations.

While granting, then, that Chesnutt takes on important social issues of his day, and at least sometimes does so realistically, McElrath contends that he addresses these issues in the form of romance, with identifiable and largely uncomplicated heroes and villains, and puts forward ideal solutions—whereas the realist must never idealize, but must portray life as he or she finds it. The "idealized" white characters Annie and John of Chesnutt's "conjure" stories, for example, are in his view no more than emblems, obviously Chesnutt's version of how white people ought to act: "The message to white readers is pellucidly clear: go forth and do likewise" ("Why" 93–94). Similarly, Chesnutt as McElrath sees him was reluctant to create a morally mixed African American character, preferring instead to subordinate aesthetic necessities to political ones by imbuing black characters with only positive traits. In other words, according to McElrath, Chesnutt consistently draws characters as "allegorical figures" rather than realistic ones (96), representing them as wholly evil or wholly good depending on which characterization suited his political message more conveniently.[10] Finally, McElrath argues that Chesnutt prioritized literary success more highly than the truthful representation of social life, adopting "the outsider's unrealistic point of view" accepted by most whites rather than developing anything that could be called an authentic African American perspective (96).[11]

Yet few characters, if any, populating Chesnutt's fiction are as stereotyped as McElrath makes them out to be. Annie and John, Julius McAdoo, John and Rena Walden, William and Janet Miller, Phil and Olivia Carteret, Henry French—you can take your pick of major characters, and any of them will be found upon close examination to demonstrate both favorable and unfavorable characteristics. In fact, the dilemmas many of them face as morally divided individuals are absolutely central to Chesnutt's fiction. McElrath errs, for example, in describing the Carterets as "punishe[d]" in the ending of *The Marrow of Tradition.* Rather, they face a punishment—the death of their son—which would serve justice but would not, as Chesnutt recognized, be realistic. Although Chesnutt appears to leave the ending of *The Marrow of Tradition* indeterminate, keeping the reader in the dark as to whether or not Dodie Carteret will die, in leading up to the final scene he strongly hints that Dodie will live, and by extension that matters will continue much as they did before. In a seemingly offhand remark, Chesnutt's narrator tips his hand. Mrs. Carteret, the unacknowledged sister of Mrs. Miller, appeals to Dr. Miller to reconsider his decision against intervening and to save Dodie's life. In doing so, she speaks to Dr. Miller "with his wife's voice,—she never knew how much, in that dark hour, she owed to that resemblance" (324). Though the last lines seem to leave the novel unresolved, to a careful reader it is difficult to conclude otherwise: Mrs. Carteret's debt is that of her son's life; he has been saved. The Carterets have not been punished at all; rather, Chesnutt ruefully acknowledges that *despite his desires* the power relationships he has drawn in this novel are unlikely to be disrupted. For this reason, the characterization of Chesnutt as a writer who depicts the world as he wishes it to be, and not as it is, seems particularly unjust.[12]

If Chesnutt's writing can seem manipulative (and it can), it is more a function of his insistence that readers *do* something—react emotionally and, it is hoped, politically to the circumstances he portrays—than it is evidence that he abandoned realism in favor of political writing. For Chesnutt, in other words, a realist aesthetic and an implied stance of political advocacy are not mutually exclusive positions. Central to Chesnutt's realism is the conviction that understanding reality rightly requires action; no one who truly saw reality for what it is could stand by and do nothing. Realism, for Chesnutt, always means getting readers to see reality differently, and the analyses provided by his novels, in particular, hinge on the assumption that people are failing to interpret properly a common reality.

Admittedly, there is the question of whether Major Carteret of *The Marrow of Tradition,* for example, is a well-rounded character or *just* an embodiment of racism, one of what Andrews refers to as "walking social exhibits" (*Literary Career* 203). As the subsequent chapter on *The Marrow of Tradition* will make clear, I find Carteret indeed to be a morally mixed character, although one who does great evil, just as individuals have done great evil in America's history of race relations. Chesnutt shows Carteret's evils to be enacted in a fog of self-delusion, the unfounded (or at least stupidly short-term) assumption that he will personally benefit thereby. Yet it is also possible, Chesnutt believed, to characterize a personality as *dominated* by racism as a defining characteristic, particularly in the milieu of the Jim Crow-era South. As Chesnutt observes, realism demands (if the reading audience does not) a portrayal of how racism has dehumanized white Americans as well as black ones.

Chesnutt's earliest priority as a fiction writer was to show how individual behavior is environmentally driven. Initially, his interest in realism was its tendency to demonstrate the entanglement of both black and white characters in a cultural milieu that defines and circumscribes their choices. Over time, he came increasingly to recognize the importance of well-rounded characters in achieving this goal. In an 1890 letter, Chesnutt (whose story "Rena Walden" had been rejected by *Century* magazine editor Richard Watson Gilder) complained to George Washington Cable that

> Mr. Gilder finds that I either lack humor or that my characters have a "brutality, a lack of mellowness, lack of spontaneous imaginative life, lack of outlook that makes them uninteresting." I fear, alas, that those are exactly the things that do characterize them, and just about the things that might have been expected to characterize people of that kind, the only qualities which the government and society had for 300 years labored faithfully, zealously, and successfully to produce, the only qualities which would have rendered their life at all endurable in the 19th century. I suppose I shall have to drop the attempt at realism and try to make them like other folks, for uninteresting people are not good subjects for fiction. (*"To Be an Author"* 66)

In the early versions of "Rena Walden,"[13] Chesnutt had attempted in a realist vein to demonstrate his characters' incapacity to transcend their social milieu. The story's characters are, borrowing terms from Pam Morris, "highly individualised, even monstrous, but simultaneously . . . embodiments of prevailing historical energies and conflicts" (74),[14] specifically those of the postslavery Southern economy. Whites, blacks, and mixed-race characters such as Rena are all defined by their economic aspirations: Rena's decision to marry for money, and her deception and exploitation at the hands of the man she marries, are thematically connected to the earlier defrauding of Rena's grandfather by a white man (and more generally, by implication, to the social-Darwinist world of the postwar South). Any sympathetic human qualities in these characters, Chesnutt suggests, arise not from their transcendence of historical conditions but from their ultimately tragic confinement within those conditions. Fundamentally, this is a world in which people exploit and betray one another for the sake of money, and in responding to Gilder's critique of his skills at characterization, Chesnutt ruefully concludes that at least one important reader has missed the point.

As he sees it, the characters have been drawn accurately, but they remain unpalatable because readers like Gilder will not choose to see themselves in such characters or to recognize the prevailing social conditions that create their avarice. As Matthew Wilson remarks, in response to Gilder's critique Chesnutt began to worry "that he might not be able to write about what he knew because of the audience's racist preconceptions" (*Whiteness* 61). Before long, however, Chesnutt had gotten over his defensiveness, writing to Cable that he had revised to provide his characters "more heart" (*"To Be an Author"* 69). His quickness to adapt his fiction to suit an influential reader might be seen as evidence of Chesnutt's desire to publish at any cost; yet the patience with which Chesnutt continuously revised "Rena Walden" during the next ten years belies such an interpretation.[15] Though he wanted, to be sure, to achieve a literary career, Chesnutt consistently subordinates the goal of commercial success to his pursuit of an aesthetic approach that will serve his ends; he is attempting to show his readers something and does not rest until he has figured out how to get the message across. As Howells recognized in his first, favorable review of Chesnutt's fiction, even when he falls short aesthetically, this is an author who knows "what he wants to do" ("Chesnutt's Stories" 53).

"Rena Walden" eventually metamorphosed into Chesnutt's first published novel, *The House Behind the Cedars,* and in the latter work we can see that he did not, after all, abandon "the attempt at realism." Instead, he draws characters that are more fully human, more easily recognizable to readers as like themselves, but who are no less caught up in, and defined by, situations out of their control than Rena and her cohorts in the earlier manuscript were. As Robert P. Sedlack explains, in the evolution of "Rena Walden" into *The House Behind the Cedars,* Chesnutt both clarifies that whites as well as blacks are implicated in his critique of racial prejudice and "soften[s] this attack" on the largely white reading audience by introducing "more complex and credible characters" with a mix of positive and negative qualities (185). Consistently throughout this period of apprenticeship, the question for Chesnutt did not concern his ends as a writer: he clearly wished to place characters' actions and choices into their proper context as part of a complicated and disturbing socioeconomic milieu. His experiment is meant to discover how to make his message palatable to a reading audience without compromising that message's challenging nature too greatly. People's blindness to the truth of their surroundings was not, in his estimation, just a personal limitation; it had a material, very negative impact on the lives of African Americans.

In his famous essay "Criteria of Negro Art" (which is also the text of his speech at the Spingarn Medal ceremony of 1926), W. E. B. Du Bois strikingly associates being African American with an ability to see one's environment with special perception: "We who are dark can see America in a way that white Americans can not" (17). Continues Du Bois,

> If you tonight suddenly should become full-fledged Americans; if your color faded, or the color line here in Chicago was miraculously forgotten; suppose, too, you became at the same time rich and powerful;—what is it that you would want? What would you immediately seek? Would you buy the most powerful of motor cars and outrace Cook County? Would you buy the most elaborate estate on the North Shore? Would you be a Rotarian or a Lion or a What-not of the very last degree? Would you wear the most striking clothes, give the richest dinners and buy the longest press notices?
>
> Even as you visualize such ideals you know in your hearts that these are not the things you really want. You realize this sooner than the average white American because, pushed aside as we have been in America, there has come to us not only a certain distaste for the tawdry and flamboyant but a vision of what the world could be if it were really a beautiful world; if we had the true spirit; if we had the Seeing Eye, the Cunning Hand, the Feeling Heart; if we had, to be sure, not perfect happiness, but plenty of good hard work, the inevitable suffering that always comes with life; sacrifice and waiting, all that—but, nevertheless, lived in a world where men know, where men create, where they realize themselves and where they enjoy life. It is that sort of a world we want to create for ourselves and for all America. (18)

This passage, delivered two decades after Chesnutt's career as a published novelist had ended and six years before his death, bears close examination in trying to understand Chesnutt's career as a realist. Just as Du Bois argues that reality is not something equally known by all, but a function of what observers are capable of *seeing*—so that not the white bourgeoisie but those who are disenfranchised have a privileged vision—Chesnutt writes on the assumption that white readers, in particular, need to remove or alter the categories of perception that blur or distract their vision before they can understand the events that his novels describe. They need to have their perspectives adjusted so that they can learn to see rightly.

As I have implied, if the question is merely one of classification, it matters very little whether or not Chesnutt is catalogued as a realist. Literary theorists have long acknowledged that the boundaries between "romance," "realism," "naturalism," and such categories are permeable anyway, and whether Chesnutt is associated with one set or another is of little consequence in itself. Nonetheless, the term "realism" seems a useful one in assessing Chesnutt's career, and I am reluctant to abandon it for several main reasons. First, Chesnutt is often regarded as a throwback to the pre-realist era, both stylistically and politically. It is just too easy to regard him as someone who rather cleverly mimicked mid-century writing modes, helped black writers to "catch up" a bit in cultural prestige, but offers little in the way of a sophisticated treatment of race. Regarding Chesnutt as a romance writer has led to two particularly unfortunate misreadings: that his fiction is rooted in an untroubled nineteenth-century conception of race, and that, writing in the tradition of romantic individualism, he fails to critique racism as a system. On the contrary, Chesnutt's novels are both sophisticated in questioning the validity of racial categories and ambitious in analyzing race in the context of cultural histories and economic conditions that were anything but simple.

I do not wish to argue that sentimental fiction or a romantic approach is artistically inferior or politically more evasive than a realist approach but merely that "realism" more aptly captures Chesnutt's literary methods. Jane Tompkins proved in *Sensational Designs* that sentimental fiction could wield substantial literary and political power. To clarify the distinction I see, I would contrast *Uncle Tom's Cabin* (which Chesnutt admired greatly) with Chesnutt's novels. Whereas the "sentimental power" of *Uncle Tom's Cabin,* as Tompkins persuasively explains, "depends upon the audience's being in possession of the conceptual categories that constitute character and event . . . above all, a set of religious beliefs" (126–27), Chesnutt relies on no such assumptions about his audience. In attempting to build common ground with his imagined readers, he does not appeal to religious beliefs or other abstractions, but refers instead to external, tangible data or visible actions: newspaper articles, factories, chains, corpses. Whereas Stowe uses spiritual referents to prepare her readers for the physical realities she wishes to present, Chesnutt makes reference to physical entities first and attempts to induce the reader to understand what these entities mean.

Admittedly, Chesnutt superficially can sound more like a product of the mid-nineteenth century than of the early twentieth, with his prosy narration and often sentimental appeal. What must not be overlooked, however, is that the sentimental strain in Chesnutt's fiction is not any sort of a stopping point; in fact, his use of sentiment is ambivalent and quite complex. On one hand, he often mocks the prose style of romance, as the over-the-top purple prose and bad poetry of *Mandy Oxendine* and the critique of Warwick's "trite" reflections in the opening of *The House Behind the Cedars* illustrate. On the other hand, he is clearly unwilling to abandon altogether the idea of some sort of unseen connection between people, including very differently situated people. One might compare Jake Barnes's attitude in *The Sun Also Rises,* in which the sterility of human existence is something one must face but must also resist and, if possible, overcome—somehow. Chesnutt presents to his readers in each novel evidence of a pragmatically minded world in which people are becoming increasingly brutal to one another, and in which romance serves mainly to overcompensate, to act as a blinder to this state of affairs, but also suggests, in a more hopeful if less certain vein, possibilities of connection that are yet to be fully imagined. Seeing him as a realist helps us to understand him as he seems to have understood himself, as a bridge between a past world—one which continues to inflect reality in ways that are important to acknowledge—and a future that is both frightening and full of possibility.

A final, and ultimately the most important, reason to insist on referring to Chesnutt as a realist is, simply put, that to speak as though race and realism are incompatible terms is an error from the standpoint of both literary theory and politics. Literary critics either must consider how the concepts of "race" and "realism" have inflected one another—work initiated by Warren, Rohrbach, and Boeckmann among others—or must abandon the term "realism" once and for all. A "strict constructionist" view, one in which the meaning of realism remains essentially unaltered and uncontested, must be rejected out of hand. Such a view is vulnerable to the major claim of those who decry the very notion of literary "realism":[16] that it retains the naïve but ultimately reactionary premise that certain people's experiences and perceptions exclusively define what's real. The problems inherent in such a notion are especially clear in considering the way in which race is constructed textually, for, as Wahneema Lubiano has written, "what is race in the United States if not an attempt to make 'real' a set of social assumptions about biology?" (98). The insight that reality is constructed, while it disallows any naïve conception of what is "real," should not cause us to step aside from the ongoing work of reformulating realities, including those of race, but should demand better-informed, more conscientious construction of them. Both "race" and "realism," as concepts, are fictive, but these terms are not meaningless: all fictions have meanings. We must not think of reality as some impermeable entity outside of culture, or dismiss it as an impossibility because we recognize it cannot be such an entity, but must reclaim it as a powerful expression of culture in which writers, critics, and those they represent have a *stake.*

"Given the constructed nature of the canon," Elizabeth Ammons forcefully asks, "what construction shall we choose? My own position is that, if American realism means anything, it means attention to the multiple realities figured in the work of the broadest possible range of authors writing in the late nineteenth and early twentieth centuries" ("Expanding the Canon" 439). A difficulty is that "the broadest possible range" is an impossibly open-ended term; somewhere, the boundary will be drawn, and numerous critics have pointed out that this drawing of boundaries renders the idea of "realism" inherently conservative. As Lubiano asserts, "[r]eality . . . is established via the consensus of a particular group [and] preserved by the absence of existing alternatives." For this reason, Lubiano argues, "realism, as a narrative form, enforces an authoritarian perspective" (104). Claims to "tell the truth" about nonwhites' lives are inherently suspect, she contends, because they represent a move "toward closure, the establishment of truth and order."

Ultimately, however, all such claims are subject to distortion, as Lubiano implies: "Realism establishes a claim to truth, but it also presents the ground for its own deconstruction—somebody else's truth" (105). Chesnutt, I have come to see, recognized more clearly than most that words employed to advance justice can, and usually will, be distorted by others to advance injustice. He was by no means naïve about the power relations at work in such a situation: his novels offer virtually no successful strategies for blacks to counter the white supremacist regime, even as they show that the whites who manipulate discourse to serve their ends are, by that very action, doomed at last. Despite this pessimistic outlook, Chesnutt also found real possibilities in the semantic richness he saw in the world and incorporated into literature, what Mikhail Bakhtin describes as "a *system* of languages that mutually and ideologically interanimate each other" (47). The novel, for Bakhtin, is characterized by a "struggle between two tendencies . . . a centralizing (unifying) tendency [and] a decentralizing tendency" (67). Every writer must come to terms with the possibility that one's words will be put to uses that are, from the writer's perspective, antithetical to his or her beliefs. But this awareness normally prompts a decision—not whether or not to continue writing, but about what type of writing to produce. In the trajectory of Chesnutt's career as a novelist, one can witness an author struggling with the basic issue: what justifies the production of fiction? And, ultimately, he leaves the answer to that question to be determined by his readers, not because he necessarily trusted them to act rightly, but because he saw he had no remaining option other than not to write at all.

This book proposes, as a partial and incomplete response to the "absence of existing alternatives" noted by Lubiano, the consideration of one African American writer as a substantive contributor to American literary realism. My primary intent is not to advocate for Chesnutt's enshrinement in the realist canon alongside Howells, James, and others. More significantly I hope that an extended reading of this author's novels will advance a conversation about non-white writers' involvement, their stake, in the debates surrounding realism, a conversation that has remained oddly stilted in previous criticism. Though readings of individual works by Chesnutt, Frances Harper, Pauline Hopkins, Alice Dunbar-Nelson, W. E. B. Du Bois, James Weldon Johnson, and others have occasionally found their way into previous studies of realism and the realist era, much more sustained work remains to be done.[17] Until that work appears, basic questions about what and how realism means remain insufficiently addressed.

Although virtually no artistic categories hold up well under close scrutiny, realism has proved a slipperier term than most. In 1894, Garland wrote that "[t]he meaning of the word 'realism' varies with the outlook of every person who uses it" (152). Nearly a century later, Eric Sundquist concurred: "No genre—if it can be called a genre—is more difficult to define than realism" (Preface vii). Because "reality" is a contested zone, realism is necessarily defined so open-endedly that the term might seem to have no use. Although I hope to have argued successfully that Chesnutt's writings are elucidated by an attempt to reconstruct his realist efforts, and more broadly that the concept of realism ought not to be excised altogether from fictions concerning race, I also concede that the ideal response is simply to resist *any* definition and read the works themselves. Ultimately, my goal is to motivate readers to find Chesnutt, and to help them read him through new eyes—seeing him as someone who was not content with social realities as he found them, but tried to refashion them. Taken to its logical conclusion, realism implies the need for not only reform but revolution: the world, known as it really is, can no longer be tolerated. As we proceed through Chesnutt's novels, we will see this author work through the problems of race and realism toward this logical conclusion.

1

Learning to Be a Realist

Chesnutt's Northern Novels

One aspect of Charles Chesnutt's career that makes it especially interesting is his frequent failure. His published writings had enough impact that he was among the most significant African American writers of the turn of the century; at the same time, his novels were rejected more often than they were published in his lifetime. Thus, he seems to exist on (and helps to define) the very edge of acceptability according to late-nineteenth- and early-twentieth-century standards, at times writing texts that met with critical and commercial approbation and in other cases not even coming close. Since Chesnutt's prominence warranted the collection of his papers by Fisk University, scholars have had access to the typescripts of his six rejected novels;[1] because Chesnutt's resurgence led to the publication of five of these novels since 1997, the public has also been able to glimpse the unknown Chesnutt. This chapter explores Chesnutt's three novels of urban Northern life: two that only recently found publication—*A Business Career* (c. 1898; published 2005) and *Evelyn's Husband* (c. 1903;[2] published 2005)—and the one remaining novel that has never been published, *The Rainbow Chasers* (c. 1900). In the following chapter, I take up the 1890s "passing" novella *Mandy Oxendine* as a precursor to *The House Behind the Cedars*, and in chapter 5 I interpret two much later novels that are currently in print: *Paul Marchand, F.M.C.* (c. 1921; published 1998 and 1999) and *The Quarry* (c. 1928; published 1999).

In the analysis that follows, I attempt to uncover the roots of Chesnutt's aspirations for realism through a close reading of the Northern novels. In a study that "focus[es] on the consequences of Chesnutt's awareness of his white audience" (*Whiteness* xviii), Matthew Wilson describes these as "white-life novels," or "novels that contain only incidental African American characters and that concentrate on depictions of white experience" (xv). Noting Chesnutt's employment of elements of "the adventure, the romance, and the melodrama" (21–22), Wilson also characterizes them as sentimental and sensational works, designed (though not quite successfully) to appeal to a popular audience.

While admiring Wilson's main argument that Chesnutt uses popular forms to work through 1890s economic and gender anxieties (which he reads in terms of the white readership's taking stock of its own racial identity), I take issue with his conclusion that the novels' references to African Americans are only incidental, and I partially dissent from his conclusion that they are best classified as romances (*Whiteness* 24).[3] It is true, as Wilson argues, that critics have neglected black authors' representations of white experience (227 n. 4), and to ignore Chesnutt's Northern novels on this basis (as virtually every critic to date except Wilson seems to have done) is unjustifiable. On the other hand, in examining Chesnutt's writing in terms of his appeal to audience, Wilson may have failed to notice some of this author's commentary that, presumably, white readers of the 1890s would themselves not have seen. As in his more explicitly racially oriented fiction, which enacts various forms of black-white contact, in the early novels Chesnutt explores racial codes, in part, by encoding a portion of his message in ways that his white readers would have been inclined to gloss over. Thus, while these novels seem unusual in Chesnutt's oeuvre in that they seem to make no mention of race, in the conclusion to this chapter I argue that the questioning of what race means—enacted so vividly in his published work—is visibly present in these early texts, and that its presence in the form of unacknowledged biracial characters is a key to understanding his career as a realist author.

Prior to Wilson's *Whiteness in the Novels of Charles W. Chesnutt* (2004), the three works considered in this chapter received virtually no attention from critics; only a very few have even acknowledged their existence. Helen Chesnutt's 1952 biography of her father documents that *A Business Career* was rejected by Walter Hines Page of *The Atlantic* in 1898 (in the same communication, Page recommended that Chesnutt undertake a book of "conjure" stories, which led to *The Conjure Woman*) and that *The Rainbow Chasers* received a cautiously favorable response from Houghton Mifflin in 1900, but ultimately was rejected in favor of "Rena Walden," retitled *The House Behind the Cedars* (91–92, 141–46). Frances Richardson Keller, in *An American Crusade: The Life of Charles Waddell Chesnutt* (1978), mentions the unpublished texts and offers a very brief synopsis of *A Business Career.* William L. Andrews's *The Literary Career of Charles W. Chesnutt* (1980) makes brief and dismissive mention of these works, describing *Evelyn's Husband* as "[u]nquestionably the worst" of Chesnutt's unpublished novels (130) and *The Rainbow Chasers* as lacking "that spark of conviction and serious purpose which appears in Chesnutt's more notable work" (122).[4] Writes Andrews, who very productively set the course of Chesnutt scholarship for decades,

> Each of these undistinguished narratives had sprung from a similar motive—to write especially for the popular market—and each was concocted only after novel-length color line stories had failed to make headway either in the publishers' offices or in the bookstores. The implications of this trend of writing alternately controversial "southern" novels of social purpose and noncontroversial "northern" novels of entertainment could not have been lost on Chesnutt. The public did not seem to favor his controversial fiction [in the form of *The House Behind the Cedars, The Marrow of Tradition,* and *The Colonel's Dream,* none of which sold as well as hoped], and his editors would not approve his noncontroversial alternatives. (131)

As bitter a pill as this must have been for Chesnutt, Andrews implies that his failure to publish the "northern" novels at the start of his career was a blessing in disguise: "Chesnutt's failure to place one of his nonracial, plainly commercial manuscripts with a national publisher prevented him from making a name for himself outside the 'problem novel' genre" (122). In other words, had Chesnutt succeeded too easily, he might never have found the incentive to take on more serious writing projects.

This assessment of Chesnutt's Northern novels seems largely to hold up upon reading these three works. The novels, each of which is populated almost exclusively by upper-class Northern whites, rarely touch on issues of race or other contemporary social problems in any overt manner, and they conspicuously break most conventional rules of good fiction: characters are flat and static; plots are either asymmetrical or overly symmetrical, fantastical, and reliant on coincidence and contrivance; endings are highly predictable. In short, it is easy to dismiss these works as mere "entertainments," and rather impoverished ones at that. On the other hand, a close look at these novels does reveal much about Chesnutt's aims and practices as a writer, confirming some conventional wisdom and requiring the alteration of some assumptions shared by critics. *A Business Career, The Rainbow Chasers,* and *Evelyn's Husband* reveal not only a writer attempting to learn his craft, but also the nature of the career he foresaw for himself: in their pages, one finds Chesnutt learning how to be a realist.

A Business Career: Renouncing Romance

Initially, that claim might seem like foolishness to anyone who reads these works: writing realistically seems to be exactly what Chesnutt is *not* doing, considering the rather outlandish stories he devises—which, if not strictly supernatural, at least come across as wildly implausible. In *A Business Career,* for example, Stella Merwin, a middle-class resident of the Midwestern city of Groveland (Chesnutt's frequent appellation for his hometown of Cleveland), is sent by an employment agency to work as stenographer for the oil baron Wendell Truscott. As it happens, Truscott acquired the business after the financial collapse, and corresponding death, of his mentor, Stella's father Henry. Stella has been raised by her mother to believe that Truscott somehow engineered her father's fall, and that they must someday expose Truscott's perfidy and reclaim their fortune. Calling herself "Miss Smith," Stella gradually gains the trust and admiration of Wendell and comes to learn that not only was her father's collapse the result of a risky (and ethically dubious) moneymaking venture, but that Truscott himself has covertly augmented the Merwins' income from her father's estate, saving them from poverty. Himself nearly ruined by a speculative undertaking that mirrors Henry Merwin's, Truscott is saved when the wealthy Matilda Wedderburn, romantically spurned by Truscott and cognizant that he and Stella have fallen in love, provides the necessary funds to complete the deal, writing, "Take the money, and take the other woman!" (213). The novel, in short, relies on at least one major coincidence, pivots on the highly romanticized gesture of renunciation by Wedderburn, and ends clearly and unambiguously with a resolution that solves all of the problems raised by the narrative—all questionable gestures, to say the least, according to the traditional tenets of realism.

So realism is not exactly what Chesnutt achieved with this novel, but it seems to have been what he was attempting in several respects, and those attempts at realism are the gestures that we see Chesnutt take up again in his more successful novels. First, and most centrally, *A Business Career* represents a clear if inconsistent attempt to replace the sentimental plot that remained highly marketable with a slower-paced, more observational approach. The novel is as concerned with the ordinary goings-on of business life as it is with extraordinary occurrences; though it relies on the latter in an effort to spark readers' interest, it seems clear that the romance plot is a means to other ends that were more central to what Chesnutt was attempting. Moreover, even as he crafts a rather turgid plot concerning Stella's attempts to learn the truth about Truscott, pumped up with subplots concerning a villainous accountant and Truscott's race to deposit Wedderburn's gift in time to save his enterprise, Chesnutt forgoes an even more romanticized, easier plot line, that of Stella's mother, Alice Merwin—signaling that his intent was to replace the gratifyingly sentimental story his novel *could* be with one that would be less evasive of social realities. The question is less his intent to produce realism than his ability to enact it.

As is often the case in Chesnutt's fiction, in which secrets and hidden papers abound, *A Business Career* is about uncovering hidden truths, and even more about interpreting truths that seem to stare us right in the face. Alice Merwin believes from the start that she knows the story that needs to be told: in it, Wendell Truscott is the villain and the Merwins' stolen riches await restoration to their rightful heirs. Says Alice, "Surely God will not let him go unpunished! Some time, in some way, perhaps from his own lips, perhaps by our efforts, perhaps by accident, the truth will become known, and he will be exposed to the scorn of all honest men; your father's memory will be cleared from all aspersions, and we shall have what is our own" (17). Although her idée fixe informs the way in which Alice interprets every datum she encounters, Chesnutt implies early in the novel that her perspective is rooted in a fantasy; she obviously has psychological and financial reasons to believe as she does. One way in which the novel is marked as an attempt at realism is its manner of flattering its readers: although Chesnutt confirms only late in the novel that Truscott is innocent of Alice's charges, the reader can easily extrapolate by the first chapters that Alice's impressions are biased and probably represent the opposite of reality. Though Alice's claims are based on evidence (the mystery surrounding Merwin's fall, Truscott's evasive comments), that evidence can logically lead to more than one conclusion. The reader, in other words, has an implicitly privileged perspective compared to the novel's characters, similar to the way in which realist novels like *The Rise of Silas Lapham, The Damnation of Theron Ware, Sister Carrie,* or Chesnutt's own *The Marrow of Tradition* work only if readers feel that they have amassed a larger perspective than the novels' characters. The purpose of each of these novels is not to reveal to the reader something wonderful and new, but to work through the meaning of an established and recognizable environment.

Like other realist novels of the era, *A Business Career* is less about describing particular conditions than about learning to interpret conditions as one finds them. Stella, although trained by Alice to accept one version of events, finds that the more she learns, the less easily she can make her mother's plot *work:*

> Stella's views in regard to the unmasking of Truscott's early misdeeds had been imperceptibly modified. At first she had seen exposure com-

> ing swiftly, like a thunderbolt, or the wrath of God, striking the usurper from his pedestal and covering him with well-merited obloquy. Now she thought of the great event as merely a retribution. Instead of an avenging fury driving the sinner to ruin, she would stand to him in the attitude of a calm and reproachful goddess. Remorse should be his portion. She would demand nothing of him but what he had taken; she would not ruin or embarrass him by exposure. She would be his conscience. (171)

As Stella comes to know Truscott better, and what she thought she knew about him becomes more complicated, her imagined plot shifts from a highly romanticized, public one to a rather more reserved, sentimental, and personal one. Eventually, she recognizes that even that outcome—in which she will act as Truscott's "conscience"—is untenable. When she locates the documents that exonerate Truscott, her reaction is less surprise than the recognition of something that, at some level, she had acknowledged to be true for some time.[5] The ways of understanding that Stella has inherited are explicitly romantic and sentimental and are vested in her and her mother's personal interests, and they do not hold up to the scrutiny of an increasing body of evidence.[6] As Alfred Habegger argues, realists were defined by their "refus[al] to give their readers the sort of satisfaction the novel generally afforded" (108), for example forsaking an "appeal to the reader's fantasies or daydreams" (106). *A Business Career* debunks its characters' daydreams but also replaces those with new, perhaps equally implausible daydreams. In the former tendency, we see Chesnutt's repudiation of romantic storytelling conventions; in the latter, we see his struggle to determine how to tell a story instead.[7]

Social life as Chesnutt depicts it in *A Business Career* is an endless series of interpretations of people and their actions, for which the act of reading a novel is a mirror. Guiding these interpretations are a whole series of assumptions, rarely acknowledged specifically, about human nature and also about gender, class, and (Chesnutt hints) race. The inflection of, for example, social class makes the quality of our interpretations especially important, in that the interpretations themselves actually make the world. It also makes the act of interpretation infinitely complex. Interpretation is, Chesnutt suggests, what constitutes the world, but the problem with such a situation is that people do not always understand what governs our readings of others; they analyze and use data in politically charged ways, even as they reveal their uncertainty about what the data might *mean* in the first place. For example, Stella reflects on Truscott's evolving attitude toward her: "He was coming gradually around to a realization of her quality. If dollars and cents had been involved, he would doubtless have detected at first sight that she was a person of superior birth and culture" (109). In our constant, almost unconscious ranking of others, the bases for comparison themselves—here, marketplace value, social class, and implicitly sexual desirability—easily become confused.

Stella's process of understanding, in which she holds onto the interpretation taught her by her mother until it can no longer withstand the weight of available evidence, is part of a larger theme developed in *A Business Career.* Frequently, empirical evidence referred to in the novel is clear enough, but what that evidence means is contested. If there is one central theme to the novel, it is that context matters. Stella's observation of Truscott's businesslike dismissal of a drunken employee and, later, of a mendicant is colored by her inherited conception of who Truscott is: his words, she reflects with hostility, are "such as she might have expected from a man of Wendell Truscott's past" (25). Words, as Truscott instructs Stella when he dictates correspondence, are not mere abstractions that function equally well in any context:

> Once he waited so long in the middle of a sentence, that Stella almost involuntarily suggested a word.
>
> "Thank you," he said, giving her a keen glance; "that would ordinarily be the proper expression. But this man would not understand it in the right way." (59)

The importance of context is heightened when one considers the amount of *reading* of one another Chesnutt's characters engage in, and the centrality of these reading acts to all other aspects of their lives. Chesnutt's characters live in what might be called a textual economy, as he shows at the most basic level when Truscott tells Stella to dismiss from consideration applicants who cannot write well or spell correctly (47). More subtly, the nature of individuals as texts is revealed in the extent to which characters' assessments of one another fluidly change according to contextual circumstances: no one's character simply *is;* everyone is constituted as he or she is *read,* which may change from moment to moment. Thus, Truscott notices that Matilda Wedderburn is aging and "growing stout" only when a union with Stella begins to seem more favorable (96), and Truscott's involvement in the Merwins' financial affairs comes to seem benevolent rather than suspicious at the exact moment Stella realizes that marriage to him is a surer route to wealth than exposure of his presumed dishonesty.

A Business Career hints at the anxiety involved in the maintenance of a shifting culture. For example, in the following passage, Alice Merwin indicates that she suffered less from the loss of her fortune than from realizing the larger implication that the social world is unstable: "I think the greatest shock I felt, when the crash came was not regret for what I had lost, but surprise at losing it. It seemed as though the bottom had dropped out of everything! It was like a dream—where one will be sailing, sailing along—on the solid earth, too, or just above it—when suddenly, without warning, the ground fails beneath one's feet, and one wakes up, trembling, as though poised on the brink of a fathomless abyss!" (81–82). What place can Stella, or for that matter Truscott, find in such a changeable atmosphere? The various, related conflicts of the novel—romance versus realism, feminine versus masculine, aristocracy versus business—constantly alter the nature of the more immediate choices the characters face.

As an aspiring businesswoman, and a fallen member of the aristocratic class to boot, Stella is ambivalently situated in a world to which she traditionally would have little access. The novel's point, however, is not to demonstrate that Stella is out of place but to question what place she (and, for that matter, Truscott) can find in this rapidly changing social world. As Brook Thomas writes, "[r]ather than prescribe a code of behavior, [a realist] work includes readers in a dialogue in which judgments of actions are constructed through a process of negotiation and exchange" (9). *A Business Career* describes an atmosphere in which the masculine realm of business seems to be crowding out the implicitly feminine aristocratic realm, upending a precarious balance and sending the inhabitants of both realms into a sort of no-man's-land.

While not quite endorsing the radical (for the 1890s) feminism of Stella's mentor, Mrs. Paxton, the novel does suggest that conventionally "feminine" qualities have something essential to contribute to the business world. Paxton argues that in order to succeed, Stella must submit herself wholeheartedly to business mores: "You'll find, my dear, that romance and business won't work in double harness" (100). The novel endorses neither this view nor Truscott's ultimately similar, though decidedly nonfeminist, assumption that business life requires the renunciation of personal feelings such as compassion. It takes seriously, instead, the notion that Stella—the representative of a younger generation, one who attempts, imperfectly, to balance sentiment and pragmatism—has something critical to contribute to this evolving social world. Stella's approach to both Paxton's feminism and Truscott's business orientation is fundamentally ambivalent; she denounces neither, and both have a striking, powerful quality that, while difficult to articulate, strikes her as compelling and discomfiting. Her basic strategy is to temper each, harnessing its capacity for potent change while moderating its potentially destructive qualities.[8]

The characters who manage to find a place in the changing corporate atmosphere presented in *A Business Career* are those, like Stella, who negotiate a successful balance between a romantic ideal of integrity as a given and, on the other hand, a fluid identity that can be responsive to the changing conditions of American life. While Stella provides the flexibility that Truscott often lacks, she in turn stands to benefit by sharing in his cultural authority, without which her qualities threaten to remain dormant. Truscott has an aura of power that captivates her: he is described as having "a virile nature radiating an atmosphere of authority" (58). His forcefulness, which translates into a blunt and unfeeling communication style, marks Truscott as nonaristocratic. Stella reflects that "[s]uch a man might possess energy and enterprise, and, by virtue of craft or force, acquire wealth and the sort of position mere wealth can purchase, without ever becoming a gentleman in even the superficial meaning of the word" (25). Truscott as arch capitalist represents a threat not only to those he exploits, but also to the gentry whom he stands to eclipse. He also, Stella senses, is capable of overwhelming her—"when he speaks, I feel as though I have to obey him—not simply because I am paid, but because I can't help it" (123)—and, given time, the entire society: "Stella felt that she had been unduly influenced by Truscott's strength of will. She would henceforth remember that craft, while commonly associated with weakness, was not incompatible with strength—such a force, indeed, as she had already dimly perceived Wendell Truscott to be in the industrial world" (131).

With *A Business Career,* Chesnutt attempts to find realism, that is, to locate a productive middle position between what Brook Thomas has described as two "ordering principles": sentimental writers' "faith in a transcendental, usually religious, moral order" and the "governing ordering principle" of determinism advocated by naturalists (10–11). Rejecting both Alice Merwin's romantic and aristocratic worldview, which incorrectly sees her loss of social position as a deprivation of her "rights" (10), and Wendell Truscott's corporate worldview, which regards every misfortune as simply the fault and responsibility of its bearer (25), it fears to reject either position too completely. Rather than retreating into romance and aristocracy, or foraying boldly into naturalism and laissez-faire economics, both of which regard all evidence as bearing only one possible interpretation, *A Business Career* attempts to mediate these competing approaches by creating a character, Stella, who comprises the best of both worlds, and imagining for her a fate (in the form of union with Truscott) in which such a character can impose herself on the social environment with a moral force. Perhaps, as Paxton claims, "romance is the death of business" (9), but Chesnutt at least attempts to find a way in which the two ideals may be reconciled, while bringing to bear a flexibility of interpretation, a resistance to a priori "ordering principles," that neither of them has on its own. Rather than pull back against impending naturalism and corporatism, Chesnutt characterizes Stella's balanced approach (which does not supercede but alters the corporate thrust to which it is attached) as the true move forward, the maneuver that, if not inevitable, at least is essential if society is not to be swallowed by an ideology that diminishes human individuality.

If the attempt of *A Business Career* to move beyond romance—to ask "what next?"—does not arrive at what we may call realism, it does point out that Chesnutt was champing at the bit of the sentimental romance plot, finding it inadequate as a forum for the questions he seems most interested in: the relative merits of aristocratic and business mindsets, the lingering presence of class in America, the economies of people and their actions as texts, and even the question that possessed Chesnutt much more explicitly elsewhere—the meaning of race. While the plot of *A Business Career* is its least interesting feature, a mere forum with which to address certain social and narrative problems that Chesnutt found compelling throughout his career, he was beginning to regard the emerging genre of the realist novel as a way of addressing the problems he wanted to address. Where would a committed realist author have taken Stella's story? Could realism do something more than merely document Stella's vulnerability? Chesnutt began to see both the potential and the limitations of realism, and while the aesthetic problems of *A Business Career* roughly match the inconsistency with which he pursued realist methods, his employment of realism in *The House Behind the Cedars* and *The Marrow of Tradition* would by no means merely follow that of Howells or James; Chesnutt was already finding, as he wrote *A Business Career,* that he would need to reshape realism to his own ends.

The Rainbow Chasers: Incorporating Characters

In *The Rainbow Chasers,* Chesnutt's ambitions to reshape realism are for the most part deferred as he attempts to polish his skill at writing realistic prose. Of the three novels considered in this chapter, *The Rainbow Chasers* is the least ambitious in terms of plot, but the most ambitious in terms of character and technique. The 188-page typescript available in the Chesnutt Collection is rough compared to those of his other novels: the main draft of *The Rainbow Chasers* is a patchwork of various fragments that he seems to have written at different times.[9] In the typescript one sees Chesnutt struggling with his novel, and while the struggle was not always successful, it is clear that he is continuing the effort to expand his abilities, and to move toward realism, that is seen in *A Business Career.*[10] Although Wilson describes it as "the least engaging novel in Chesnutt's oeuvre" (*Whiteness* 36), in some ways it is the most compelling of Chesnutt's three Northern novels. *The Rainbow Chasers* is the only one of Chesnutt's nine novels that is written in first person, and in it he experiments with the unreliable narrator, with nonintrusive narration that shows more than tells, and most of all with the development of a variety of characters while relinquishing a sensational plot.

An incidental summary of a popular novel read by one of the novel's characters reveals something of Chesnutt's own aims: "It was a pathetic tale of a worldly man, who, after many years of selfish indulgence, is brought through the gentle influence of a child to realize the emptiness of such a life. After a few months of strenuous efforts to redeem himself, he receives a fatal injury in an act of self-sacrifice, and dies in the confident hope of a glorious here-after" (52). The first sentence of this description loosely plots *The Rainbow Chasers,* whereas anything resembling the second sentence with its "glorious here-after" is not to be found. In truth, not much happens in *The Rainbow Chasers.* The narrator (for whom Chesnutt considered various appellations; he most often used "Quilliams," which is what I shall call him) is a forty-one-year-old scientist who has inherited enough income to conduct his experiments in isolation, without need of a position in industry or academia. He learns, however, that—like Edward Olney in Howells's *An Imperative Duty*—he has unfortunately allowed his inheritance to remain in railroad stock that now has nearly gone bust. On the advice of an old school friend, he invests his remaining fortune in a rubber plantation in Nicaragua, which he is assured is about to explode in value. Meanwhile, Quilliams nears completion of his project of the last fifteen years: he is in hot pursuit of a modern form of alchemy, an efficient method of separating gold and other valuable metals from ore. The discovery, upon its perfection, is sure to make Quilliams celebrated and rich; thus he feels assured of two sources of wealth within a matter of weeks.

Again like Howells's Olney, as a result of straitened circumstances Quilliams must find inexpensive lodging, and he ends up in a working-class neighborhood as a boarder of Julia Gray, a young working woman who supports her blind mother and her lame younger brother, Jimmie. In this setting, Chesnutt puts the good-natured but remote Quilliams in productive contact with various types of people he would not normally encounter: the Grays, an honest but simpleminded carpenter named Bowles, a rector named Jordan with "six motherless children," a midlevel machine politician named Nutter, and others. Quilliams's position in this community, in his own and others' perception, is one of detachment: he observes but is not really a participant. As an impartial outsider, Quilliams is prevailed upon by Bowles, Nutter, and Jordan: each wants to marry Julia and asks Quilliams to intercede on his behalf. The agreeable Quilliams plays Cyrano on behalf of each man in succession, but also finds himself growing increasingly attracted to Julia, due to her practical nature, he claims.

Gradually, Quilliams allows himself to realize that he is falling in love with Julia. He develops a bond with Jimmie and nobly helps the family deal with the return of their profligate father, who must avoid the police in order to die at home rather than in jail. In successive drafts, Chesnutt tried out, and apparently rejected, numerous plot twists, including the kidnapping of Jimmie by his father and Jimmie's death at a baseball game upon being hit by a line drive. While a few gaps are apparent in the plot of the most recent draft—we do not know how Chesnutt resolved some of the loose ends before sending the manuscript to Houghton Mifflin—it seems that he was working to extract sensational events and let a more plausible story unfold. He apparently could not, however, bear to leave his characters penniless: the novel ends with Quilliams, now destitute as a result of the failure of both his scientific and his investing enterprises, becoming engaged to Julia and learning that she has inherited a fortune in the form of a gold mine obtained by her father.

The Rainbow Chasers clearly is designed to follow Howells's tenet that in realism character takes precedence over plot. Quilliams's main preoccupation, whatever happens to him, is that of his identity; from the beginning, he is spinning events of his life to reinforce his conviction that he is a "practical" man. Underneath this mask of practicality is Quilliams's anxiety that he will be overwhelmed by some unanticipated change: "Any ripple of disappointment, any wave of misfortune, that has disturbed the current of my life—there have not been many, I am glad to say—has always broken harmlessly against the rock of practical philosophy opposed to it" (2). This self-assurance is belied by Quilliams's behavior, which avoids human contact and other prospective sources of upheaval as much as possible.

Naturally, Chesnutt's main goal as a novelist is to give such a character something to do. And, if one imagines some of the adventures he might have been tempted to craft for Quilliams, his intent to pursue a character study is clear. In comparison to *A Business Career,* in which characters are largely static (although new facets are revealed by changing circumstances), *The Rainbow Chasers* uses external events not only to reveal elements of its protagonist's personality but to dramatize its evolution. Chesnutt has taken his pursuit of realistic narrative one important step forward.

Like other works of the realist era, the novel responds to what Alan Trachtenberg describes as "the emergence of a changed, more tightly structured society with new hierarchies of control," which Trachtenberg calls "the incorporation of America" (3–4). Not only did the rise of the corporation change society; as Walter Benn Michaels has indicated, it changed people. Following a 1905 analysis by John P. Davis, Michaels articulates the turn-of-the-century anxiety that the corporation's "effect on the human beings who own it or are employed by it is to recreate them in its own image—to deprive them of their 'sympathy'" (200). Even as the concept of the corporation as legally an artificial person gained currency, people's identities were coming to seem equally artificial; as Michaels illustrates, the boundary between a human and a business was becoming problematic. Quilliams, at the outset of the novel, resembles the naturalist character Michaels finds in the fiction of Frank Norris, whose "immun[ity] to loss" and lack of agency render him a "corporate personality" (201–2). The quest for identity in which he inadvertently finds himself, a direct consequence of his investment activities, illustrates the detachment, the lack of sympathy, that corporate life seemed to promise. The question for Chesnutt, then, is whether such a character can be incorporated in other ways as well. Given the encroaching, seemingly unavoidable, specter of economic determinism, what other possible ways are there (if any) of embodying a human character with identity?

The Rainbow Chasers is preoccupied with this question, and with some success it portrays characters as sites of complex interaction between various ideas in the air during the 1890s. How these characters are constituted—by their self-image, by their social status and the surrounding culture, and especially by their interactions with others—is more central to the novel than what happens to them. In this way, it fits the model of realist characterization described by Thomas: realists recognized that "human identity is always historically constituted" but also insisted that "it is not completely determined" (282). People's identities are constructed, but the question is, to what degree are individuals able to participate in their self-construction? Quilliams, for example, constantly refers to his own identity as a "practical" man, whereas events quickly prove that his motivations are as sentimental and self-involved as the next person's, or more so. Julia, in fact, is a much more practical individual, for the simple reason that—as the sole provider for her family—she has to be. While the pose of the "practical man" does not hold up, Quilliams is much more successful at forging an identity for himself when he moves from the realm of contemplation to that of action, when he leaves his laboratory and becomes involved in people's lives. He and other characters are developed as conglomerations of personality and circumstance—a mingling that is suggested symbolically by Quilliams's obsessive quest for an efficient means of extracting metals from ore. For the novelist Chesnutt is trying to become, such a separation of traits is no longer desirable: the point is not to separate individuals and their motives from society, but to make their mutual enmeshment the basis of the narrative.

Ideas and events are in the air: the novel makes reference to Darwinism, the exploitation of natural resources in Nicaragua (and, by implication, colonialism), stock scandals, and Tammany Hall–type political machines. These do not just provide a backdrop; together they constitute Chesnutt's main interest, as he shows such social forces to be the materials that make up individuals' lives. How, the novel asks, can an individual maintain a coherent identity amid such a rich proliferation of discourses? A fundamental error of Quilliams's is that he fails to recognize his interconnectedness—with others and with the social fabric more generally—until it is too late, a theme Chesnutt also explores productively in *The House Behind the Cedars.* For example, in typical solipsistic fashion, Quilliams dismisses the newspaper, with headlines such as "The war in Africa," as irrelevant until it speaks directly to his situation. When it reveals that his quest for a world-changing invention has been trumped by a younger scientist, Quilliams finds out that his mistake has not been one of scientific method or logic—"Every step was correctly taken, and led logically to the next" (185)—but that he has erred by assuming that he operated in a vacuum: "I had vainly dreamed—I who had stupidly imagined myself to be a practical man!—that I alone, of all the thousands of learned and ambitious scientific students, was seeking the key to this treasure-chamber of the world" (184).

More than anything else, the 1890s atmosphere of *The Rainbow Chasers* is one of permeating change. New industries rise with unprecedented rapidity; new medical procedures, unimaginable just a few years before, are curing the blind and the lame. The result of such developments, despite obvious benefits, is not confidence but increasing cultural anxiety, as the novel illustrates. Rapid fluctuations in industry ruin people as quickly as they enrich them; new cures are available only to the moneyed. The main theme of the novel is that of the inherent uncertainty of life. *The Rainbow Chasers* mocks its protagonist's claim of certainty. Quilliams reflects that Nutter's field of politics is inferior to "the clear, calm atmosphere of scientific truth, where I had taken up my abode, [and] there are no clouds to obscure, and no vain hopes to delude!" (48).[11] His success, he believes, is "as certain as the immutable law of nature on which my method was founded" (51). His folly is brought home most forcefully near the end of the novel, in which a competitor's achievement renders his own life's work useless, just as the Nicaraguan stock he has purchased turns out to be a fraud. But his limited perspective is also represented by his attitude toward Julia, whose main flaw, from his perspective, is her excessive zeal to make money, which causes her to stay up catching up with her stenography work. "I did not like this feverish love of gain," remarks Quilliams, failing to notice that Julia's work is not a choice but an economic necessity. "It was unnatural in so young a woman" (55). What might be an indication of her dedication to her family's well-being is seen instead as evidence of Julia's avarice.

The ending of the novel—in which the moral weight of Quilliams's past decisions seems to be alleviated by an unexpected fortune, shielding him and Julia from past consequences and future risks—complicates Chesnutt's attempt at realism. On one hand, the implausible occurrence seems to trivialize the novel; on the other, the ending accentuates Chesnutt's point that what had once seemed essential now is acknowledged to be trivial. The novel does not depend on the infusion of money to end successfully; if anything, the introduction of the lost-fortune contrivance is disappointing rather than gratifying. The receipt of a sudden fortune via Julia's father, of course, is no more fortuitous than Quilliams's own inheritance from *his* father, the loss of which instigates the novel's plot. The difference is that readers can now more easily recognize that, rather than completing the person, money prevents an individual from amassing an identity in a healthy way. If Chesnutt's narrative strategy has done its work, the cheeriness of the novel's ending is undercut by readers' recognition that Quilliams's and Julia's newfound fortune in fact compromises the seemingly happy ending.

Evelyn's Husband: Encountering Naturalism

Chesnutt's pursuit of an economic insight into his characters' moral qualities continues in *Evelyn's Husband.* This novel describes how abstractions such as love can be communicated only using terms of economic exchange, but does not argue that eradicating such pragmatic concerns as money and status is possible or necessarily desirable. Chesnutt sidesteps such a romanticized conclusion by offering, in the second half of the novel, a qualified naturalistic argument that individuals' brutal true selves become apparent once social inhibitions lose their force. Ultimately, however, he seems to reject the naturalistic thesis as well, concluding that how people would treat each other in their natural state is unknowable, since our knowledge is always predicated upon social convention. Overarching insights into human nature are not possible; the best one can hope to achieve is a momentary glimpse into human behavior, taking social context into full account.

In *Evelyn's Husband,* even more than in *A Business Career* and *The Rainbow Chasers,* one finds Chesnutt resisting, but ultimately succumbing to, sensationalism. As a work of sentimental romance, the plot is easily summarized: Edward Cushing, a middle-aged, wealthy Boston dilettante, wishes to marry Evelyn Thayer, the nineteen-year-old daughter of his onetime friend, now deceased. With the encouragement of her mother, Evelyn reluctantly agrees to become engaged to Cushing; although she feels favorably toward him, she is not certain she loves him and believes she has not yet experienced enough of the world to marry. Into this situation arrives Hugh Manson, a brash and promising young architect who has not yet made his fortune. Although Evelyn's mother, Alice, prohibits Evelyn from meeting with Hugh, he secretly courts her; meanwhile, Cushing fears that Evelyn's heart will stray and pushes for a prompt wedding. All hope seems lost for a successful coupling of the young lovers when the reader begins chapter 9, titled "Evelyn's Marriage." Chesnutt, however, has a surprise in store for us: Evelyn has not wed Cushing; instead, she and Hugh have eloped.

If this were all there was to *Evelyn's Husband,* it would not be worth much attention. The segment of the plot summarized above, however, comprises roughly one-third of the 289-page novel. Continuing the experiment he initiated with *A Business Career,* Chesnutt provides his readers with the sort of neatly wrapped, satisfying sentimental plot that they had been trained to consume, and which they might well have rewarded. In the remaining two hundred pages, he attempts to unravel this romance story by exploring more difficult questions: Were Hugh and Evelyn ever really in love? What part do economic concerns play in matters of the heart? And, most importantly, what might human nature reveal itself to be like, if somehow it could be stripped of the influences of social convention?

Attempting to answer these questions, and more generally rounding out the plot of *Evelyn's Husband* so that it pushes well beyond the sentimental story he was clearly uninterested in replicating intact, leads Chesnutt to a series of desperate maneuvers—most notably the coincidental shipwrecking of Cushing and Manson on the same island for most of the last half of the novel—which disallow us from considering the work an accomplished example of realism. Still, as with *A Business Career,* Chesnutt is attempting to move past the romance and figure out what might come next. How could he take the sort of heart-wrenching romance stories that, admittedly, do occur in life and show how such stories are inflected by the culture, by the worlds of commerce and social status? Recognizing what his characters do not—that money and status, more certainly than love, shape the world—Chesnutt, with clear vision but occasionally extravagant imagination, tries to account for this fact in a way that would not be altogether paralyzing. Given a situation that, if fully acknowledged, must lead to pessimism, he nonetheless tries to chart a course for his characters in which such blissful abstractions as "true love" could be made to count in the "real" social world.

Even more than *A Business Career* and *The Rainbow Chasers, Evelyn's Husband* is a novel about interpretation, one in which characters' main preoccupation is analyzing visual data for their significance.[12] The central point in his scheme is that interpreting is what people do, unconsciously, all of the time, and that acts of interpretation are ways of maintaining hierarchies. In the first chapter, Cushing contemplates what's revealed by photographs of the Thayers: in Alice's "clear eyes could be read loyalty . . . patience . . . cheerfulness," although the narrator suggests that "[a] more astute physiognomist than Cushing might have read there still other qualities—a fine pride, a delicate reserve, and a firmness of character—which to him had been swallowed up for the most part in the refulgence of her more obvious virtues" (6). Henry Thayer's portrait reveals "curly hair—a sign of energy; a square jaw, which would denote pugnacity, endurance . . . though a close scrutiny revealed certain lines of weakness" (6). Of course, these particular interpretations can only be made retrospectively. Cushing knows (or believes he knows) that Alice Thayer is loyal, patient, and cheerful; that Henry Thayer was energetic but had a hidden weakness (which in Cushing's mind accounts for his economic and then physical downfall); and so on. Other matters are more open to interpretation, and Chesnutt reveals an interest (later to become one of his trademarks) in symbols that may be interpreted more than one way, depending on the perspective and context of a given moment. An extravagant pearl necklace given to Evelyn by Cushing, and later the offer of a Mediterranean cruise, under different circumstances would have been received with pleasure, but now that Manson is in the picture they are markers of Evelyn's discomfort with Cushing. The necklace, for example, "would be the badge of her servitude, which already she was finding irksome. It ought to be the token of her loyalty, but it was not; to wear it otherwise was disloyal" (63–64). Alice, similarly, wonders "why the same words meant such different things in the mouths of different men" (97).

Language—or, more generally, symbols, which for Chesnutt include objects and especially people—is fundamentally unstable; nothing simply *means* outside of particular circumstances that inflect or even create words' meaning. For the novelist, this state of affairs presents a distinct problem: on what basis can he communicate with his readers? In rejecting romance and attempting realism, Chesnutt reveals his answer: feelings and other abstract ideas cannot suffice; they are too liable to be distorted in the transference from one mind to another. If there is a basis for reliable communication, it must be economic in nature: only something like money seems to have the necessary stability to provide meaningful exchanges.

Although *Evelyn's Husband* is ostensibly a romance story, economic matters fuel the story more reliably than feelings of love do; certainly, for Chesnutt, economic motives may be defined and quantified much more certainly than abstractions like love can. Most notable in this regard is Cushing's pursuit of Evelyn, which is treated as essentially a business transaction. Because most of the Thayers' fortune was lost shortly before the death of Evelyn's father, Cushing (like Wendell Truscott in *A Business Career*) has covertly supplemented Alice and Evelyn Thayer's income. After travelling for a year, Cushing discovers that his goddaughter, a mere girl when he departed, has changed: "Evelyn's skirts had lengthened, and her childish angularities were rounding into delicate curves." After another year's travels, he finds that "Evelyn had become a beautiful woman" (13). So Cushing resolves, for the first time, to marry, and he approaches Evelyn's mother: "After a few words with Alice had convinced him that her daughter's heart was entirely free, it seemed to him that his wooing ought not to be difficult. He had much to offer a woman. Possessing Evelyn's confidence and respect, it ought not to be difficult to win her love" (13).

Although Chesnutt does not overtly emphasize Evelyn's relative powerlessness in this arrangement, he does elucidate the pragmatism that necessarily guides her thought process. Upon hearing of Cushing's proposal, Evelyn reflects:

> The prospect was not unpleasing; many women would have thought it alluring. Mr. Cushing was rich, and a young woman reared in the full tide of contemporary American life would scarcely despise its deity. Mr. Cushing was cultured and kind; she had been trained to regard him as the ideal man. From infancy her childish tricks and graces had been rehearsed with a view to their effect upon him. At school the hope of his approval had been an incentive to industry. To marry him would raise her from a position of genteel poverty to one of opulence and large outlook and leave to her mother what had been spent upon her maintenance and education. (14)

Interestingly, the narrator, with the reference to the "deity" of "contemporary American life," suggests that not money per se, but a zeitgeist in which money is pursued with almost worshipful zeal, is what influences Evelyn. She is not calculating so much as she is the product of American culture in the Industrial Age, allowing Chesnutt to portray her sympathetically while also accounting for her realistically mixed motives. Evelyn is not the prime mover in her fate; although her decision carries great stakes, she has no control over the consequences it will have. When Evelyn, attempting to preserve a modicum of independence, accepts Cushing's proposal but defers setting a wedding date, Cushing agrees, though he "felt a sudden and fierce impulse to foreclose his claim upon Evelyn" (15). With this choice of phrasing, the economic nature of their relationship cannot be made more clear.

Chesnutt does not attempt with this romance to achieve transcendence; Evelyn's love relationships are firmly pragmatic, which is not to say necessarily that they lack love but that they reflect a love that cannot be expressed in altogether nonpragmatic terms. For Chesnutt, feelings such as love surely exist, and perhaps even exist outside of worldly concerns such as economic survival, but they cannot really be known or expressed in other terms: the only language we have amounts to commercial language, the terms of exchange. Nor is it possible to abstract emotions from circumstances. Complicating Evelyn's decision is a fact of which Alice informs her after Manson has entered the scene as a rival: Cushing has contributed a large part of the Thayers' income since Henry Thayer's death some eighteen years ago. Though the practice is supposed to be a secret, Alice has silently been aware of it and accepted the gift, knowing just how vulnerable she—as a single mother—and her daughter are without the income that Cushing provides. Were Evelyn to reject Cushing, Alice's honor demands that the money be considered a loan rather than a gift, and she would have to spend the rest of her life repaying it. This state of affairs accentuates just how much Cushing's pursuit of Evelyn is like the purchase of a wife (he is owed a refund on his down payment), but it also binds Evelyn yet more strongly, since in rejecting Cushing she would exchange her happiness for her mother's misery. So, in terms anticipating Jake Barnes's in *The Sun Also Rises*—"Just exchange of values. You gave up something and got something else" (152)—Evelyn weighs her options: "If by marriage with her guardian she could repay the debt which burdened them, she would drive from her heart this sudden love, this delight to which she had just awakened. It had possessed some of the bitter sweetness of a forbidden thing. She could now look forward to the exquisite suffering of a martyr; it would be some compensation" (88).

If Cushing's pursuit of Evelyn is businesslike, Manson's is in its way no less possessive. His initial appeal to Evelyn is characteristically laconic and bold: "I want you for my own" (54). Like Truscott in *A Business Career,* Manson exhibits a magnetic power that distinguishes him from the aristocratic class among whom he seeks status; he is the proud descendant of backwoods Kentucky folk, and his feelings are described as "primitive" compared to Evelyn's (107). Despite his cocksure attitude, as a character suspended between two ways of life Manson represents Chesnutt's ambivalence about contemporary culture. His character anticipates that of Hurstwood in *Sister Carrie,* spurred on by motivations that are often obscure to him. In the following passage, the narrator summarizes Manson's perspective, but with an insight to which Manson himself presumably would not have access:

> To him Evelyn was a woman—*the* woman, of course, the one woman—to be loved and cherished; but, after all, merely subsidiary to her husband; an object to be sought, but, once she had become his, to be held in assured possession while the man put his energies at work to acquire other and more serious things—wealth, reputation, social position. Wives are not hard to find, for the qualified man who seeks one: a man may marry several—consecutively, of course, with the entire approval of society. He can scarcely hope to make more than one reputation; and it is rarely that having gained and lost wealth or social standing, he can regain either. (107–8)

To a contemporary scholar, what is important in *Evelyn's Husband* is its exploration of what a novel does; it is best read as a meta-text. As in a novel by Jane Austen (cited by Howells as the consummate realist[13]), for the perceptive reader the basic plot issues raised by the novel are resolved early on, and the remaining question is a writerly one: how can the parts of the story be sorted out so that they fall into what we implicitly may agree to be their rightful place? For a writer who wishes merely to entertain, the question is primarily one of effect; any of a number of narrative tricks might enable the "correct" pairings to come about. For a committed realist, however, the resolution cannot come too easily; questions of human nature, of rational cause and effect, of probability and plausibility must be addressed. Moreover, beyond (or within) even these considerations, a realist must not, as Chesnutt foresaw in composing *Evelyn's Husband,* allow complicated feelings and relationships to appear overly simple; complication itself is valuable because the part of life in which the realist is interested is complicated. Some novelists may tend to make life seem reassuringly simple, but realists tried to reject this tendency and restore to the genre its tenor of uncertainty and doubt.

The trick is to accomplish this without lapsing into absurdity, and it is here that *Evelyn's Husband* runs into trouble. As I have stated, the basic principle of the novel is to initiate a romance plot but then extend the narrative by a couple of hundred pages in order to complicate and interrogate how such a plot does its work. Chesnutt initiates the post-marriage plot by employing a fine novelistic device, perfectly suited for realism: lacking a complete perspective, Evelyn and Hugh interpret one another's intentions wrongly. Manson, distracted by a variety of monetary entanglements, neglects Evelyn, who in turn travels to New York to aid her ailing brother, Wentworth, leaving a deliberately vague note as retribution. When Manson, following up on the note, thinks he sees Cushing departing on a cruise with Evelyn (it's actually Alice, seeing him off), he assumes that Evelyn has left him for Cushing, and purchases a ticket on the next available steamer in order to pursue them.[14]

The second half of the novel rounds out the consequences of that decision: coincidentally, both Manson (whose ship was downed in a storm) and Cushing (who jumped overboard trying to save Wentworth, whom he escorted on the cruise for its palliative effects, from a suicide attempt) are stranded on the same small island. The remainder of the novel is disappointing but does reveal some interesting facets of Chesnutt's project. Having demonstrated, in a realist vein, that abstractions such as romantic love are always tinged by the social, he now attempts imaginatively to discern what the result would be of removing the element of the social. That is, he switches from a realist critique of romance to an exploration of what human nature is like in an imagined native state. The turn away from realism and toward an exploration of naturalism may be seen in this passage, which occurs at the novel's midpoint: "The great storm of that season is a matter of marine history. It is written in the records of insurance companies, some of which kept no more records thereafter. It is written in the registers of almshouses, and asylums for sailors' orphans. It worked widespread havoc, after the manner of Nature when she wishes to assert herself and teach man his true place in creation; and among other things, it sunk the *Adelaide*" (151). In the first half of this passage, the narrator relies on the equipment of a realist author: external, quantifiable data such as "the records of insurance companies." But within a few sentences, Chesnutt largely abandons that approach for one that relies instead on a worldview which—although it too seems to be supported by evidence—can really only be hypothesized. He continues to refer to evidence, such as maps and sailing charts that might identify Cushing's and Manson's position precisely, but only to note their inadequacy to tell the story that he now seems intent on telling. Abandoning the precise economic observation that marks the first half of the novel, he now attempts to articulate perceptions like that of blindness, things readers must ultimately take on faith if they have not experienced them personally.[15]

The second half of the novel is engaged with this question: in men (the use of the masculine noun is deliberate, reflecting the question as Chesnutt seems to ask it), is the tendency toward love or the tendency toward hate stronger? Both instincts, as they surface in Cushing and Manson on the island, are magnified; or rather, in the absence of other influences that might mitigate them, they loom larger than ever. Cushing notes that "[t]he primal instinct, which had impelled him to feel, a year before in the full tide of his newborn passion, that he could kill anyone who should rob him of Evelyn, now returned with redoubled force" (170). Interestingly, it is his imagination—even more than his emotions—that seems dangerously unfettered: "Under the circumstances, it was inevitable that to an active, imaginative mind, smarting with a sense of outrage, every selfish consideration should present itself with unnatural force" (177). With apparently unintentional irony, given the rather outlandish turn the plot has taken at that point, Chesnutt identifies the unleashed imagination as a threat to human decency.

Cushing resolves to have his revenge on Manson, but finds that civilization is still "in possession" of him, and that his conscience will not allow him simply to kill his foe (177). Instead, he will conduct an experiment. Rather than reveal his identity to the now-blind Manson, Cushing takes on the persona of "Singleton" and nurses him back to health. In a sequence of numerous, ironic statements, Manson swears eternal friendship to "Singleton" but also vows to have his revenge on Cushing at the next available opportunity.[16] Intones the narrator, "[s]eldom does it fall to the lot of a man to be at one and the same moment loved and hated by the same person—to be simultaneously the object of two great passions which are direct opposites. . . . What might result from the clash of two antagonistic feelings, both in full flower—hatred and friendship, gratitude and revenge, would be a curious problem. What would a man do, who should discover that the friend to whom he owed his life was the enemy whose life he had sworn to take?" (197–98). In an apparent plea to prospective publishers, the narrator concludes this monologue by noting, "[t]he problem would interest almost any one."

Continuing his self-referential approach, and confirming that he had a sense of how odd his narrative must be starting to look to its prospective publishers, Chesnutt offers a defense of coincidence in literature:

> We often speak of coincidences as strange; but the narrow margins by which related events sometimes fail to coincide are quite as remarkable, the difference being that we know of the one and seldom of the other. The material world is [one] of orderly development; left to itself, it works steadily towards its predestined end. The moral world, whose laws are less well known, and which involves the uncertain element of free will, seems often a world of chance. It was indeed wonderful that Cushing and Manson should have come together on a lonely island in the Atlantic ocean; but it was no less strange that they should not have met in New York [thus resolving their misunderstanding before their ships departed]. The chances were a thousand to one in favor of the latter contingency. Had chance put Cushing in touch with his pursuer, instead of keeping them apart, this story could never have been written. (226–27)

As a defense of the far-fetched developments of the latter half of the novel, this statement is weak, even desperate. As a fragment of a literary philosophy, it carries more interest. Chesnutt indicates that coincidences necessarily happen; while some can be observed, others (such as the failure of two individuals to meet) cannot. A realist author, concerned with both the observable and the truthful, must nevertheless make choices; not every contingency, or possible contingency, can or should be recorded. However realistic, a novel cannot shirk from its duty of providing some compelling interest to the reader—if the novelist somehow evaded the responsibility of making narrative choices, no story would be possible at all. A degree of coincidence, from a realist's perspective, is not only allowable but unavoidable; the question is how, and to what degree, coincidence is employed. And, although Chesnutt's use of coincidence in

Evelyn's Husband stretches beyond reason's and realism's limits, one must keep in mind that, at this point, he is learning and extending his craft. By way of comparison, in *The House Behind the Cedars,* he uses coincidence skillfully, as P. Jay Delmar argues, "to emphasize the role played by forces external to the characters in the downfall of the characters themselves" (97).

Evelyn's Husband, however, once again reveals Chesnutt's distrust that realism could pay the bills. The thematic complexity of the novel dissolves into incoherence even as the novel's plot winds toward its conventional, happy resolution. The men are finally rescued and taken to Rio de Janeiro, where (fortuitously) a world-renowned surgeon is able to restore Manson's eyesight. "Singleton," therefore, brings his experiment to fruition by arranging for Manson to meet Cushing in a duel. Upon learning that his sworn enemy is also his savior, what will Manson do?[17] At last seeing all, Manson finds that he cannot kill Cushing; but, believing that his life must end if he cannot avenge his enemy, he uses the pistol provided for the duel to attempt suicide. Evelyn, who is in Rio de Janeiro to attend to her brother (who has ended up there after surviving his attempt to drown himself), arrives just in time to deflect Manson's hand as he fires; the bullet strikes Cushing but not fatally. Cushing considers that he has been "justly punished" for deceiving Manson (283), while the moral Manson articulates is so petty as to seem anticlimactic: it is that "[s]ecretiveness with those we love is a dangerous game" (280).

The results of Cushing's (and Chesnutt's) experiment may be even less definite than they appear. Does Manson's decision to forgo revenge prove that love instinctively trumps hate, or merely that Manson is more enduringly socialized than he seems? For that matter, what is the source of Cushing's solicitousness toward the helpless Manson—is it nature or nurture?[18] Ultimately, although Chesnutt does not develop the point overtly, the only conclusion that may definitively be made is that the answers remain elusive; they cannot be found with recourse to the imagination alone, nor arrived at empirically. The real question addressed by the last half of *Evelyn's Husband* is a question about authorship: how, by whose authority, can this story be told? The delicate negotiation undergone by Cushing and Manson on the island—one literally blind, the vision of both figuratively obscured by lack of perspective—has to do, at its root, with the nature of the story they tell: for Manson, the tale is that of a wronged husband who must attain revenge, but for "Singleton," it is that of the loss of a beloved woman to a "coarse, unselfish" youth (212). Ironically, in the absence of clarifying contextual information, Manson is perfectly willing to accept, and even to identify with, Singleton's side of the story; he goes so far to remark that "[y]our position seems so much like my own!" (212). But Chesnutt shows that it's an open question whether Evelyn ever loved either man, although each man's version of the story depends on the assumption that she loved *him.* Undercutting the attempt at a naturalistic experiment which digs beneath social convention is the conviction, subtle but always there, that the experiment itself is impossible: society remains even where its trappings do not. And society is defined by, in, and through its participants' narrative choices, even as those choices are limited, ironically, by social convention.

The Presence of the Unsaid: Reading Race Back into the Early Novels

As we have seen, in his early career as a novelist Chesnutt is preoccupied with the question of what makes an identity, especially in a world of encompassing change. As Eric Sundquist writes, in the realist era, "an age of love with competing systems and transfixed by the inevitable importance of exact detail, the problems of the novelist and the man in the street alike are dispiriting: How can life be organized, governed, made plausible?" ("Introduction" 11). Chesnutt, although he was initially reluctant to define his career as an extended commentary about race, saw that the organization of life was a constant concern, one visibly manifested by unceasing acts of interpretation, of establishing and reasserting hierarchies. And he saw that heredity generally and race specifically were central organizing principles of American life at the turn of the century. In the remainder of this chapter, I explore the subdued presence of blackness in *A Business Career, The Rainbow Chasers,* and *Evelyn's Husband.* These novels not only offer somewhat realistic portrayals of upper-class, urban, Northern white culture at a particular moment in history; they also suggest that this culture, which defines itself by its assertion of exclusivity, is in truth more mixed than its members are aware.

Understandably, as one of only a few African American authors who attained literary success between the end of Reconstruction and the Harlem Renaissance, Chesnutt has been scrutinized for his willingness to use fiction to uplift the race. As we will see in the next chapter, some critics have regarded his works as politically counterproductive or evasive of racial realities. Yet even the early novels discussed in this chapter, easily dismissed as apolitical entertainments, are not entirely escapist. In subtle but, I argue, significant ways, *A Business Career, The Rainbow Chasers,* and *Evelyn's Husband* are altered by inconspicuous references to their characters' multiracial makeup.

In a study written when Chesnutt still had "scarcely been read with anything approaching the seriousness he deserves," Sundquist defends Chesnutt against the argument that was then more current: "If it is objected that, after all, he wrote 'only' about race, one would have to bear in mind that . . . it was nearly impossible for the minority writer to do otherwise" (*To Wake* 12). It should be noted that the characters and scenes employed in these early, rejected novels probably are drawn more closely from Chesnutt's own life experiences than the novels that deal overtly with racial issues. And, if the audience he sought in the late 1800s and early 1900s expected African American authors to write about race, contemporary criticism has not been much more broad-minded, rarely taking note of black authors' portrayals of "white" culture such as Richard Wright's *Savage Holiday* and Zora Neale Hurston's *Seraph on the Suwanee.*[19] Chesnutt's motives in attempting to avoid overtly racial themes in *A Business Career, The Rainbow Chasers,* and *Evelyn's Husband* can only be speculated upon: perhaps he wished to move past what he saw as the confinement of racial themes, or perhaps he imagined that writing about Northern white characters was a surer path to success.

Whatever Chesnutt's motives, the theme of interracial contact is not so much absent as it is subdued in these novels. Each centers around a marriage plot, and in each pairing there is a broad hint, subtle enough to go unrecognized by a casual reader, that one of the participants in the desired marriage has African American ancestry. Interracial marriage, or miscegenation, was of course anathema to mainstream white sensibilities when Chesnutt wrote, and to portray such an occurrence casually, or outside the accepted (but still controversial) genre of the "tragic mulatta" plot, would have been professional suicide for an author. So Chesnutt's flirtation with such a theme in each novel is compelling evidence that literary politics—the question of exactly how much he could get away with—was very much on his mind. If one were to imagine a version of *The House Behind the Cedars* in which all direct references to passing are omitted, and neither Tryon nor the reader ever learns directly that Rena is partly African American, the result might be similar to Chesnutt's ostensibly "white" novels.

Each of the three novels thematically explores the matter of interpretation: individuals are treated as texts to be read, and the act of reading one another is both culturally pervasive and integral to the maintenance of social hierarchies. In *A Business Career,* for example, physical characteristics are scrutinized for signs of "character," even though Chesnutt demonstrates that in discerning "character," one generally finds what one looks for in the first place (23). That this theme intersects with the novel's commentary on gender and class is easy to see: characters frequently hone in on the data that they believe will confirm the assumptions to which they are predisposed. But the hint at a presence of blackness is much more subtle. Wendell Truscott, the object of Stella Merwin's evolving acts of reading and eventually the object of her love, is described in the opening paragraph as a gentleman "of dark complexion, with coarse, dark hair growing slightly grey about the edges, square shoulders and large hands" (3). Though far from definitive evidence that Truscott is part black, the description of his "dark complexion" and "coarse hair" is at least comparable to the description of William Miller in *The Marrow of Tradition,* whose "swarthy complexion and his curly hair revealed what had been described in the laws of some of our states as a 'visible admixture' of African blood" (49)—not to mention the description of one of that novel's white characters, Tom Delamere, as "dark almost to swarthiness" with "black eyes [and] curly hair of raven tint" (15–16). For Chesnutt, the distinction between a black person such as Miller and a white one like Truscott or Delamere is social and political, not biological, although he recognized the radicalism of this idea in his time and frequently made the point obliquely.

Rather than leading to a definite conclusion that Truscott is or is not of mixed race, the physical description should cause us to consider what Chesnutt may have meant in introducing such ambiguous evidence, particularly at a moment in American history when racial ambiguity was a potentially explosive topic. Certainly, the introduction of a seed of doubt as to Truscott's racial "purity" is in sync with Chesnutt's overall intent of questioning the habits of interpretation by which people make the world. That is, if readers—relying, of course, no less than the book's characters upon physical characteristics as a basis for judgment—assume that they know Truscott wholly, the joke may be on them. Very possibly, the datum that many would regard as outweighing every other consideration—that of the protagonist's race—is, if they could know it, staring them in the face. Chesnutt's unwillingness to remark directly on Truscott's possible racial indeterminacy might be explained by his recognition that most readers, if clued in, would miss the point, fixating instead on the question of his racial heritage. If, on the other hand, they get the right point—that Truscott is, despite initial appearances, a worthy man—only by *not* noticing the physical suggestion of mixed race, then Chesnutt's agenda is neatly (if secretively) fulfilled.

Unlike *A Business Career, The Rainbow Chasers* includes an acknowledged black character, Quilliams's former servant George. In some respects, George comes across as a stereotypical portrayal, one that mimics racist tropes current in Chesnutt's day. His most notable characteristic is his doglike fealty: even after Quilliams fires him due to his newly straitened circumstances, George continues to oversee his former employer's meals and dress for no pay. Recalling that Quilliams once saved his life, George explains: "I won't have no trouble to get another job, suh, with yo' recommen' but I don't like to leave you, for I'm used to you an' you're used to me, an I'm sho' you ain't goin' to find nobody to look after yo' vittles an' yo' clo's an' ten' to yo' ores and acids an' reto'ts as well as I does—you sho' ain't" (8). Additionally, as the above quotation illustrates, George's dialogue seems meant to tap the white readers' market for stereotypical depictions of dialect rather than to convey vernacular speech accurately.[20]

George's loyalty, at any rate, is at least not without an explanation: he sticks with Quilliams out of a sense of obligation, Quilliams having once saved his life. Quilliams is eager to dismiss the debt—he claims saving George was "[a] simple act of humanity . . . which any man would have performed for another" (8)—characteristically preferring the "practical" or rationalist explanation to the sentimental one. He attributes George's loyalty to his "simple African intellect" (62). His main rationale in interpreting his relationship to George as he does is to justify an ideology that separates him from people like his servant, propping up social hierarchies as though they are an unavoidable consequence of individual autonomy. Rather than conceding their common human impulse, Quilliams insists on characterizing his own generosity as merely rational and George's as simply irrational. Acknowledging George's debt to him would, from a broader perspective, force awareness of the social debt that he, as a privileged white, owes to George and other African Americans. As a corporate character, Quilliams's stance of detachment is integral to his status in the social hierarchy.

With momentary candor, Quilliams explains: "I am friendly to the colored race. My father fought to give them freedom. I sympathize with their higher aspirations, and would willingly see them attain, by worthy effort, to actual equality with the more favored race among whom their lot is cast. But personally, I must confess, I like them better as they are. The equality of all men is a beautiful theory; the unquestioned superiority of some is a comfortable fact" (62). Quilliams equivocally accepts the notion of equality as a "theory" even as he confesses relief that the theory has not yet been proven in fact. His subscription to the capitalistic ideology of autonomy and self-reliance informs his thinking: George is free to chart his own course, but what Quilliams assumes to be his inherent qualities—even his sense of obligation to Quilliams, dismissed as innate ignorance—necessarily validate things as they are, belying the faith in self-reliance and racial uplift to which Quilliams theoretically subscribes.

In other words, Quilliams assumes, as a white man and heir to a fortune, that the hierarchy as it exists is just, based on the circular reasoning that its very existence proves its justice. He is willing to concede that his perspective may be biased: "[A] Negro, I imagine, might think differently. There is everything in the point of view" (62). Even such an admission is risky: in acknowledging the contingency of his perspective, Quilliams subtly undercuts the tenuous logic of capitalism, which depends on the autonomy of individuals and therefore is threatened by the mere consideration of someone else's viewpoint. Quilliams's position at the top of the cultural hierarchy, in short, depends on regarding himself as entirely autonomous, separate from others, and on remaining as detached as possible from the circumstances that constitute his life.

Quilliams often assumes that events occur fortuitously; his consistent good fortune seems to endorse his cultural status. Ironically, were he to act more industriously, he would undermine his own capitalist stance by acknowledging that his place in the economic order must be earned. In contrast to the detached Quilliams, who simply lets things happen to him, is the assiduous George, who is constantly (as readers are occasionally allowed to see) working behind the scenes to ensure a successful outcome of events. Not only does he secretly arrange to have Quilliams fed and clothed properly, but he is integral to Quilliams's successful negotiation of the returning-father subplot, as he gets a suspicious neighbor drunk to keep him from revealing that Julia's father has returned.

The last scene in the novel clarifies Chesnutt's analysis. Quilliams and Julia have become engaged, and George happens to arrive on the scene with a bouquet of flowers to present to Julia. Reflects Quilliams, "I do not know what George's thoughts may have been. Doubtless he had never thought of me as a possible married man, but as a practical man he rose to the occasion" (188). The reader, however, recognizes clearly that George has not merely risen to the occasion spontaneously; having a bouquet at the ready, he must have predicted the engagement was about to occur. As the character who has covertly directed the plot to a successful resolution (and thus can correctly predict the outcome), George has revealed himself to be both the best capitalist and the best craftsman. While Quilliams and other characters (such as the politician Nutter) confidently anticipate success arising naturally from their efforts, George actually makes things happen in the world. That his social position does not match his talents and abilities indicts the faulty logic by which capitalism and its hierarchies are perpetuated. George does not fail in the capitalist system, but is failed by it.

In addition to sketching out an analysis of economic racism through the character of George, in *The Rainbow Chasers* Chesnutt continues the pattern of *A Business Career* in subtly implying miscegenation. Quilliams, the narrator, seems semiconscious of the issue when he first describes Julia "Gray": she is "dark, *not too dark*, with brown hair, verging upon black" (26; emphasis added). An earlier typescript reveals that Chesnutt took pains with this initial physical description of Julia, for example crossing out "of complexion" after "not too dark" and changing "eyes of gray that at times flashed almost black in their intensity" to "grey eyes that at times flashed almost jet in their intensity." In another version she is "a brunette, not too swarthy, with brown hair verging on black, and grey eyes that at times flashed almost jet in their intensity." In yet another draft, he omits altogether any description of Julia. It is as if Chesnutt is attempting to figure out exactly how many hints he can insert about Julia's racial heritage without getting caught.[21]

The description of Julia is, in fact, reminiscent of Howells's description of Rhoda Aldgate in *An Imperative Duty,* which (as we have seen) is alluded to in Chesnutt's novel. Through the eyes of his protagonist, Edward Olney, Howells describes "the particulars of [Rhoda's] beauty; her slender height, her rich complexion of olive, with a sort of under-stain of red, and the inky blackness of her eyes and hair. Her face was of almost classical perfection, and the hair, crinkling away to either temple, grew low upon the forehead" (147). In the case of Rhoda Aldgate, readers know (or quickly learn) that this vision of beauty is racially mixed. Knowledge of this sort is a thematic key to the novella. The actual presence of African American "blood" in Rhoda, Howells shows, is immaterial; what matters is people's knowledge (or lack of knowledge) of Rhoda's real heredity. Were her secret to be revealed, Rhoda and Olney recognize, she would be unable to maintain her position in society. On the other hand, both assume that Rhoda's suitor Bloomingdale would not change his attitude upon learning the truth, an (untested) assumption by which they recognize his inherent nobility.

Given the centrality of the theme of possession (or dispossession) of knowledge in *An Imperative Duty,* and Chesnutt's apparent mindfulness of Howells's novella as he wrote *The Rainbow Chasers,* a significant difference between the works is that Howells shares with his readers the knowledge of his heroine's mixed blood, whereas Chesnutt does not. Readers of *An Imperative Duty* are given a privileged perspective in that they can see more than the characters can at a given moment. Olney, for example, seems dense in not grasping the situation accurately in chapter 5, given the broad hints provided by Rhoda's aunt concerning her racial heritage. Chesnutt seems less apt to trust his readers with similar knowledge about his heroine, perhaps reasoning that most of his readers would respond like Howells's average Bostonian—as if that one piece of knowledge signified everything—and not like the broad-minded Bloomingdale. Or perhaps the response he feared to provoke in his readers is that of Edward Olney, who shares Howells's relative liberalism on race but changes his behavior, subtly but significantly, upon learning Rhoda's secret. Immediately after Olney's illumination, the formerly unattainable Rhoda becomes the almost fetishistic object of his desire—a consequence, it seems, of the strong hand his new knowledge has given him in manipulating events to his advantage.[22]

In *The Rainbow Chasers,* I have argued, Quilliams's increasing agency in the ongoing development of a "self" is enabled by his willingness to sacrifice a static concept of his identity and embrace the possibilities and risks of interaction with others. Identity, in other words, must be adaptive and fluid in order for one to negotiate the precarious changes of late-nineteenth-century culture. Regardless of his liberalism, Olney shows little of this adaptability. Quilliams's willingness at the end of *The Rainbow Chasers* to be satisfied in an anticipated life of poverty with his loved one rings truer as a moral gesture than Olney's commitment to Rhoda in *An Imperative Duty.* In refusing to be dissuaded from pursuing Rhoda's hand, Olney retains his integrity but risks nothing. Just the opposite, he navigates the safest possible route in enacting his desire, and superfluously enhances this self-protection by moving with Rhoda to Rome, where no one will suspect or care about her racial heritage—even though no one has ever suspected the truth in Boston, either.

Howells flatters his readers by implying that they can share the broad-mindedness of individuals such as Olney and Bloomingdale, avoiding the prejudiced attitudes of Meredith Aldgate and others. Although his approach may be in some respects more realistic than Chesnutt's, its realism is compromised by this attitude toward the reader, since it seems illogical to suppose that the average reader of *An Imperative Duty* differs so substantially from the typical individual within the novella. As Cathy Boeckmann points out, Howells makes a potentially subversive message safe for these readers by banishing his characters to Rome (154), thus protecting himself in exactly the way Olney does. His thesis is that a sense of moral "duty" is misplaced when performing that duty does not have moral consequences; despite its topicality in dealing with a racial theme, nothing in *An Imperative Duty* is presented so as to persuade readers to abandon racist habits of interpretation. Nor does *The Rainbow Chasers* attempt to make a case against racism; but in writing it Chesnutt seems cognizant, at least, of his audience's limitations. Even though *The Rainbow Chasers* does not directly thematize the issues of power that surface in Howells's work, Chesnutt is more clear-eyed in assessing how those issues encompass the reading audience itself.

The technique of withholding knowledge, and therefore a certain amount of power, from the reader continues in *Evelyn's Husband.* In writing these works, Chesnutt is aware that introducing a racial theme would provoke a reaction among his readers, but he shows little confidence in his own ability to channel this reaction in productive directions. Thus, his commentary on race remains covert. *Evelyn's Husband* is concerned with the reliability of physical and hereditary factors as determiners of character, though it barely mentions race directly. As learned by George Tryon in *The House Behind the Cedars,* whose pursuit of marriage as (at least in part) a sort of economic speculation brings him to grief, the mere possibility of a presence of blackness in a prospective mate undercuts the logic by which the dominant class maintains its power. The white, aristocratic class represented in *The House Behind the Cedars* knows this very well, which is why it so forcefully denies even the possibility of an African American drop entering the bloodline. *Evelyn's Husband* does not seem to be concerned with such a lofty analysis, but it does enact the marriage of Hugh Manson, a "primitive" white man who aspires to a position atop the hierarchy, to aristocratic Evelyn Thayer, accepted unquestioningly as white despite "her rich southern coloring—the belated inheritance of some distant ancestor" (25). It is hard to imagine, knowing what we do of Chesnutt's thoughts on race and ancestry, that this reference to the physical manifestation of Evelyn's heredity (and several other references to her dark complexion) is accidental. Rather, it is part of a theme the novel develops concerning people's subscription to dubious hereditary principles, which again are seen as tools to maintain power.

If people are willing to overlook the "weakness" presumed to be inherited genetically from "some distant ancestor" which has manifested itself in Evelyn's dissolute brother, Wentworth, on what basis can one maintain that heredity matters in the first place? The anxiety displayed by the white, aristocratic characters of *Evelyn's Husband* seems to stem from the possibility not that a genetically weak person will somehow find his or her way into the upper classes, but that one of their own might be exposed as already the carrier of a culturally undesirable trait. Heredity is treated by the characters in *Evelyn's Husband* as an influence on behavior, but one that can be mitigated. Wentworth, though he will always struggle with the gene that supposedly induces him to go on drunken sprees, is redeemable for one simple reason: he is a member of the privileged class; for that class to maintain its privilege, it is *necessary* that individuals like Wentworth be redeemed. On the other hand, Leonie, the white (but "dark-haired" and "black-eyed") maid, is seen by the aristocratic characters as much more a product of her heredity, and less redeemable: "If she had not profited in every way by the training [provided by the Thayers], it was certainly not the fault of her mistress; heredity has a way of intruding its claims, now and then, against the influences of environment" (5). Though talented (at the end of the novel she has become a vaudeville performer), Leonie is regarded as inherently sinful and a burden on her employers, whereas Wentworth, though he is indirectly responsible for the family's calamity in the South Seas, ends the novel in his "rightful" place as family heir. Chesnutt exposes the logic of such a situation not in order to appeal to some imagined, "rightful" hierarchy of talents, but to complicate the meaning of heredity to a point where it can no longer be meaningful at all. Wentworth, Evelyn, and Leonie all might be biracial, or none of them might be, and each has weaknesses and gifts. It is, Chesnutt hints, simply illogical to try to account for such character variances systematically, given the number of variables that actually are in play—though this form of illogic carries considerable cultural force.[23]

As he does later in *The Quarry,* Chesnutt gives some credence to hereditary principles, but concludes that, in the end, the contradictory nature of the available data makes such principles functionally useless. Despite many people's unquestioning adherence to such principles in their speech, in practice everyone implicitly acknowledges that heredity is a deeply problematic way of making judgments. Ultimately, people do not use hereditary principles to make judgments about individuals, but always to enforce class distinctions that favor their own interests with a minimum of cultural disruption. And, although he does not dare to introduce the factor of race directly as he employs this insight, race is unavoidably part of the discussion, which is why Evelyn's dark complexion carries interpretive weight.

In his controversial series of essays for the *Boston Evening Transcript,* published under the title "The Future American" in 1900, Chesnutt asserts that racial amalgamation is not only likely in the future, it is already occurring much more often than whites acknowledge or, in many cases, are even aware. The series' thesis, which can seem retrogressive from a contemporary perspective, was potentially radical for his contemporary readers: as Dean McWilliams states, it "proposes as the twentieth-century's savior the nineteenth-century nightmare. The Future American is the mulatto" (51). In his fiction, Chesnutt advances a similar thesis, but is more interested in exploring the psychology of white resistance to this apparently inevitable occurrence. In the short story "White Weeds," for example, a Southerner, Professor Carson, "worrie[s] himself into an early grave" due to his suspicion (unfounded, it appears) that his wife is part black (*Short Fiction* 403). His wife, offended at learning that Carson's love depends on her racial makeup, had refused to deny the truth of his suspicion. Chesnutt's main point does not seem to be that unacknowledged amalgamation occurs; as "The Future American" essays demonstrate, that is easily enough proven. The real target of his fiction is the cost in anxiety of the constant scrutiny caused by the cultural aversion to mixed-race couplings, especially considering the dubious rewards received in turn. Explains one of his colleagues, Carson's "exaggerated race feeling . . . is more than a healthy instinct for the preservation of a type; it is more than a prejudice. It is an obsession" (403). The longer works *Mandy Oxendine* and *The House Behind the Cedars* extend this analysis of cultural attitudes toward racial intermixture through the motif of the "passing" novel.

A Business Career, The Rainbow Chasers, and *Evelyn's Husband,* despite their initial appearance as exclusively white-oriented "entertainments," should be read into the tradition of Chesnutt's writing that explores the psychological and cultural cost of maintaining a facade of racial integrity. It might reasonably be argued that Chesnutt's employment of potentially mixed-race characters is so subtle as to be meaningless; certainly, readers who were not alerted to Chesnutt's interest in interracial themes would not notice their employment in these novels. If, in other words, Chesnutt had continued with the pattern suggested in *A Business Career, The Rainbow Chasers,* and *Evelyn's Husband,* he would not have come to be known for important commentary on race in America. On the other hand, these novels do provide to Chesnutt scholars some important hints about the themes that would continue growing in importance during his writing career. If nothing else, they represent his consciousness of the degree to which race, even when it is not the ostensible topic of conversation, subtly permeates American discourse; race is never more than an inch beneath the surface. And they demonstrate to the careful reader an awareness, central to his later fiction, of the politics that underlie such a situation.

In his notes for the novel that would be a follow-up to *Invisible Man,* Ralph Ellison suggests that whites who preach racial purity are often, unconsciously, repudiating their own identities: "[M]any who think they don't [have African American heredity], do" (362). Perceptively, Ellison regards the abhorrence of mixed blood as an instrument of power: more significant than the question of having or not having "Negro blood" is one's "manipulation of race," which for the dominant group means denying the diversity that, in Ellison's view, fundamentally shapes and creates American culture (361–62).

Chesnutt shares Ellison's analysis, but he does not share, at the turn of the century, Ellison's ability or willingness to articulate that analysis forcefully. As I will take up in the next chapter, a fundamental difficulty Chesnutt faced as a writer was how to negotiate the bold indictment he wished to serve up to his audience, especially the white readers who would make or break his career, and the need to please those same readers. In *A Business Career, The Rainbow Chasers,* and *Evelyn's Husband,* one sees Chesnutt being analytical but not yet bold. His preoccupation with questions of racial identity—what constitutes it, and how does it function politically?—is demonstrated, instead, in the way he slips hints of these questions into his narrative, not to be noticed except by the reader who has learned to look for them.

2

Time Passing

Chesnutt's Revisions of the "Tragic Mulatta" Tale

Debates about the "tragic mulatto" or "tragic mulatta" genre of fiction and its uses have centered on its realism, or lack thereof. Sterling Brown, identifying the genre as the source of a pervasive stereotype in his 1937 survey *The Negro in American Fiction,* pointed out that the genre tends to rely more on popular white perceptions of mulatto life than on the lived experiences of mixed-race individuals; as Werner Sollors puts it in his summary of Brown, these characterizations were often "merely derived from convention and not from life" (223). For his part, Sollors is largely unconvinced by Brown's reasoning that the genre is inherently contaminated by its stereotypes. The danger, Sollors argues, is that *no* depiction of biracial people's lives will be found acceptably to detach itself from available stereotypes, "making any representation of biracial characters appear to be 'unrealistic' and potentially dangerous hetero-stereotypes" (232). All characterizations are in some sense conventional, and in Sollors's view it makes sense to evaluate the work performed by individual representations of mulattos, but not from any imagined purist position. Although he does not make much of it, implicitly Sollors seems to believe that Brown's argument is based on an appeal to racial authenticity, a fictive convention no less stereotypical or hazardous than those surrounding the figure of the mulatto. To an extent, Sollors seems unfair toward Brown, who does not argue against representations of mulatto characters per se but against the "tragic mulatto" as a stereotype. Still, the point is well taken that even a seemingly conventional portrayal, firmly within the genre, might have subversive possibilities: "[I]t is possible to see the outline of a less visible counter-tradition in which the Mulatto actually appears as a most upsetting and subversive character who illuminates the paradoxes of 'race' in America" (234).

In his first long works that focus on African American characters, the long-unpublished novella *Mandy Oxendine* (which finally appeared in print in 1997) and the successfully published novel *The House Behind the Cedars* (1900), Chesnutt seems both to subscribe to and to "illuminate the paradoxes of" the standard conventions for racial fiction at the turn of the century, especially those concerning mixed-race people. Critics of *The House Behind the Cedars,* in particular, have debated whether or not the novel qualifies as subversive or is merely a conventional, stereotypical portrayal.[1] That his novel resides on the border between these interpretations illustrates, at least, that Chesnutt was not strongly or openly able to decimate the genre and its harmful stereotypes. On the other hand, he was very much engaged with what was then a largely unacknowledged problem within realism: given that our notions of "reality" are substantially infused with conventions of thought, how can a writer—even assuming he was able to imagine himself, to a degree, out of the boundaries of these conventions—induce his readers to see things through new eyes?

This philosophical problem was for Chesnutt also a practical one. Although he assumed that a sympathetic audience, consisting of some black readers but primarily liberal whites, was capable of supporting his writing career, he also seemed to sense that this audience would react favorably only to an approach that was reassuring rather than challenging. He writes implicitly with the attitude that his white, Northern readership will welcome an exposé of racism in the South, but might squirm if asked too directly to regard their own implication in racial injustice or to consider their own responsibility to act. Such an approach as his readers would find acceptable could not satisfy Chesnutt's desire to be a politically effective writer unless he managed to exercise great care and skill, and his attempts to negotiate the problem of audience carefully and skillfully account for much of what can be seen in his fiction.

In *Modernism and the Harlem Renaissance,* Houston A. Baker, Jr., takes on the twinned questions of how African Americans may survive and how they may create new representational spaces for themselves by defining two major strategic categories: "mastery of form" and "deformation of mastery." In the former, any subversive intent is deeply masked, and a writer narrates experience in a seemingly conventional matter in pursuit of "some intended gain" (31). In the latter, one "distinguishes rather than conceals . . . secures territorial advantage and heightens a group's survival possibilities" through a more disruptive, less conservative narrative form (51). Though Baker describes mastery as normally preceding deformation, a compelling understanding of these two early works arises when *Mandy Oxendine* is regarded as Chesnutt's deformation of a form he could easily have mastered, the "tragic mulatta" story, and *The House Behind the Cedars* as his concession (though not without posing challenging problems) to his audience as he mastered the established tradition.[2] Both are conspicuously attempts at a story in the "tragic mulatta" tradition, in which biracial heroines were "either 'tragically' torn emotionally in their racial identity or victims of a 'tragic' flaw which ultimately led to an unpleasant ending for themselves or the people that surrounded them" (Watson 48). Although *The House Behind the Cedars* is by nearly any measure the more successful book, at least a brief exploration of the earlier work may prove fruitful, if for no other reason than to explore what is meant by "successful." An analysis of *Mandy Oxendine* both enables a stronger understanding of *The House Behind the Cedars* and, in its own right, reveals some salient features of Chesnutt's literary approach to social problems.

Mandy Oxendine: The Unsentimental Sentimental Tale

Mandy Oxendine, Chesnutt's first work of long fiction, was submitted to editor Walter Hines Page in 1897 to be considered for publication either as a serial in the *Atlantic* or as a single volume with Houghton Mifflin. It was rejected, and there is no indication that Chesnutt submitted it elsewhere (Hackenberry xv). That is not entirely surprising, since *Mandy Oxendine* comes across as an uncontrolled mess of a book. While William L. Andrews cites it as "a prototype of a new brand of African American literary realism in the early twentieth century" (Foreword x), others such as Charles Hackenberry and Matthew Wilson have faulted the novella for abandoning the realism of the early chapters in favor of audience-pleasing melodrama. These critics tend to agree that the difficulty Chesnutt faced in writing *Mandy Oxendine* is that of audience: as Hackenberry writes, the novella remains "just within the limits of what popular race fiction would allow" (xxiv). Wilson concurs, stating that Chesnutt's "artistic ambitions" in this book "were almost impossible to realize" (*Whiteness* 46). The interesting question, then, is whether or not Chesnutt's failure with this book was, in some sense, purposeful—whether his uncontrolled, haphazard appeals to readers' hearts and heads are a result of his immature development as an artist or, just possibly, a more sophisticated attempt to work through the uncontrolled, ugly nature of the world he was depicting. In any case, by the time of the novella's rejection Chesnutt was on the verge of breaking out as a mature writer whose publications little resemble what is found in *Mandy Oxendine,* which finally appeared in print a century after Chesnutt had submitted it.[3] He had learned to produce writings that would be palatable to audiences, though whether the result was a stronger or a weaker vision is subject to debate.

Mandy Oxendine is the story of two light-skinned African Americans: Tom Lowrey, a young schoolteacher who has returned to North Carolina after being educated in the North, and Amanda (Mandy) Oxendine, Tom's onetime love who, feeling herself spurned by Tom's longer-than-promised absence, elects to pass as white and is secretly engaged to a wealthy white rapscallion, Robert Utley. Presence and absence are constructed by the novella's characters as near-absolutes. When Tom is away, his devotion to Mandy withers away rather quickly, and yet upon his return he fully expects their romance to pick up right where it left off. Mandy's perspective is similar: although her attachment to Tom appears to fade somewhat more slowly, by the time of his return she is fully divested of longing for him, but also willing to consider marriage to him as a sort of backup plan: "[S]he would hold Lowrey in reserve, and if Utley married his cousin, she would take Lowrey, after making him do reasonable penance for his former neglect" (41). Instead, as the result of a chain of events in which both Tom and Mandy end up suspected and then absolved of Utley's murder, Mandy is exposed as a mulatto, marries Tom, and embarks with him to an uncertain future. For a work that seems firmly rooted in the sentimental tradition, this is a remarkably unsentimental story.

Critics have disagreed about the degree of challenge *Mandy Oxendine* presents to its readers. Andrews, in his foreword to the 1997 edition, finds the work politically "reticent" compared to Chesnutt's subsequent novels and speculates that Chesnutt "may have been trying to determine for himself just how far a writer in his position should go in representing forthrightly and objectively the complex web of personal desire, racial obligation, and socioeconomic ambition that held the mixed-blood in social suspension in the post–Civil War South" (x). Hackenberry, on the other hand, describes *Mandy Oxendine* as a more challenging book than *The House Behind the Cedars,* especially to its original intended audience: "[I]n its day, only a decade after the violence accompanying the collapse of Reconstruction, *Mandy Oxendine* would have been considered shocking. Chesnutt's endorsement of such a route to opportunity [as passing] would have offended almost all of the white reading public no matter how successful his method of amusement" (xviii). For Hackenberry, however, Chesnutt's initially uncompromised vision ends up being muted by his desire to please his audience: in particular, "[h]is introduction of a popularizing device, the mystery form, two-thirds of the way into *Mandy Oxendine* dilutes its themes of injustice and thwarted opportunity" (xix).

In reading the book, one can see how it might come across as either shocking or tame; considered in historical context, it is oddly both of these. A nineteenth-century white reader content to assess what *is* would find little objectionable, beyond the simple fact of racial passing being introduced as subject matter: a young woman passes because she can, and because she cherishes the economic American dream as she imagines it to be; meanwhile, her suitor declines to pass, despite nourishing similar dreams, pragmatically reasoning that hard work and education are a surer route to success. After a certain amount of turmoil and appropriate punishment for their indiscretions (punishment which—importantly, as we will see—is bestowed on *others*), the couple emerge wiser and more accepting of their lot in life. The woman is exposed as a black woman, she marries her black suitor, and that is that. If, on the other hand, a reader mentally inquires into what *might be*—into the world that *Mandy Oxendine* merely suggests as a possible consequence of American social mores—then a more disturbing vision emerges. An unseen world, barely suggested in any given instance but hinted at repeatedly throughout the text, is the key to any full understanding of *Mandy Oxendine* and its themes. Chesnutt cleverly attempted to write the novella in a way that would be palatable at a superficial level but which would reward a closer reading with uncanny depths.

Despite Hackenberry's claim that the novella's late movement toward the mystery genre represents a falling-off, in fact motifs of mystery and spying pervade the novella throughout and are thematically central. In what might initially seem like a ham-fisted attempt to build suspense, chapters often end at moments of uncertainty, instances when motivations for people's actions seem mysterious to other characters and the reader alike. Nearly half the chapters end with a character—usually Lowrey—hurrying with some (momentarily unexplained) purpose or else being hindered from doing so by the knowledge that someone is watching. Often, readers are also informed that the hurrying character is being spied upon by some other. These chapters also, for the most part, end in the piney woods that separate the black and white communities of the town, highly suggestive of Chesnutt's interest in the inarticulate, indeterminate borderland between two cultures. It is these indeterminate moments that the chapters, with their abrupt endings, draw us *toward,* deferring resolution but compelling the reader to continue on toward a hoped-for resolution that never really comes.

A close examination of the structure of *Mandy Oxendine* reveals perhaps more artistic care than will be obvious at first, and roundly illustrates Chesnutt's preoccupation with the *mysterious* aspect of his topic, race relations in the South; the mysteries of the novella are not so much a means to an end as they are an end in themselves, what the author seems to wish his readers to pay attention to. In order to make sense of race relations, observers must substantially come to terms with cognitive dissonance, must accept certain absurdities as the deepest truths and take the answers to many questions as merely given. To make sense of this world, in other words, its absurdities and mysteries—the parts of it that require interpretation—must be dismissed as invalid or, more properly, ignored. Most obviously, perhaps, one must discount the question of the "color line": the fact that an individual with only a fraction of African American ancestry is legally or culturally described as "black," with no accounting for complexity, is an oddity that Chesnutt, along with peers such as Mark Twain, found endlessly fascinating.

Chesnutt's fictions are often described as "problem novels," meaning that they highlight political problems and advance possible solutions, but *Mandy Oxendine* offers little in the way of a conscious argument about the plight of biracial people. It is a "problem novel" in a different sense: its main theme is the problematic nature of reading itself. Readers are inclined, as Chesnutt surmises, to seek narrative coherence, and thus to gloss over the many possible disruptions that—if scrutinized—might provoke consciousness of a narrative's underlying incoherence. In *Mandy Oxendine*, the disruptive moments that inevitably occur in any text are more difficult to ignore than usual because they are so central to the novella's thematic core. Consider, for example, three significant disruptions that belie the seeming resolution of the plot:

1. In ending the novella, the narrator admonishes readers that the remainder of Tom and Mandy's life together is beyond the scope of the present work: "Whether they went to the North, where there was larger opportunity and a more liberal environment, and remaining true to their own people, in spite of some scorn and some isolation, found a measurable degree of contentment and happiness; or whether they chose to sink their past in the gulf of oblivion, and sought in the great white world such a place as their talents and their virtues merited, it is not for this chronicle to relate. They deserved to be happy; but we do not all get our deserts" (112). While mildly subversive in that it asks white readers to understand that continuing to live in the South as black people is not a viable option for Mandy and Tom, talented and virtuous individuals who can pass, this passage amounts to little more than a conventional assurance that the important events of these characters' lives have now been chronicled. It offers a conventional form of closure even as it denies that the story is closed.
2. The identity of Utley's killer is never made definitively clear. The omniscient narrator carefully avoids informing the readers directly of what happened, and so readers must rely on characters' own variously motivated accounts. It's entirely conceivable that Lowrey, Mandy's white suitor Elder Gadson, or

even Mandy killed Utley.[4] That this crucial question remains unanswered, and that no one appears especially concerned by the lack of a definitive answer, testifies to Chesnutt's interest in the disparity between what we accept as appearance (Gadson is, acceptably to all parties, acquitted on a self-defense plea, closing the case) and murky reality. It also makes clear that Chesnutt is quite willing to distract his readers (if they wish to be distracted) from some of the harder questions that might really matter. Knowing that most readers prefer tidy resolutions to unsettling questions, Chesnutt packages the story with both, and allows readers to find what they seek.

3. The ending relies on at least two substantially implausible occurrences, the improbability of which must have been evident to both Chesnutt and his prospective readers. First, given the confessions of both Gadson, a white man, and Lowrey, a black man, the lynch mob that has formed to murder Utley's killer accepts Lowrey's story at face value and frees him, despite the plea of a lone vigilante who acknowledges, "[i]t's true the nigger didn' kill Utley," but wishes to lynch Lowrey anyway (110). Chesnutt's interest in a realistic assessment of race relations cannot withstand scrutiny at this particular moment. Nor can it when, in the final chapter, Mandy's indiscretion of passing is forgiven by the community: "[H]er youth, sex, and beauty excused in Mandy what would ordinarily have been regarded as an almost unpardonable social crime" (111). Dean McWilliams notes that "[o]ne of the most important features in American stereotypes of the mulatto female was her sensuous beauty," and that, in the cultural economy of the South at the time Chesnutt wrote, "[t]he strong sexual desires evoked by dark blood must be repressed" (124–25). The narrator of *Mandy Oxendine* confirms this, remarking that Mandy "seemed destined to pay dear for her fatal beauty" (95). Mandy's beauty makes her more dangerous in the eyes of the white community, not more understandable and acceptable in her decision to pass, and Chesnutt's remarkable (but not remarked-upon) inversion of dominant cultural practices suggests he is after something deeper than an exposé of these practices. He wants readers to recognize not just that they exist, but *why* they exist.

Although these incidents might be taken to add up to a lack of artistry, my contention is that they mean something. In his tying up of *Mandy Oxendine,* Chesnutt exhibits only limited artistic control as he plays with possibilities that, in their conspicuous illogic or implausibility, highlight their negative image, the stupid consistency of racial categories as they are enacted in the South. His narrative gives us a villain, a victim, and a victor, and if that's what readers want—if, beyond that, they are uninterested in the *meaning* of the relationships portrayed in the book—then that is what they will find. If, however, they find themselves unsatisfied with the way in which events are wrapped up in *Mandy Oxendine,* then there is at least the possibility that their perturbation will extend itself to the larger discursive world Chesnutt is portraying.[5] Of course, what happened instead is that Chesnutt's editorial readers were simply unhappy with the novella and recognized that prospective readers would be as well—a lesson Chesnutt appears to have taken to heart as he continued his career.

For the author of *Mandy Oxendine,* abstract terms such as "injustice" do not adequately define the nature of the racial problem in the American South. The problem, as it unfolds discursively, is much deeper and messier than that; we don't really have the vocabulary to speak of what's wrong, of how far removed our habits of interpretation are from anything like lived reality: discourse *makes* reality but is, paradoxically, inadequate to describe it.[6] Language is a social contract, but in the deconstructive world presented in *Mandy Oxendine*—in which resolution to any of the novella's ruptures is deferred, even by its last words—whether or not anything more nourishing than plain, abstract power underlies words and their meanings is a matter of faith. That is, if readers wish for something more heartening than a pragmatic explanation of the discursive world to which the novella is a referent—if they wish to believe that words such as "love" or "justice" mean anything beyond *what people are able to do to each other in order to advance their own interests*—then they will merely have to have faith; nothing more is available, but it had better be more than the sort of sloppy and thoughtless faith that easily categorizes experience into "hero," "villain," and such trivial shells of words.[7] The faith of the romance reader, that which easily puts every datum into its place and finds all's right with the world, is scrutinized by Chesnutt with the purpose of asking: is any more reasonable, productive form of connection, of communication, between people to be had?

The "tragic mulatta" tale is an appropriate vehicle for Chesnutt to explore these types of questions, first because his primary interest is in deconstructing racial categories, and if possible altering their significance; and second because the figure of the mulatto or mulatta offers an excellent analogue of the disruption between "signifier" (i.e., one's visual appearance) and "signified" (what that appearance is taken to mean). The narrator clearly makes the point that one's skin color is essentially meaningless. For all that, however, it is meaningful as well—that is, despite Chesnutt's philosophical belief that race ought to carry no meaning, he is well aware that in lived reality it does, and that racial categories, like any words, subsume and obscure complexities. Words are powerful in exactly this way. Perhaps, then, he can harness this power toward new ends: by exploring the ability of words to connect individuals—even though, in an abstract sense, they may be little alike—it seems just possible that Chesnutt can combat racism with the very same discursive forces that currently perpetuate it.

"Is you a *rale* black man?" Rose Amelia, Lowrey's devoted student, asks him soon after his arrival at the school (15). Though Rose Amelia means "real" to be taken in its absolute sense—you either are or you aren't—Lowrey elects to interpret it as a relative term: "Not *real* black. I was left out in the rain an' got some of it washed off. But I'm black enough to teach you." The philosophic, pragmatic Lowrey knows that the signifier "black man" carries no transcendent meaning—clearly, in his mind race is an arbitrary construction perpetrated upon him by others—but in this case, it is Rose Amelia who instructs her teacher. Over the course of the narrative, Lowrey fails to the extent that he cannot find personal meaning in his racial identity or in anything else.[8] McWilliams aptly glosses Rose Amelia's question as meaning "are you truly committed to your black identity?" (128), but also highlights the novella's apparent frustration with a paradox of communication: words yoke us together in uncomfortable, even oppressive ways, but their ability to connect us is also prospectively our salvation. So how can one tell the difference?

Whether or not words mean anything other than themselves and whether or not the life of an individual person is meaningful in itself are parallel questions in *Mandy Oxendine.* At one level, the pragmatic one, only power is meaningful in the novella: only the exercise of power explains people's actions, and it underlies every other concept, from "race" to "love" to "justice." The romance between Mandy and Tom, for example, easily can be read along a pragmatic line: they are almost wholly unconcerned with each other soon after Tom's initial departure, and upon his return each correctly surmises that the relationship may be resumed as it was unless a more convenient arrangement presents itself. Though Mandy explains that her current, realistic attitude replaced a naïve one—"I thought then that men were faithful and true, and that love meant somethin' great and grand and lastin'" (43)—in fact, little about the outcome of this book would be different if Mandy had *not* so adapted; the world is the same cold place regardless of how she feels about it. Passing, as has been noted, is likewise a matter of pragmatic ratiocination: Mandy passes because she believes she will benefit from it, and Tom does not because he believes he will not benefit. In such a world, why should anyone feel connected to other individuals, much less make decisions on the basis of such an imagined connection? What misguided sense of racial loyalty, the narrative sometimes seems to ask, would require one *not* to pass?

Thus, when the most shocking feature of *Mandy Oxendine*—the death of Rose Amelia—occurs, one must question its meaning, indeed question whether it has any meaning. Her death seems capricious: it does not advance the plot and remains essentially unexplained by the narrative: "Whether Rose had fallen in a fit, and in the helplessness of unconsciousness had perished; or whether she had run until exhausted, and falling, had not had strength enough left to extricate herself; or whether in her remorse and despair [at Lowrey's presumed lynching] she had taken her own life, no one of course could know" (106). Nor does anyone much seem to care: at her funeral, Lowrey drops a single tear "at the thought that here lay one who had been fond of him," having never learned of the extent of her devotion to him (112). In another sense, however, Rose Amelia's death is very necessary, in that the genre in which Chesnutt is writing demands that *someone* pay for Mandy's indiscretion, and since "*Mandy Oxendine* tries to uncouple the adjective and noun, 'tragic' and 'mulatta'" (McWilliams 131), Mandy needs to live. Rose Amelia very literally dies for Mandy's sins (and in a narrative with frequent references to Christianity, the religious undertones of this eventuality need hardly be mentioned). The stage has also been set for Rose Amelia's death by Chesnutt's employment of a motif of characters standing in for one another—as when Utley replaces Tom as Mandy's suitor, for example, or when Tom and Gadson both offer to stand in for Mandy after she confesses to murder. Given that no one within the narrative understands Rose Amelia's death, or can find meaning in it, is it—and was her life—meaningful? Or do the characters inhabit a world in which people are basically interchangeable, like workers on an assembly line, and one death will serve about as well as another? The difference between these two possible interpretations—in which Rose Amelia is essentially a Christ figure or else she is basically a cog in a machine—is dramatic, of course, and so it is illustrative that the difference appears as subtle as it does in *Mandy Oxendine.* The question is one for the novella's readers—what will *they* take the meaning of her death to be?—and in this may be seen the roots of an appeal to an imagined readership that will be developed in each of Chesnutt's remaining novels.

The House Behind the Cedars: The Future Is Now

The House Behind the Cedars attempts a similar deconstruction of racial categories to *Mandy Oxendine* but is more normalized in form. How, Chesnutt's first published novel asks, can people make reliable ethical decisions based on uncertain, often contradictory data? The world inhabited by the characters of *The House Behind the Cedars,* although part of the social order its initial readers might have recognized as reality, is a radically illogical one in which the central characters, Rena and John Walden (later "Warwick"), are legally either black or white depending on whether they happen to be in North or South Carolina.

Chesnutt puts Rena and John in the teeth of this society's illogic by having them insistently but somewhat blindly act in accordance with the Enlightenment values—equality, rationality, justice—by which the culture claims to define itself. That is, they act as though these values really are prized above all others, and the novel documents their respective initiations into a more realistic, cynical world.

The novel does not, however, advocate a path by which the culture should reorient itself in accordance with its stated ideals. Rather than making its case from an idealistic position, *The House Behind the Cedars* places a high value on the insight that comes with experience. Human behavior is seen as part of a complicated social milieu; rather than describing the ability of exceptional individuals to transcend that milieu, it demonstrates their enmeshment within historical events that are larger than they. The characters' agency is, as the novel portrays it, exceedingly limited: the best one can hope to do is to capture a glimpse of the forces by which he or she is constrained, but even that insight is likely to carry a heavy cost. Because Chesnutt wished to convey this message, he wrote the novel as a tragedy; but, reluctant to invest his writing with unleavened pessimism, he balanced the heavily deterministic perspective that had marked his earlier drafts of the story with an undercurrent of hope. Perhaps, though Rena herself dies, others can benefit from her experience: the students for whom she hopes to open, "if ever so little, the door of opportunity" (164) or the novel's readers themselves.

The ability of the latter group to benefit from Rena's education, however, seems questionable given the novel's attitude toward the knowledge gained from books. Educated by romantic works such as *Ivanhoe, Gil Blas, Robinson Crusoe,* and the *Arabian Nights,* Rena's brother John emerges as a deeply impoverished moral agent. He and another character Chesnutt introduced late in the composition process, George Tryon, are the objects of the novel's satire of romanticism, which is condemned for its tendency to separate ideals and experience. Both men are characterized as having the "imagination" necessary to understand Rena's experience, but as lacking the ability to act upon that understanding.[9] A moral vision can come only with experience, but can that experience be approximated in the process of reading? That question lies at the heart of *The House Behind the Cedars.*

As I discuss in the introduction to this book, *The House Behind the Cedars* was the result of more than a decade of revisions to an early story Chesnutt prized highly, "Rena Walden." In 1890, its rejection had caused the author to consider "drop[ping] the attempt at realism" he had undertaken in it. It seemed to him that the "amorphous" nature of the story, as *Century* editor Richard Watson Gilder had referred to it in rejecting the piece, was a consequence of this representative reader's habit of seeing race in strictly binary terms: because whites habitually regard biracial people as "amorphous" in the first place, it may be impossible to represent them acceptably in fiction. Concluded Chesnutt in 1890, "I fear there is too much of this sentiment to make mulattoes good magazine characters" (*"To Be an Author"* 65). Instead of abandoning the piece, however, Chesnutt continued working on it with the advice and guidance of George Washington Cable. At some point during the revision process, he developed a minor reference to one of Rena's siblings who "changed his name, and was lost to his people" into the main thread of the novel (Andrews, *Literary Career* 148). In *The House Behind the Cedars,* Rena's brother is identified as John Walden, a bright young resident of Patesville, North Carolina, who reasons that "[a] negro is black; I am white, and not black" (113). Although legally defined in his home state as entirely African American due to his "one drop of black blood" (113), John decides to take advantage of the fluidity of legal conventions by moving to South Carolina, where he is legally white and where—more importantly—his history as an African American will be unknown.

The House Behind the Cedars exposes the legal hypocrisy that sends John (who changes his last name to Warwick) away from his home and family, that of the "one drop" rule. The novel begins with his return home to his mother, Molly, and to Rena. John has become a respected lawyer and has married a wealthy white woman: though he lacks social pedigree, he has overcome this barrier, ironically due to the cultural upheaval caused by the Civil War. In the period of economic desperation in the Southern states following the war, nearly any such shortcoming except racial "impurity" can be overlooked by the old aristocracy. John's wife, however, has now died, and he arrives in Patesville hoping that Rena can be convinced to join him in passing as white, and that she will follow him to Clarence, South Carolina, to care for his young son. Shaming their mother into accepting that she "must not bar [Rena's] entrance" into privileged white society, John as well overcomes Rena's reluctance to leave Molly (19). In her new identity as a white woman, Rena is wooed by the aristocratic Tryon, and is persuaded by John that to acknowledge her racial heritage would merely cause pain to all parties without producing any corresponding good.[10] Due to a series of coincidences, however, Tryon discovers Rena's secret shortly before their anticipated wedding and breaks off their engagement while also declining to reveal the Warwicks' family secret publicly. Rena then declines John's offer to be educated among whites in the North, stating, "God is against it; I'll stay with my own people" (121).

The preceding two paragraphs summarize the first two-thirds of *The House Behind the Cedars,* which describes a world suffused with romantic ideals. This portion of the novel, which ends with Tryon wondering if he has made the correct decision in rejecting Rena, comprises most of what Chesnutt added to his original story "Rena Walden" to round it out to novel length. In these first twenty chapters, Chesnutt depicts an appealing environment in which the richness of the past seems to be coupled with a sense of the world's newness. The main representative of this social environment, Tryon, easily adopts two contradictory personas, that of the youthful representative of an aristocratic order which self-consciously adopts Arthurian pageantry and that of the modern, egalitarian rationalist who believes that individuals, more than families, possess traits such as honor (57). Tryon is capable of stating with evident sincerity that he would love Rena even if she were black—"True love has no degrees; it is all or nothing!" (59)—and of regarding a white-supremacist editorial as "well-considered" (71). Moreover, he is aware of no contradiction in these two forms of behavior because nothing in his experience to date has made its contradictory nature evident. Neither Tryon nor anyone else in the novel can understand abstract ideals without their being driven home by practical experience. In Chesnutt's restrained portrayal, Tryon's bifurcated personality makes him come across as not monstrous but realistic, to a degree even sympathetic. He depicts Tryon less as hypocritical than as someone whose aristocratic "sensibility" is "curiously inconsistent with his most positive convictions" (151). Although his actions are the instrument of Rena's downfall, in a larger sense he and she are mutually victims of the same tragedy.

Darryl Hattenhauer describes *The House Behind the Cedars* as a mixed-genre work: "[T]he sentimentalism and melodrama overlaying this text are underlaid by the thematic complexity of realism and tragedy" (43). Comparing the published version of *The House Behind the Cedars* to earlier versions of the "Rena Walden" story yields some insight into Chesnutt's method of "overlaying" a realist narrative with sentimental conventions that might be more palatable to his audience. The final third of the novel, chapters 21 through 33, is roughly equivalent to much earlier versions of "Rena Walden" and (with the admitted exception of the melodramatic ending) comprises the novel's realist core. The plot concerning Tryon is grafted onto this part of the story, while John disappears entirely from the novel. In these chapters, Rena (like her counterpart in the earlier versions) is wooed by the discreditable Jeff Wain, a middle-class mulatto commissioned to hire a schoolteacher for Sampson County. Rena in *The House Behind the Cedars* is more sophisticated than she appeared to be in earlier versions—a result, it seems, of the worldly education she has received in her dealings with Tryon. She is also more socially conscious; whereas in "Rena Walden" she agrees to marry Wain in pursuit of wealth, in *The House Behind the Cedars* she accepts the opportunity merely to serve other African Americans by becoming a teacher. Wain, for his part, is equally vulgar and dishonest in both versions, but the novel's narrator now attempts to make him understandable and even sympathetic to a degree, for example by explaining that the crude pass he makes at Rena is no more than an attempt "to declare his passion in what he had hoped might prove a not unacceptable fashion" (166). Rather than an embodiment of evil, he is—like Tryon—someone who seems to be the product of a particular environment, and understandable only in terms of that environment.

The two parts into which *The House Behind the Cedars* is divided—Rena's respective encounters with Tryon and with Wain—might be seen as her songs of innocence and experience. In the latter segment, Tryon (though with noteworthy equivocation) now wants Rena back. Like John before him, he resolves to "make [Rena] white" and have her come away to live with him in some new land (140). Whereas John had asked the "innocent" Rena to abandon ties of family, what Tryon now asks of Rena is that she leave behind the knowledge she has acquired, and this knowledge is yet more precious to Rena (who still finds it acceptable to leave Molly behind, as she does in accepting Wain's job offer). Though her loss of innocence is lamentable, Rena prizes the insight she has gained as a result, explaining portentously that she "would rather die of knowledge than live in ignorance" (120). Rejecting Tryon's proposal of a final meeting, she writes: "You are white, and you have given to me to understand that I am black. I accept the classification, however unfair, and the consequences, however unjust, one of which is that we cannot meet in the same parlor, in the same church, at the same table, or anywhere, in social intercourse. . . . As a white man, this might not mean a great deal to you; as a woman, shut out already by my color from much that is desirable, my good name remains my most valuable possession" (172–73). Rena here voices two of Chesnutt's fundamental attitudes about race: it is artificial, what today would be called a social construct, and it is meaningful in that it carries social weight. It is a mistake for race to carry such heavy significance as it does in American culture, but it would also be a mistake to do as John has done and behave as if it does not carry such significance. The former is the culture's error, about which Rena can do little; the latter has been her error, and she has learned from it. In this way, Chesnutt seeks to resolve a difficult philosophical and aesthetic question: he wants to give his character a degree of agency (if not, then her behavior might come across as racially determined, exactly what Chesnutt thought it was *not*), but he also wishes to convey the very serious historical boundaries around that agency. As a realist, Chesnutt portrays his heroine as *relatively* bound by her environment. Her behavior is not biologically driven—as Tryon assumes it has been, concluding that "her brief association with white people . . . had evidently been a mere veneer over the underlying negro" (150)—but it is constrained by historical circumstances. Rena has free choice only within historically determined boundaries, and so it becomes important to her to make the most of the choices she has.

Given her limited choices, Chesnutt prioritizes Rena's moral agency. Like John, she could continue to pass, and if she did so would have better material prospects than she does in her chosen role teaching in an African American school. John, however, has not (as he seems to believe) trumped an unjust political situation by adhering to a natural-law conception of right and wrong; instead, he has rendered himself a product of and a participant in the racist legal system that previously had disadvantaged him. He has not sidestepped the political reality but is firmly ensnared within it. As Brook Thomas writes, John's rationalist ethic paradoxically advocates "concealment" rather than openness: for John, "[e]nlightened reason might be a force against prejudiced custom, but prejudice—at least in terms of race—has its revenge by forcing reason to advocate repression" (166). John's mistake comes in regarding his choices in isolation from the larger consequences in which they occur: quoting Longfellow, he sums up his ethic by saying "[l]et the dead past bury its dead" (54). Chesnutt clearly shares John's belief that individuals *ought* not be condemned by their ancestry, and that morality is a matter of present behavior and future consequences rather than of past events, but unlike John he regards an understanding of the past as essential in evaluating behavior and its likely consequences. If nothing else, one must learn from past mistakes, as John has failed to do.

It is Rena, however, who most directly suffers from John's lapses in judgment, despite her capacity to learn from mistakes in a way he does not. Faced with a literal and metaphorical decision between two paths, one occupied by Tryon and one by Wain, she risks (and loses) her life rather than choose either alternative, jumping instead into the briars and consequently dying of exposure. Before interpreting her death, however, it is appropriate to acknowledge that Chesnutt has provided Rena a third marital option, that of Frank Fowler, a dark-skinned African American who for years has loyally loved her from afar. The novel, in fact, ends with the dying Rena acknowledging that Frank "loved me best of them all" (195). According to critics such as Trudier Harris, the fact that Frank is never presented as a viable suitor for Rena—that Chesnutt has her die rather than unite with Frank—reveals a political blind spot of the novel and its author. Chesnutt's description of Frank, asserts Harris, "is not that of a man who has virtues of his own," but one that shows the influence of, and that ultimately participates in, available stereotypes of blackness (216). Concludes Harris, "Chesnutt has not been able to lift himself far enough above his own prejudices to convincingly make the case that all blacks are to be included in the grand adventure" (228). Hattenhauer, on the other hand, claims "it is the critics, not Chesnutt, who turn Frank into a stereotype," noting that he is ascribed the characteristics of intelligence, morality, and even heroism (44).

Frank, however, is neither a spoof of blackness nor the embodiment of African American heroism. He is instead a manifestation of the values of Booker T. Washington, an intellectual sparring-partner of Chesnutt's around the turn of the century. Chesnutt felt that Washington was too willing to back down from demanding full voting rights for African Americans, overly emphasizing the alternatives of vocational education and property acquisition. He wrote to Washington in 1903, "I appreciate all you say and have written about education and property, but they are not everything. There is no good reason why we should not acquire them all the more readily because of our equality of rights" (*"To Be an Author"* 182). Although Rena's values, like Washington's, focus on the education of Southern blacks, it is Frank and his father, Peter, who most completely represent Washington's ideal of incremental progress for African Americans, an ideal Chesnutt regarded as a dead-end compromise. The Fowlers have pieced together a relative degree of prosperity in their business as coopers, but their security is threatened by encroaching industrialization as a new barrel factory eats into their business (85), possibly illustrating a limitation of Washington's "bootstraps" approach as Chesnutt saw it. Moreover, both Frank and Peter unreasonably valorize whites' behavior in spite of the evidence offered by their own experience. When John buys Frank a new mule and cart, his father remarks, "Now dat . . . is somethin' lack rale w'ite folks," failing to consider (as the narrator points out) that "[n]o real white person had ever given Peter a mule or a cart" (125–26). For his part, Frank is enamored of the Waldens' mixed-race gentility to a degree that even his father regards as servile (26). Ultimately, Chesnutt does not locate Rena's salvation in marriage to Frank because neither his path, nor John's, nor Wain's is conceived as the most productive model for African Americans. All three of these characters are faulted for miming white-modeled patterns of success. Of the novel's characters, only Rena ends up asserting that there is value in claiming a black identity. If there is an African American role model in the novel, it is she.

In ending the novel as he does, then, Chesnutt highlights the dearth of viable options for someone like Rena, whose behavior is circumscribed by both her cultural identity and her individually chosen moral code. As Cathy Boeckmann writes, "[w]hen she rejects both men and both paths and sets off into the uncharted swamp, she succumbs both to the powerlessness of her gender position and the liminality of her racial identity" (166).[11] Chesnutt thus uses a contrived ending to make a realistic point. In Boeckmann's words, the ending, "though sentimentally conventional and appropriate, is employed as a means toward a representation of mixed-race character" (167). The novel employs established aesthetic codes to bring new insights to light. Similarly, John Sheehy notes that it may appear as though "Rena *must* die to satisfy the needs of the novel's sentimentalism." However, Sheehy contends, the novel's ending works to open up as well as close off meaning: her "death at the end of the novel brings our sentimental reading to a neat close, [but also] leaves the novel's simultaneous Signification on its own racial preoccupations spinning in space, unresolved and unresolvable" (413).

The meaning of the novel is "unresolvable" only in the sense that one cannot imagine a successful resolution outside of a particular historical moment. The novel, in other words, is designed to signify differently depending on the manner in (and the cultural position from) which it is read. The commentary on racism in *The House Behind the Cedars,* for example, has proved a continuously divisive issue precisely because the novel is capable of being read in diametrically opposite ways. Several critics have faulted *The House Behind the Cedars* for its failure to indict racism, or more precisely for limiting its indictment to racism encountered by those who are legally black but appear white. One such critic, SallyAnn H. Ferguson, with a considerable measure of justice reads *The House Behind the Cedars* mercilessly as a statement of Chesnutt's "apparently unshakable belief in the principle of unitary racial development," in a doctrine—expressed in Chesnutt's nonfiction writings of the period—that called for racial amalgamation until racial differences ceased to exist ("Rena Walden" 204). The stance is problematic, Ferguson argues, in what it calls on African Americans to give up, beginning with identity. As Ferguson demonstrates, Chesnutt's essay series on "The Future American" (1900) suggests that Chesnutt saw little inherent value in African American identity as such, apparently considering identity a necessary sacrifice as he combated Anglo-Saxon notions of "purity": "Chesnutt asserts that any dream of a pure Anglo-Saxon type for the United States should be abandoned even though the future race will be predominantly white, call itself so, and will likely conform closely to the white type. But this race will have absorbed and assimilated the other . . . races" (198). Thus, Ferguson writes, in electing to pass, John Warwick is portrayed as having "no identity problems whatsoever" (199).

In Ferguson's reading, Rena's main problem, then—her tragic flaw, as it were—is that she insists sentimentally on retaining a semblance of racial and familial identity, one which by rights she may abandon at will. "Her death . . . punishes one who cannot conform to Chesnutt's racial ideas," which imagine that whites, due to environment, really are superior to blacks ("Rena Walden" 203). According to Ferguson, she is made out to be a victim of her choices and not of society, and thus the main problem Chesnutt has with romanticism is that it has led her toward sentimental loyalties and away from John's hard-boiled, pragmatic, and self-interested realism.

Numerous other critics have defended the novel against the charge of colorism. For one of these, Dean McWilliams, Chesnutt's "The Future American"—in which McWilliams concedes "colorism is present" (54)—must be read differently from his novel *The House Behind the Cedars.* "An author's essay," he writes, "is not a template for understanding his story for the simple reason that each is a separate text. . . . We cannot substitute one for the other, as tempting as that may be" (21). McWilliams ponders, as does Ferguson, the disturbing nature of Chesnutt's reasoning in "The Future American," but sees him as much more likely in his fiction to attempt to burrow underneath his readers' guiding assumptions about race. In the fiction, Chesnutt may seem to take a more indirect approach to social issues, but the level of critique tends to be deeper. This explanation strikes me as adequate to explain some of the more disturbing content of the "Future American" essays and to sanction a reading of *The House Behind the Cedars* that is capable of moving beyond Chesnutt's rather reductive approach in the essays. On the other hand, the "Future American" essays offer an important contextual reference for readers of Chesnutt's novel of the same year. It is too easy to regard *The House Behind the Cedars* as a novel preoccupied with the past, and thus of only historical interest to those who read it from a contemporary perspective. Chesnutt, however, in both the "Future American" series and *The House Behind the Cedars* means to use the lessons of the past to shape an uncertain future. In a deterministic fashion, the novel demonstrates how individuals' behavior is driven by their cultural environment. Its hope lies in the fact that, were the environment to change, the future to which the novel's events seem to point could be altered as well. But to influence the trajectory of history, people must learn to understand the past and to benefit from its lessons. Rena is a qualified role model in that she is able to learn from her experiences but dies before this knowledge can be put to use.

McWilliams wisely brings up, from a post-structuralist perspective, a fundamental problem within any articulation of an imagined future: "We try to look past the present with the lenses of the present, but we see not the object upon which we train our gaze but the lenses themselves. The lenses are the constructs—the language and the categories—we use to organize our experience" (56). Unsurprisingly, then, given the limitations of perspective, Chesnutt's "fictions capture the problems of the present more accurately than his essay predicted the future" (56). As McWilliams writes, "long-term looks into the future are almost always futile" (56). Quite true—if by "futile" one means "of dubious accuracy"; however, accurate or not, such attempts to glimpse the future certainly perform cultural work. The interest in the future in Chesnutt's novels is at the heart of their disruptive possibilities, and so it is critically important that *The House Behind the Cedars* does more than document the circumstances of an already realized moment. By placing his readership of 1900 in the novel's "future," Chesnutt uses the theme of time in an attempt to make the novel's events personally compelling for readers, something in which readers are involved rather than a document to be inspected from an abstract, detached position.

The past and the future are dominant motifs throughout the novel. In an essay that appeared early during Chesnutt's revival as an important writer, William L. Andrews argues that, in "focusing on the physical setting of Patesville as a tangible indication of the survival of the past in the present, Chesnutt [found he] could go further to show how traditions and customs, like the old town structures and landmarks, could remain unaltered despite the change in the times" ("Chesnutt's Patesville" 285). As it is in the works of a later writer to whom Chesnutt is often compared, William Faulkner,[12] the past is very much a central entity in *The House Behind the Cedars.* But an equally significant referent in describing Chesnutt's approach might be Nathaniel Hawthorne, who writes in *The House of the Seven Gables* of "a mysterious and terrible Past, . . . a blank Future . . . [and the] visionary and impalpable Now, which, if you once look closely at it, is nothing" (113).

That "nothing" is, from a post-structuralist point of view, where meaning occurs: as Houston A. Baker writes in an essay concerned with the usefulness of post-structuralist theories in the criticism of African Americans' texts, "[s]igns are founded in difference—distinctions marked by phonemes and the infinite deferral of meaning, which is always indeterminately suspended between past and future" ("Theoretical Returns" 433). If we are to look within a narrative for political possibilities, then, we must remember that language does not primarily function as a record of thought but actually carries meaning only in an unrecordable instant, which cannot be reproduced precisely (though it may be approximated in some sense) by a sign. A reading experience, thus, carries most possibility when it is one of active engagement, not a mere attempt to decode what signs mean in some abstract, permanent sense. Notes Baker, "Derrida reminds us that repetition alone maintains presence, and repetition's motivation is preeminently a system of signs whose very possibility is founded on absence" (433). In other words, the relationship contained within a sign—that between signifier and signified—is, we are told by deconstructive theory, arbitrary: theoretically, the relationship could be disrupted and the sign could *mean* very differently at any moment, though a dramatic, wholesale disruption of meaning is unlikely at any given period of time.

Things—which are mediated, available to us, through language—are as they are not due to an inherent permanence but due to constant repetition; our contact with language requires us to repeat the patterns that shape reality for us over and over again, for the most part unthinkingly. Thus, for example, Rena exults in hearing statements about her beauty "repeated and itemized and emphasized" (14); her beauty does not exist in any permanent, abstract sense, but carries meaning only through repetition and reassurance. Whereas, in *Mandy Oxendine,* Chesnutt attempted (for the most part unsuccessfully) to break the chain of signification and render a thoroughly deconstructed world in which events are often unhooked from their traditional meanings, in *The House Behind the Cedars* his tack is both more subtle and more sophisticated.

Chesnutt suggests from the start of *The House Behind the Cedars* that the social world tends, admittedly with fits and starts, toward fluidity and not fixedness. He introduces social change as a guiding theme in, as well as a setting for, *The House Behind the Cedars* when Warwick strolls through Patesville, the abandoned home of his youth:

> There had been some changes, it is true, some melancholy changes, but scarcely anything by way of addition or improvement to counterbalance them. Here and there blackened and dismantled walls marked the place where handsome buildings once had stood, for Sherman's march to the sea had left its mark upon the town. The stores were mostly of brick, two stories high, joining one another after the manner of cities. Some of the names on the signs were familiar; others, including a number of Jewish names, were quite unknown to him. . . .
>
> A few moments later, Warwick saw a colored policeman in the old constable's place—a stronger reminder than even the burned buildings that war had left its mark upon the old town, with which Time had dealt so tenderly. (2–3)

Readers are not privy to Warwick's opinion of the landscape he mentally documents, but the scene does seem to demonstrate an important, easily overlooked, premise of the novel: that even a world that appears to be entrenched in the status quo may, in reality, be in the process of stark change. Though its old buildings are fewer in number, Patesville may seem to the casual observer even to have escaped the most drastic effects of Sherman's onslaught; Warwick sees "little that is not familiar" (2), and the sleepy Southern town seems ready to go on with life approximately as it has for decades before. However, on closer examination, the important changes are those that might seem the most subtle: names on buildings reveal that Jewish merchants are now able to do business in the town, and the appearance of the black constable signifies that African Americans are now able to occupy at least some tenuous positions of authority.

The remaining old buildings seem to signify stability and resistance to change, but the people who occupy and surround them suggest that such visible realities are deceiving: consistently, Chesnutt portrays the social world as a socially constructed one whose status is characterized more strongly by people (and their discourse) than by mute things. Like an organism that is constantly but imperceptibly shedding and replacing its cells, to the knowing mind the social world is metamorphosing even as it appears to be in stasis.

Just as appearances may belie the transitions a locale is undergoing, there is a gap between appearance and reality when it comes to race. Chesnutt's writings, as numerous readers have observed, reflect a deep interest in how race is constructed in America, especially given the insistence, enshrined in law and culture, on rigidly classifying individuals into one of two categories: black or white. What, he repeatedly asks, about a person who fits neatly into neither category, or who (like Chesnutt himself) appears to refute the classification system because his appearance is deceptive, who appears white but is legally black? In a 1901 essay titled "The White and the Black," Chesnutt recounts his quizzing of a railroad conductor as to just how Jim Crow laws are put into practice:

> "Do you ever," I asked, "have any difficulty about classifying people who are very near the line?"
>
> "Oh, yes, often."
>
> "What do you do in a case of that kind?"
>
> "I give the passenger the benefit of the doubt."
>
> "That is, you treat him as a white man?"
>
> "Certainly."
>
> "But suppose you should find in the colored car a man who has a white face, but insisted that his descent entitled him to ride in that car: what would you do then?"
>
> "I'd let him stay there," replied the conductor, with unconcealed disgust, which seemed almost to include the questioner who could suppose such a case. "Anyone that is fool enough to rather be a nigger than a white man may have his choice. He could stay there till h_ll froze over for all I'd care." (*Essays and Speeches* 141–42)

As this passage illustrates, the abstract idea of racial categories—that an individual may be only white *or* black—is *not* necessarily put into practice if the person in question appears racially ambiguous. What the system asks of people in this equivocal middle group is *mental* compliance to the social order, obeisance if not strict obedience; and this is exactly what Chesnutt conspicuously refuses to give. The conductor makes clear that neither a light-skinned black person nor a dark-skinned white person will be troubled to change cars, assuming they accept their classification into one of two established racial identities. His annoyance, moreover, is not so much provoked by the hypothetical idea of being (as it were) "deceived" as it is by Chesnutt's probing questions. That is, the conductor—as a representative of society—clarifies that those "near the line," those capable of passing, may largely live whatever lives they desire, *so long as they do not call the line itself into question.* It is a tricky but important point: the segregation of the races is not what it may seem to be, an end enforced by certain means; it is rather a means to an end. Classification is not a means toward the end of racial purity, but the reverse: the ideology of racial purity is a function of, and follows from rather than precedes, the classifying impulse itself, and the power relations that underlie this impulse. In short, Chesnutt exhibits a deep but subtly expressed awareness that racism is, at bottom, an exercise of power, and nothing else.

The distinction becomes important because the nature of Chesnutt's commitment to the cause of all African Americans, as opposed to the narrower plight of those (like him) who are near the "edge" of the color line, has long been debated. The question of whether Chesnutt ultimately identified as a white person (who was pushed into a black identity by historical circumstance) or as a black person (who circulated in a largely white world) may, given his take on the meaning of race, be overemphasized. The ambiguity surrounding Chesnutt's personal attitude toward race—as someone who consciously chose not to pass in most instances, but who also admitted the desire to pass on occasion[13]—might be converted from one that restricts his writings' political work to one that enables that work, once it is kept in mind that a defining goal of his was to trouble the nature of the "color line" itself.

Chesnutt's mulatto characters, then, are best seen not as models of how some African Americans might (if circumstances, such as skin color, permit) evade their fellow blacks' misfortunes and achieve a properly "white" life, but as devices for making racial categories less rigid and more complicated, a progression that potentially could benefit all African Americans, and indeed white Americans as well. He insisted repeatedly throughout his career that the categories as they are presently constituted, indeed the rigorous impulse to categorize itself, hurt whites as well as nonwhites, if not with equal pressure: understandably, he writes in "The White and the Black," a white person "can endure, with considerable equanimity, restrictions which make him superior whether he will or no. The brunt of the separation falls upon the Negro, but the white man does not escape" (*Essays and Speeches* 140). In time, whites will learn that they suffer along with blacks as the result of a historical legacy of slavery and oppression; if reading cannot teach them this lesson, then they are bound to learn it through painful experience.[14]

Chesnutt troubles racial categories in *The House Behind the Cedars* in recognition that the world of tomorrow may be radically different from the world we inhabited yesterday. For this reason, racial categories—"black," "white," "mulatto," etc.—being constructions, and philosophically troubled ones at that, may come to carry much different meanings (ideally, less meaning, but Chesnutt is not that optimistically idealistic) than they do today. Cultural fluidity is a defining characteristic of the world he paints in *The House Behind the Cedars*—the South, he suggests, cannot long resist the sorts of rapid change witnessed in the North[15]—and so parties interested in racial justice, or even merely in self-protection, are best advised to be alert and prepared to help shape the coming change. Although the immediate problem Chesnutt takes on in this novel, as in almost all his fiction, is racial injustice, his commentary is best seen as focused on the exercise of power, a neutral concept that may create justice and injustice but may not itself be characterized by those terms. While Chesnutt may understandably be seen as a writer who rests his case for racial justice on the bourgeois abstraction of a color-blind society, a world where race does not matter, in fact his argument is more radical and historically engaged than that: it is not an argument that race should not matter so much as a statement that race *will* matter *differently* in the future, for better or worse, and that upending readers' assumptions about race might well be a way of nudging such changes along in productive paths.

In the deconstructive world of *The House Behind the Cedars,* language, like the signifier of skin color, is unreliable from a logical point of view—and logic is, likewise, unreliable from a linguistic point of view. John Warwick is the preeminent example of a character whose point of view seems perfectly logical, as long as the terms by which he lives are as transparent and uncomplicated as he asserts them to be. In all his actions, Warwick assumes that he can control his world by making it *mean* less: race, in particular, should be meaningless in his view, so he structures his life to make its meanings hinder him as little as possible. He is adamantly disinclined to seek out complexity. "Once persuaded that he had certain rights, or ought to have them, by virtue of the laws of nature, in defiance of the customs of mankind, he had promptly sought to enjoy them. This he had been able to do by simply concealing his antecedents and making the most of his opportunities, with no troublesome qualms of conscience whatever" (53–54). As long as he can maintain the semblance of a philosophically uncomplicated world—which he does primarily by referring to a simplistically capitalist ideal of individualism and free enterprise—then he remains successful. Clearly, from his perspective, notions that fail to serve this ideal, such as family ties, are unworthy of much consideration, as in chapter 2 he shames his mother into allowing Rena to depart in order to seek better chances in life. The novel, however, demonstrates that his desire to extend his lifestyle to include his sister, Rena, and thus provide for his son after his wife's death, causes his life (and others') rather quickly to unravel.

Cautions the narrator, accordingly, "[m]en who have elected to govern their lives by principles of abstract right and reason, which happen, perhaps, to be at variance with what society considers equally right and reasonable, should, *for fear of complications,* be careful about descending from the lofty heights of logic to the common level of impulse and affection" (19; emphasis added). A central question for any reader of *The House Behind the Cedars,* then, is this: does Chesnutt share Warwick's investment in capitalistic free enterprise, and his attendant suspicion of complication?[16] Consider, for example, a seemingly incidental early passage in which Warwick reflects on the antebellum "curfew bell, which at nine o'clock at night had clamorously warned all negroes, slave or free, that it was unlawful for them to be abroad after that hour, under penalty of imprisonment or whipping" (2). Simply in the employment of the words "all negroes, slave or free," Warwick (and possibly Chesnutt) casts the injustice primarily as one against freed blacks; the implication is that it is unfair to treat freed and enslaved people similarly. Thus, simply in a small nuance of expression, Warwick has revealed his investment in a logic and language of Western rationalism, one that calls on whites to apply their assumptions universally (in other words, the concept of "slave"/"free" implicitly requires that distinctions between these categories be upheld), but does not trouble the nature of the assumptions themselves (why must the distinctions exist as they do in the first place?). So right from the beginning, the nature and depth of the novel's attack on racism are subject to question. Is racism—which is obviously incompatible with Warwick's individualistic assumptions—an impurity in, or a consequence of, capitalist rationalism? Just how deep is the critique being offered here?

I believe that Chesnutt extends his critique beyond one that picks at capitalism along its edges, and that in *The House Behind the Cedars* he attempts to attack the capitalist system at its very heart. In the quotation above concerning "the lofty heights of logic," the narrator seems not to be saying with a straight face that "the common level of impulse and affection" ought to be eschewed; instead of such a literal reading, it ought to be taken as a warning that actions chosen according to "the lofty heights of logic" must pass a more rigorous test: can such actions sustain a lifetime of real experience; can one take such an abstract, logical path and continue to live in the world with any fulfillment? In addressing this basic question, Chesnutt completes a key maneuver:

having attacked sentimental or romantic ideologies (such as those displayed in the ludicrous feudal-style tournament in which Tryon does homage to Rena) from a realist perspective—demonstrating that they cannot sustain a prosperous future—he goes on to attack pragmatic realism, such as Warwick's, from a sentimental perspective. Typically enough, Chesnutt here is attempting to have it both ways. The pitfall of such an approach, of course, is that he might end up with not the best, but the worst of both worlds—appearing, as some have taken him to be, invested in a romanticized view of the Old South that excuses its racism but also in a callously realistic determinism that sees no room for affinity with other (particularly darker-skinned) black people.

It seems possible to describe Chesnutt's approach in *The House Behind the Cedars* as sentimental realism, the goal of which is to locate ways of existing in the world that rely, selectively, on carefully constructed and nourished connections with other people: seeing the world not through rose-colored glasses, but with a clear view of how interdependent each of us is, how we contain meaning not within ourselves, but only as part of a system. Kenneth W. Warren describes the difference between sentimental romance and realism as follows: while "the sentimental romance assumed that the redemption of the social world lay with the individual[,] . . . the realistic novel, albeit with great ambivalence, asserted precisely the opposite: the redemption of the individual lay with the social world" (*Strangers* 75–76). Chesnutt's works blur this boundary: for him, it may be said that the redemption of each lay with the other.

This state of affairs, however, leaves us in the grips of a paradox. No one is an island; we depend upon others for existence and for our very identities. But the judgments of others are most often superficial and even bigoted, and thus our interdependence may be construed as a kind of tyranny. Consider this description of how Rena's decision to pass creates a great deal of unwanted complexity, and stress, for her:

> Rena's shrinking from the irrevocable step of marriage was due to a simple and yet complex cause. Stated baldly, it was the consciousness of her secret; the complexity arose out of the various ways in which it seemed to bear upon her future. Our lives are so bound up with those of our fellow men that the slightest departure from the beaten path involves a multiplicity of small adjustments. It had not been difficult for Rena to conform her speech, her manners, and in a measure her modes of thought, to those of the people around her; but when this readjustment went beyond mere externals and concerned the vital issues of life, the secret that oppressed her took on a more serious aspect, with tragical possibilities. (50)

Our interconnectedness with others defines us; in itself, that's not a bad thing, and John's resistance to this fact is his downfall. However, in Rena's case the novel illustrates how passing—which, from John's perspective, is an assertion that identity does *not* depend on others' valuations—intensifies her susceptibility to the whims and perceptions of others. Rather than stripping down her identity to an essential self, as John believes himself to have done, Rena has become more detached from the possibility of such an essential self than ever. Even her *thoughts* are now largely determined by the role she is playing.

So where does one draw the line, achieving an identity that is acceptably rooted in connections with others but also adequately grounded in some form of an authentic self that is at least relatively detached from others' valuations? It appears, based on both his portrayal of Rena and his self-portrayal in his letters and journals, that Chesnutt saw identifying as an African American as a partial, provisional answer to this question.[17] To be more definitive, one must be vaguer: for Chesnutt, the question of identity is one that must be solved ad hoc, with whatever materials make themselves available. In such a situation, appeals to abstract, permanent ideals are virtually useless in that they cannot answer the questions that are really important in a given moment, the questions Rena and others need answered in order to make enlightened decisions. "Would [Tryon] have loved me at all," she needs to know, "if he had known the story of my past?" (50–51). Although a number of observations are possible based on Tryon's eventual response to Rena's secret, there is no absolute answer to Rena's question.[18] His response depends on a number of variables (such as how he learns of her secret) and changes over time. The narrator informs us that "his liberality was not a mere form of words" (97), but clearly it has been retarded by social conventions that he is, for the moment, unable to break out of. A definite answer (which the novel never provides) could only, hypothetically, be achieved by disruptions of the social fabric and of time that are not possible—we can only move forward in time, and so Tryon's eventual response of devotion to Rena is absolutely useless because it comes too late, just as his earlier profession of love is useless for having come too early, before he knew of Rena's past.

What fuels *The House Behind the Cedars* is the sense that what its characters believe to be a completed story is actually dramatically in flux. As an abstraction, time is a nearly empty signifier, nothing more than the ticking-off of seconds on the town clock, "which so long as it was wound up regularly recked nothing of love or hate, joy or sorrow" (97). However, time is a serious factor in determining what concepts such as "love or hate, joy or sorrow" mean—these words signify differently based on perspective, and time is Chesnutt's primary metaphor for how the meaning of words necessarily depends on personal and historical contexts. Even within the mind of a given individual, such as Tryon, "love" means different things based on a perspective that changes over time; one reason his romance with Rena cannot be fulfilled, from a narrative point of view, is that his eventual coming-around to a stance of devotion cannot be trusted to last. To the extent that words are regarded in a cultural vacuum, as stable and permanent entities, they cease to carry meaning; if the concept of "love" presumes permanence, then Chesnutt, in the vein of documentary realism, professes that it does not exist. His commentary, however, is more sophisticated than that, and allows for more possibilities than the documentary stance alone can provide. *The House Behind the Cedars* depends on what its readers take to be the meaning of certain key concepts: "love," "black," "white," "freedom," "identity"—the list closely resembles a standard enumeration of what are often taken to be the central themes of American literary and cultural history.

Consistently, the novel invites readers to become engaged in recasting the meaning of these terms, and demonstrates that, absent such ongoing cultural and discursive work, such words will cease to mean anything—or, more likely, will continue to be defined by power relations which may not always protect the same readers in the same way they do now. Although a critique of capitalism may not seem as central to *The House Behind the Cedars* as it does to, say, *The Colonel's Dream,* here as elsewhere in Chesnutt's oeuvre, a pragmatic and dehumanized capitalist nightmare underlies the novel's anxieties. Every one of the events in the novel that refute idealism—starting with the disastrous death of Molly Walden's father described in chapter 18, and continuing on into John and Rena's abandonment of Molly—is rooted in economic pursuits somehow. The Jim Crow–era law that "[o]ne drop of black blood makes the whole man black" is itself explained by Judge Straight as simply being "more profitable" than its alternatives (113). The choice available to us is not between stable, traditional meanings and chaos; it is between an engaged realism that will create meaning in the ongoing historical—not the ideal—world and an alternative in which human life—*all* human life—will eventually cease to carry meaning or value.

As Stephen P. Knadler writes, "Chesnutt's novels . . . are oriented toward the future destabilization of nostalgic identities" (438). Though Knadler locates Chesnutt's interest in "future destabilization" of identities primarily in *The Marrow of Tradition,* I would argue that it fuels *The House Behind the Cedars* more completely than any other work by Chesnutt. Like "The Future American," which argues that racial amalgamation is not only likely but already in progress, *The House Behind the Cedars* strikes a tone of social possibility by pointing out not that change ought to occur but that it *is* occurring. The initial readership of *The House Behind the Cedars,* it is important to remember, was—due to a clever but overlooked narrative maneuver—not a readership of the present but of the future. From our vantage point a century later, it might be easy to forget that Chesnutt is not writing, in 1900, of his contemporary social world. Instead, the novel is set in about 1868, and its characters are anxious about their future—a future that the novel's readers are experiencing and enacting even as they read. If the novel is considered as social commentary, at least some of the unanswered questions it poses—especially questions concerning the nature of Southern life after Reconstruction—would seem, by 1900, to have been answered. Moreover, any sense on readers' part that the inevitable change Chesnutt refers to will mean progress is soundly refuted by the narrative. Change is inevitable, according to the novel, but progress is not. For example, in contemplating the white murderer of a black man who was sentenced to life imprisonment, Warwick, being "neither a prophet nor the son of a prophet, . . . could not foresee that, thirty years later [or, in the readers' 'present'], even this would seem an excessive punishment for so slight a misdemeanor" (3).

Rather than an idealistic appeal to an imagined future, then, Chesnutt borders on a pessimistic documentary realism, positing a world that is embroiled in change, but whose changes tend to be mechanistic ones that dehumanize people by placing them in rigid social roles, parts in a machine. Chesnutt subtly mocks the misguided hopefulness that drives readers' experience, much as Edgar Allan Poe deconstructed the detective-story genre even as he invented it, engaging his readers' attention in elaborate mysteries whose outcome is fixed and immutable. Like sports fans watching a previously recorded baseball game, readers foolishly invest their hopes in Rena, feeling hollow emotion when informed of what they might have predicted from the very start: she dies in the end. The book, the acts of writing it and reading it, cannot change the fact that the racism portrayed in *The House Behind the Cedars* has not been alleviated in thirty years' time, but has worsened; no more can Chesnutt (as he unsuccessfully attempted to do with *Mandy Oxendine*) write a "tragic mulatta" tale that is both intelligible to its readers and non-tragic.

But Chesnutt calls upon his readers to question whether that is the world they really want to live in, and to consider that the dismal history of the past thirty years need *not* continue to be plotted along exactly the same path: the future, as he suggests, is wide open. The trick is in making readers, by the novel's end, *want* the novel to have achieved something that initially they would never have contemplated, much less advocated. Chesnutt lets the careful reader know that Rena has died for *you*, to fulfill your demands, and encourages that same "you" to create a new mental space in which the Renas of the world might live and prosper. In one of the novel's few moments of intrusive commentary, the narrator instructs the readers that they must evaluate the characters' actions from a position other than detachment: "If there be a dainty reader of this tale who scorns a lie, and who writes the story of his life upon his sleeve for all the world to read, let him uncurl his scornful lip and come down from the pedestal of superior morality . . . and put himself in the place of Rena and her brother" (86). The work the novel shows to be necessary is, in a very literal sense, work for its readers: the novel deconstructs the "tragic mulatta" genre by demonstrating to an attentive reader its limits. It is, however, a progressively minded sort of deconstructive act, aimed at breaking down our reading habits and expectations—and the social world that these habits and expectations help create—in order to rebuild them better than they were.

As William L. Andrews compellingly argues, for Chesnutt "the real is not a constant but a function of words like 'Negro' and 'white' which are themselves but traces of racial *différance* in the cultural text of the racist American reading community" ("Slavery" 74). Chesnutt's realism is not an attempt to reflect or stabilize "reality" in words that somehow exist outside that reality, but to work through some of the problems of contemporary reality by working with words, the material of which it is constituted. In *Playing in the Dark: Whiteness and the Literary Imagination,* Toni Morrison concludes that "for both black and white American writers, in a wholly racialized society, there is no escape from racially inflected language, and the work writers do to unhobble the imagination from the demands of language is complicated, interesting, and definitive" (13). To recognize the possibility of "unhobbl[ing] the imagination" from the given possibilities of language emphatically does not cause Morrison to attempt an escape from history or culture; in the same breath she articulates her view that "[a] criticism that needs to insist that literature is not only 'universal' but also 'race-free' risks lobotomizing the literature" (12). Yet historical and cultural evasiveness, mistaken as they are, are not the only possible threats. On one hand, it seems true—as critics such as Matthew Wilson have pointed out—that Chesnutt's narratives might well refute his intentions, leading to stasis or even more racism rather than less ("Who Has the Right" 31–32). On the other, it seems equally true—as his more sympathetic critics have often argued—that his works contain a power that is exciting in its potential to cut through layers of racist discourse and arrive at politically powerful truths.

These are not necessarily two Chesnutts, and neither of the two interpretations is necessarily incorrect; certainly neither is complete. The problem is one of language, and of literary theory: Chesnutt's commentary in *The House Behind the Cedars* comes about indirectly, by means of what Mikhail Bakhtin describes in "Discourse in the Novel" as a "fusion of voices" and of genres that makes his intent harder to pin down but renders his text fuller with life, with possibilities (however uncertain of being realized) of continuing dialogue (315). Chesnutt asks much of his readers—in some ways, more than his contemporaries among the realists who invite their readers to gaze through a mask of presumed objectivity—and, in return, he offers them a dramatic, risky degree of control over what his writings will mean.[19] As Morrison powerfully explains, works of literature are revitalized by an active, process-oriented reconsideration of their boundaries and meanings, and Chesnutt has only recently begun to take his rightful place among American authors whose richness of imagination—not despite but *because of* his sense of political urgency—allows for stimulating, productive, and potentially transformative readings.

Chesnutt appears to have crafted a novel that takes a supposedly simple cultural narrative—that of the "tragic mulatta"—and subtly warps it into a more complex statement about race. The result is one that careful, critical readers can respond to with attention and delight: as Ferguson notes, "critics claim that *The House Behind the Cedars* is the most artistic of Chesnutt's published novels" ("Rena Walden" 204). Yet, as she points out, the politics of the novel's reception are more complicated, and in some respects troubling, in that reading the novel aesthetically may require one to "ignore the extent to which the author uses it as a vehicle for racial propaganda" (204). While I think Ferguson's argument is essential, a necessary corrective to political readings of Chesnutt's work that are too facile, I also see more possibility than she does of the novel being used toward better political ends—not as a means to the end of African Americans' absorption in white culture, as she fears, but potentially toward a more diverse, complicated world of the sort Ferguson herself might accept as a goal. Readers, I argue, have a responsibility to find in Chesnutt's texts the challenge that he presents to them: that of seeing the world as it is, but also as it can be, and taking upon themselves the work of remaking it. Imagining a world that is truly diverse, however, requires more capacity for self-reflection than readers in Western culture typically exhibit, and we will see in the next chapter that Chesnutt became partially disillusioned with complexity as a goal for his narratives. Readers of elaborate, realist literature, one would expect, are especially capable of embracing the needed complexity in the very act of reading the world; but if the complication of a reading act is exhausted during the process of reading—if, as aesthetes, readers revel in it, only to emerge once again into an external world of reassuring simplicity—then they do both the text and the extra-textual world (the larger, social text) a disservice.

In other words, if readers can recognize the complexity of *The House Behind the Cedars* but remain incapable of *doing* anything with it, then the reading experience becomes worse than useless; it becomes counterproductive.[20] If, as Ferguson suggests, the novel has a simple—and troubling—message but disguises that message through a series of feints and maneuvers, making its readers feel as if they have undergone real mental or imaginative movement while in fact asking very little of them, then it would not be worth reading. If, however, it truly is capable of motivating readers fundamentally to reimagine how race is and could be regarded—of influencing readers to enact a future that is not simply a recycling of the past—then this power remains available for readers to find and use. The success of *The House Behind the Cedars* remains, inevitably, up to its readers. Recognizing that his contemporary readers were depressingly incapable of the sort of response he hoped to invoke, yet apparently hoping that a future readership would be up to the task (the jury's still out), Chesnutt worked, in his following novel, toward a yet more challenging approach to the problem of racism in the United States. In *The House Behind the Cedars,* Chesnutt manages to demolish romanticism as a mode for thinking about racial politics, opens up a new space, but struggles to find anything to put in that place. He figuratively throws up his hands, leaving the remaining work to future readers and authors. The novel is a work of realism, but fails (as other realist works failed, in dealing with race) to do much more than document a situation and begin to wiggle our understanding of it, to "unhobble the imagination" from the limitations seemingly set by language and culture as they are presently constituted. In *The Marrow of Tradition,* he begins more substantively to explore not just the limits of romance, but the possibilities of realism.

3

Simple and Complex Discourse in *The Marrow of Tradition*

~

> Literature may be viewed in two aspects—as an expression of life, past and present, and as a force directly affecting the conduct of life, present and future. I might call these the subjective and objective sides of literature—or, more lucidly, the historical; and the dynamic, the forceful, the impelling. History is instructive, and may warn or admonish; but to this quality literature adds the faculty of persuasion, by which men's hearts are reached, the springs of action touched, and the currents of life directed.
>
> —Chesnutt, "Literature in Its Relation to Life" (*Essays and Speeches* 114)

Evidence of Chesnutt's always tenuous but enduring faith in the power of literature can be found in a 1909 letter he wrote to William M. Brown, a Southern bishop who had the temerity to send him a copy of his white supremacist volume *The Crucial Race Question.* After calmly but forcefully castigating Brown's views, Chesnutt concludes the letter by explaining, "I take pleasure in sending you a copy of a book from my own pen, which treats the same general subject in a very different manner" (*Exemplary* 73). We do not know which of his books Chesnutt mailed to Brown, but it can be said with certainty that a decade earlier, as he observed (via news reports, personal interviews, and his own research travels) the violence inflicted upon African American residents of Wilmington, North Carolina, which would become the basis for his novel *The Marrow of Tradition,* he saw a situation in which the power of abstract concepts such as justice, and of the words to describe such concepts, was sorely tested.

For Chesnutt, untruthful literature must be countered by truthful literature. Yet the events of November 1898 in Wilmington seemed to demonstrate that the power of words, like any source of power, will be exploited best by those who are strongest to begin with, in this case the town's white Democratic-party leadership. A pretext for the Wilmington "riot" was a lucid, forceful editorial by African American newspaper editor Alexander Manly arguing (in H. Leon Prather, Sr.'s words) that "[not] every sexual contact between black men and white women [was] an act of rape" (23). Moreover, the white rioters' ability to translate Manly's words and other texts into physical and economic violence against Wilmington's blacks rested in their control of the media but also, as Leslie H. Hossfeld writes, in their intended audience's receptiveness to loaded language regarding white superiority and African Americans' political participation. The white supremacists of Wilmington were able to employ fraught words from the Revolution and the Civil War—"beauty (white womanhood), courage, honor, virtue, and independence" (Hossfeld 36)—in a way that the town's African Americans could not. As a result, Wilmington's black population was terrorized, deprived of their rights, and in many cases driven out of town, and numerous among them were murdered in what Prather more properly terms a "massacre" (20). The massiveness of the task Chesnutt undertook for himself, to wrest away some of the discursive control that the white "victors" in Wilmington had successfully asserted, must not be overlooked.[1]

What, then, convinced Chesnutt that such a discouraging discursive environment would prove fertile soil for his second novel, one intended not only to sell much better than *The House Behind the Cedars* but also to stand with Stowe's *Uncle Tom's Cabin* and Tourgée's *The Fool's Errand* as formative texts in "depicting an epoch in our national history" (*"To Be an Author"* 162)? Certainly, the manifest injustice of what happened in Wilmington struck Chesnutt as a powerful story, yet he cannot have failed to note the grim lesson learned by Manly, that appealing forthrightly to readers' sense of "justice" can be hazardous. Nor could he count on a Northern white readership to be entirely free of the blind spots of their Southern counterparts. If one of his novels was to succeed commercially, it must be "in spite of his subject, or rather, because of its dramatic value apart from the race problem involved," as he had become convinced by the time he composed the novel (*"To Be an Author"* 150).

Nonetheless, to achieve what he wanted to achieve with the novel, Chesnutt knew he must rely on his audience. "It is true," he wrote to his editors at Houghton Mifflin, "that I have not been writing primarily for money, but with an ethical purpose entirely apart from that; yet I have always hoped that I might perchance strike a popular vein, for unless my books are read I shall not be able to accomplish even the ethical purpose which I have in view" (*"To Be an Author"* 171). Rather than pandering to either their interests or their emotions, however, he challenges his readers to rise to the occasion of his troubling and realistic portrayal of the events in Wilmington. More than a political novel, *The Marrow of Tradition* is written as a work of realism, based on the assumption that truths made understandable to a reading audience must tend toward morality.

It would be accurate to say that Chesnutt did not accept this guiding principle so much as attempt to test it out in composing *The Marrow of Tradition.* The realism of someone like Howells, which in Henry B. Wonham's description "never commits itself to an identifiable moral or political vision" but instead points out "the limitation of any view of reality that forecloses some other view of reality" (51), may seem in some ways foreign to a reader of Chesnutt's novel. Can a person successfully read *The Marrow of Tradition* without sharing its author's moral and political vision? To some, as Brook Thomas points out, realism's detachment from "preconceived principles" makes it seem "unreceptive to novels with a purpose" (278), and *The Marrow of Tradition* certainly appears to be a "purpose" novel. The novel is written from a point of view, but more significant (and harder to notice) than its political commentary is the test case Chesnutt provides for realism: can realist methods be applied successfully to the sorts of events that occurred at Wilmington—events that, although shocking, would have been hardly new to any black Southerner at the turn of the century, a violent undercurrent of reality that was always present in its potential, if not its realization? Could any words represent even a semblance of the reality of the Wilmington events to someone who did not experience them?

Is realism, in other words, up to the job of representing racial existence in the South? As Daniel H. Borus writes, realism as Howells saw it was meant to overcome the culture's "divisiveness" by presenting "a unifying picture of . . . common life" (172). In painting this picture, however, the realist must eschew an overtly political stance; he or she "could not adopt the people's causes personally but must instead ruthlessly and unemotionally fictionalize them" (173). A standard reading of *The Marrow of Tradition* is that Chesnutt does indeed take up the cause of Wilmington's African American citizens, shaming the white rioters of Wilmington and directing his readers to recognize the inherent nobility of its principal black spokesmen, the brave insurgent Josh Green and the restrained pragmatist Dr. William Miller. Although there is a grain of truth to this assertion, critics who read *The Marrow of Tradition* as propagandistic neglect to notice just how restrained Chesnutt actually is in presenting to his readers the events of Wilmington and, more generally, the interactions that occur on the "color line." As Ernestine Williams Pickens argues, the novel has suffered from a double bind: attacked as melodrama on one hand, its artistry has been neglected due to Chesnutt's fidelity to historical events on the other (50–51).

Given the nature of the historical events he was describing, if anything it is remarkable that Chesnutt retains as much detachment as he does. Indicates

Matthew Wilson, "if one compares his performance in this novel to [Thomas] Dixon's in *The Leopard's Spots,* which was published a year later, Chesnutt is the model of restraint" (*Whiteness* 234 n. 6). If there is a superfluity of emotion involved in the experience of reading *The Marrow of Tradition,* perhaps we must consider that this emotion is not directly a function of Chesnutt's carefully controlled technique but a response to the nature of the events he depicts. In Chesnutt's design, *The Marrow of Tradition* is a novel to which readers must respond, and if it has done its work, they respond not only to the particular manner of depicting reality, but to the depicted reality itself. Yet a novel's ability to instill in readers the proper response to such events as the Wilmington riot is vexed, as Chesnutt saw, by the tangled forms of discourse available for talking about race. If language is the medium for representing reality, and yet our language reflects pernicious habits of mind concerning race, then by what possible route may the novelist compel readers to accept the responsibility, and the risk, of seeing past the standard categories to something like the truth?

The Marrow of Tradition attempts to give a physical presence to realities that a Northern audience might otherwise understand only as abstractions, depriving the massacre "of all its poetry" (253) by putting the lie to the revisionist accounts available from the Southern media. Well aware of the Southern establishment's efforts to palliate its racial situation in Northerners' eyes by means of selective presentation (efforts he derisively describes in chapter 13, "The Cakewalk"), Chesnutt attempts to get at the reality of facts such as Jim Crow segregation laws. What happens if a train passenger, such as Dr. Burns, resists the law? Explains a conductor, "[t]he law gives me the right to remove him by force. I can call on the train crew to assist me, or on the other passengers. If I should choose to put him off the train entirely, in the middle of a swamp, he would have no redress—the law so provides. If I did not wish to use force, I could simply switch this car off at the next siding, transfer the white passengers to another, and leave you and your friend in possession until you were arrested and fined or imprisoned" (54–55). Passages like this one are designed to get at the nuts and bolts of segregation; in them Chesnutt refers not to concepts like justice or equality but to physical events: here, the removal by force and the abandonment of train passengers.[2] Similarly, aware that the meaning of the whites' "race riot" would be shaped in Northern readers' minds by the public relations efforts of its perpetrators (313–14), the author counters these efforts with a grisly description: "At the next corner lay the body of another man, with the red blood oozing from a ghastly wound in the forehead. The negroes seemed to have been killed, as the band plays in circus parades, at the street intersections, where the example would be most effective" (287).

The murder of African Americans on the city streets is both a bodily and a textual act, a killing but also a spectacle and a warning to others. Chesnutt attempts to reclaim the symbolism of this violence in the interests of African Americans' rights, and does so consistently with detached description rather than intrusive commentary. But could such descriptive details do their proper work? To put it another way, might such a description be discounted by Chesnutt's readers as mere words—no more (and likely less) authoritative than contemporary newspaper accounts that attempted to palliate the violence? The textually mediated nature of the events at Wilmington, in which the ability to control discourse created the ability to inflict violence, is the subject of considerable ambivalence on Chesnutt's part, providing him with both an obstacle and an opportunity. As in *The House Behind the Cedars,* he recognized in writing *The Marrow of Tradition* that in order to achieve realism, he would first have to get at the roots of racial discourse. One reason, perhaps, he selected the Wilmington "riot" as his topic is that it provided an opportunity to thematize the power relations underlying such discourse, which in turn could be upended only by a virtuosic performance such as he attempted to pull off in this novel. By directly portraying the Southern whites' insidious use of discourse to augment their power, he attempts to exert at least a degree of constraint upon that power. In this undertaking, simply describing the events would be inadequate. He would have to demonstrate to his readers the relativity of perspective while also inviting them somehow to share in a perspective that, at least provisionally, exists outside of the particularities of time and space.

In other words, the novel Chesnutt set out to write must be rooted in its historical moment while also, paradoxically, unconfined by that moment. As Ian Finseth points out, *The Marrow of Tradition* is engaged with "abstract issues" concerning race and language as they "play out in a particular moment of American history" (3). Recognizing, as Finseth writes, that "the struggle for racial justice would be waged, and could only be won, on the field of common discourse" (3), Chesnutt attempts to determine what sort of language would be most advantageous in this struggle. An illustrative technical question he encountered in writing the novel, which I explore in the present chapter, is this: should the discourse surrounding race become more simple or more complex?

In a sense, Chesnutt's answer to this question seems easy to discern: a notable achievement of his writing is to complicate matters that may seem simple, showing, for example, that social structures and discourses are infiltrated by racial concerns more often than people usually realize. As the title of *The Marrow of Tradition* itself suggests, one goal of the novel is to get at the marrow of practices that people enact seemingly without a thought, and Chesnutt repeatedly sheds light on the often covertly racialized history behind practices that seem, from a casual viewpoint, merely natural.[3] He announces this aim in the opening chapter of the novel, in which Jane Letlow, nurse to the infant Dodie Carteret, explains the history behind Olivia Carteret's separation from her half-sister Janet, a history that bears upon much that happens later in the novel: "[I]t goes fu'ther back, suh, fu'ther dan dis day er dis year" (4). Everything does. In this regard, the novel is justly viewed as a masterpiece in the realist tradition, showing as it does the occult significance of seemingly unremarkable events. Yet a significant strain of *The Marrow of Tradition* interrogates the efficacy of this sort of realism as a political instrument, and suggests the strong possibility that, in endlessly complicating our understanding of the world around us, writers risk producing a form of discourse that is verbose, cyclical, and ultimately passive—one that, Chesnutt seems to fear, merely replicates the discursive world of the Southern racists portrayed in the novel, for whom the seemingly obvious nature of injustices is obviated by the claim that every act is something *other than* what it appears to be.

The Marrow of Tradition tracks the intersecting fates of two families, the Millers and the Carterets, which are bound up by family ties (the white Olivia Carteret and the biracial Janet Miller are unacknowledged half-sisters) and, eventually, by the "Wellington" racial massacre provoked in part by the newspaper writings of Olivia's husband. In the novel's design, every event is subtly connected to a tangled series of past and future events in ways of which the characters are often unaware. Chesnutt's narrator frequently references past occurrences that provide the events of the novel's "present" with textures of meaning. The narrative (including many of the characters' speech) slides easily and almost imperceptibly between the present and the past, as in this typical passage from the first page: "The stifling heat, in spite of the palm-leaf fan which he plied mechanically, was scarcely less oppressive than his own thoughts. Long ago, while yet a mere boy in years . . . " (1). Besides being rooted in the past, the novel's events are connected to the future: nearly all of the subplots, from the serious (the near lynching of a black murder suspect, Sandy Campbell, on spurious evidence) to the frivolous (the rivalry for Clara Pemberton's hand in marriage), have at least an indirect impact on the way in which the so-called "race riot" plays itself out in the final six chapters. A central issue in the novel is the characters' ability or inability to maneuver this tangled web of events to suit their own ends. Phil Carteret, the character Chesnutt treats in most detail, attempts to manipulate events (and it is significant that, as a newspaper editor, he attempts to control events *textually*), but ultimately sees the violence he has instigated flare out of his control, as the attempt to intimidate African Americans devolves in the mob's hands into indiscriminate slaughter.

The unsuccessful attempt to leave behind a troublesome past and to enact some control over one's future is, in one way or another, the fatal error of each of the novel's major characters. Tom Delamere attempts to cover up his past misdeeds and retain the respectability that will gain him Clara's hand by murdering his aunt, Polly Ochiltree, for money. William Miller chooses to overlook what he knows to be the bloody "history of his country" and attempts to enact the Booker T. Washington–endorsed path of professional education, even as it becomes evident that this route will not protect him and his family from racial violence (278). And Phil Carteret (even as he indulges in nostalgic fantasies of re-creating an idyllic South that, in Chesnutt's analysis, never was) pulls himself out of postwar poverty and attempts to start a dynasty that his son, Theodore Felix ("Dodie"), will extend by purchasing a newspaper and using it to ensure Democratic party dominance over state politics. Miller and Carteret invest a great deal of symbolic capital in their infant sons, as does Chesnutt—with a somewhat different purpose. Although Carteret, dismayed by the devastating consequences of his efforts at political control, purports to "wash [his] hands" of the massacre (307), he soon learns that the tendrils of his actions extend into his family and threaten his most cherished goal. His sickly son, Dodie, left unattended because the Carterets' black servants have fled for home during the massacre, has developed a deadly case of croup and can be saved only by Miller, a highly qualified African American surgeon. All other qualified doctors in Wellington either have fled town or are attending to casualties of the violence.

The Millers, however, have lost their own son to the massacre: the doctor's wife and child were caught in the streets during the violence, and the boy has been killed by a stray bullet. Initially Dr. Miller declines to attempt to save Dodie, but at the behest of Olivia Carteret's entreaties he defers to the decision of his wife, Janet, who grants her half-sister's request in order "that you may know that a woman may be foully wronged, and yet may have a heart to feel, even for one who has injured her" (329). Although it correctly will seem that the Millers have the moral upper hand in this exchange, their suffering also suggests a deeper point. Parallel characters to the Carterets, the Millers are characterized as aloof from—and implicitly as holding themselves superior to—the rest of the black community, and while Chesnutt does not dwell on the comparison, it seems that their son occupies a similar importance in his parents' aristocratic sensibility as Dodie Carteret does in his. Both the Carterets and the Millers learn—or at least are provided the opportunity to learn—a critical lesson: that their actions cannot be isolated from the larger social context in which they take place. Prior to learning that the Millers' child is dead, Phil Carteret predicts that Dr. Miller will accept the call to treat Dodie, and had the Miller child not been killed, there is no reason to assume that his prediction would have proved wrong. Whether to operate on Dodie is a moral dilemma for William Miller: he must determine whether cooperation with the white community makes moral sense any longer. But the dilemma is not caused by his own son's death—only his awareness of it *as* a dilemma is. It is keeping with Chesnutt's analysis that a black family is more severely punished than a comparable white one for a similar limitation of perspective: the price paid differs although the underlying lesson is the same. Chesnutt faults the residents of Wellington for failing to understand that they share a common—not individual—future, one less susceptible to their control than they appear to believe. A minor white character, Dr. Burns, characterizes the novel's guiding perspective when he remarks that the future of African Americans "is a serial story which we are all reading, and which grows in vital interest with each successive installment. It is not only your problem, but ours" (51).

As the preceding synopsis suggests, the vulnerability of children is full of symbolic resonance for Chesnutt. The endangerment of Dodie Carteret, in particular, structures *The Marrow of Tradition,* as Dodie's life is in jeopardy in the beginning (chapter 4), the middle (chapter 11), and the end (chapter 36) of the novel. The first occurrence of this motif, which I wish to examine closely, provides a suggestive allegory for the challenge Chesnutt saw himself as facing in rendering the Wilmington violence in the form of a novel.

In the three chapters leading up to the scene, Dodie has been found choking on a small piece of ivory. Dr. Burns, a specialist from Philadelphia, has been summoned to the Carterets' home in Wellington to carry out a delicate, risky operation that will remove the offending material from the child's throat. Upon arrival, however, Burns nearly refuses to operate because Dr. Miller, a former protégé of Burns, has been refused entry into the Carteret home, in keeping with Major Carteret's well-known advocacy of white supremacy. Burns finally succumbs to Carteret's claim that his bias against Miller is not only racial but personal, and he prepares to operate. Chesnutt describes the preparation for the procedure, which itself is life threatening for the patient, in riveting terms: "The implements needed for the operation were all in readiness—the knives, the basin, the sponge, the materials for dressing the wound—all the ghastly paraphernalia of vivisection" (78). Following this buildup of carefully controlled intensity, Chesnutt elects, at the last moment, to spare little Dodie the trauma of having his throat surgically cut. Burns, the now somewhat compromised hero of the scene, notices that "[t]he obstruction seems to have shifted."

Continues the narrator, "[a]pplying his ear again to the child's throat, he listened for a moment, intently, and then picking the baby up from the table, gave it a couple of sharp claps between the shoulders. Simultaneously, a small object shot out from the child's mouth, struck [local physician] Dr. Price in the neighborhood of his waistband, and then rattled lightly against the floor. Whereupon the baby, as though conscious of his narrow escape, smiled and gurgled, and reaching upward clutched the doctor's whiskers with his little hand, which, according to old Jane [Letlow], had a stronger grip than any other infant's in Wellington" (78). While hardly central to the novel's plot, this scene is important for an array of reasons. The story of Miller's refused entry into the Carteret home as an attending physician, and the related sequence in chapter 5 in which Miller is humiliatingly forced to leave a "whites-only" railroad car despite Burns's protestations, are among the most powerful scenes of the novel, anticipating the striking ending in which the moral dilemmas surrounding race relations in America are vividly enacted. Yet the easily overlooked description of Dodie's "narrow escape" is itself worth close attention if one considers that Chesnutt's novel is not so much an attempt to expose racism as it is an exploration of racial discourse, to examine how we talk about race and the implications of our manner of talking. As Finseth argues, "the novel's conflict of race emerges in large measure as a conflict of language" (2). While Chesnutt generally seems to assume that any solutions to the problems facing the nation must be complicated, carefully controlled, subtle, and enacted over a long period of time, some part of him seems to feel—or, at least, strongly hope—that an end to racial injustice can be enacted swiftly and with minimal disruption of the social structure as it exists.[4] Just as Dodie evades an operation that is complicated and risky, and which carries no guarantee of success, Chesnutt appears to hope, despite his realist methods and his realistic understanding of the nature of power, that the nation's race problem can be corrected with a strong, precisely applied whack on the back.

Designed to produce just such a whack, *The Marrow of Tradition* may have been an easy novel for a Northern white audience to agree with, but Chesnutt seems to wish his readers to do something much more challenging than merely agree. Chesnutt was well aware that most of his likely readers were not racists, at least in theory. The problem is that, while a reader may be moved emotionally by reading literary scenes such as those Chesnutt presents in this novel, spurring readers into action is a trickier matter to achieve. *The Marrow of Tradition* is not clearly intended to convert racists into nonracists; it seems meant instead to change nonracists into antiracists—that is, to make the fight against racial injustice no longer an abstraction, but central to one's consciousness, and as a result to one's decisions and actions as well. This remains, in my view, a contribution this novel has the potential to offer.

Reinforcing Chesnutt's apparent conviction that racism demands a more substantive response than abstract belief is the principle that even white Southern racists typically do not *believe* what they say about African Americans. Were we to probe just a little beneath the surface, the novel suggests, we would find, if not a spirit of egalitarianism, at least a grudging acknowledgment that racial hierarchies are nothing more than a seemingly convenient (to themselves) social arrangement. No one who knows oppression for what it is truly believes in it.[5] Susan Gillman is precisely correct in stating that "[f]or Chesnutt, white supremacy is a slogan, not a belief" (1081). Carteret's fellow white supremacist General Belmont, for example, upon reading the "frank and somewhat bold" antilynching editorial in the local black newspaper, says privately that "there's some truth in it, at least there's an argument" (85). Furthermore, despite his apparent conviction that Miller cannot be an effective doctor, at the novel's end Carteret clearly knows that Miller can save his son's life. Particularly among the wealthy, middle-aged cynics such as Carteret whose power against African Americans seems most pernicious, an ideology is something that can and will be dropped as soon as its costs outweigh its benefits in the assessment of its bearer—although it must be kept in mind that those benefits include psychological as well as more obviously material ones.[6] Ideological positions such as Carteret's which to their bearers seem fixed and immutable, part of one's very identity, are shown in the novel to be tenuous and relative, after all.

The inveterate nature of racism is central to the novel; as the narrator remarks, "[t]he habits and customs of a people were not to be changed in a day, nor by the stroke of a pen" (7). Yet this remark summarizes the perspective of Dr. Price, a white Southerner, and it is fair to say that Chesnutt only reluctantly agrees with it. Racism, he contends, is both enacted through individual acts and a system that exists at a deeper level than any specific act, and its slippery nature makes it all the more difficult to slay. Recognizing that in many ways the racists' tactic has been to oversimplify racial discourse, Chesnutt unsurprisingly contends that the proper response is to reinstitute the real complexity of the matter, to examine the history of each act. Yet Chesnutt, who admired *Uncle Tom's Cabin* for its treatment of "deep-seated, fundamental realities" (*Essays and Speeches* 521), seems to wonder if the power of simplicity, so ably exploited by the white power structure, ought not to be employed by the antiracist faction as well. Why not simply expose racism for what it is?

An answer to this question is provided by the events in Wilmington: any representation of reality is deeply saturated in power relations that are not easy to recognize, let alone control. To get a sense of the discursive difficulty *The Marrow of Tradition* is contending with, consider once again the exchange between Major Carteret and Dr. Burns concerning Dr. Miller's presence at the operation. Carteret convinces Burns to operate on his son by making the matter both less and more complex: more so, because what Burns had originally regarded as a straightforward matter of racism is now explained to be about both race *and* personal history (Dr. Miller is a reminder to Mrs. Carteret of her own troubled family past); the major convinces Burns that the issue is not as simple as it had seemed. Yet, ironically, this maneuver actually makes the decision simpler for Burns, since he suddenly (to his evident relief) does not have to consider any factors beyond the word of Major Carteret. In this sense, Carteret's ability to restrict the meaning of words to suit his purposes becomes the very definition of his authority, an authority that Chesnutt appears to associate with authorship. Burns no longer has to examine the complexities of his own implication in racial injustice, something he has been forced to contemplate while in the South, and may simply act according to traditional, comfortable patterns.[7]

While Burns is left with the impression that Carteret's words have altered a simple matter (standing firm against racism) into a complex one (a mixture of racial and personal histories), readers can recognize that the reverse is, in fact, more accurate: Carteret has slyly made Burns's decision to operate easier by reducing the factors that Burns must consider. Making the choice more complicated actually makes it easier, since Burns, predictably, shies away from the complexities of the matter and, rather than inquire further into the history of Carteret's prejudice, simply takes him at his word. This scene represents Chesnutt's view on Southern racists' methods: they have managed to negotiate complex and simple answers to their antagonists' objections quite adeptly, as it suits them. In many ways, Chesnutt seems to aspire to a way for antiracist agents to become similarly adept and fluid at controlling discourse to suit their ends. And he saw *The Marrow of Tradition* as a contribution to this strategy, as can be seen in his efforts to send copies of the novel to a number of prominent American political leaders (Sundquist, *To Wake* 427).

Like Howells and other realists of his day, Chesnutt was convinced that representing the world accurately and fully was inherently a morally significant act; yet he also recognized that the efficacy of such an act of representation was problematic if others were not mentally prepared to recognize the truthfulness of his words. As Finseth writes, "[h]is well-known goal to effect a moral revolution in his readers . . . depended in large measure on an *intellectual* approach to the problem of racial division" (3): he could not bring his readers to the emotional response he wanted them to have if he did not, first of all, persuade them of his logical premises, in particular the premise that racism harms the perpetrator as well as the victim. The novel's emotional, ostensibly manipulative, and inexact treatment of the Wilmington massacre has been the subject of much criticism since its publication. Rather than evidence of Chesnutt's inconsistency of method, the mingling of historical data and emotionally resonant material ought to be seen as the result of a struggle—successful, in my reading—to make the intellect and the emotional faculty work in concert: to make the novel not only a representation of but an integral part of the "currents of life" to which the author alludes in this chapter's epigraph. The realism of *The Marrow of Tra-*

dition is designed to uncover genuine (though normally unexpressed) dilemmas and possibilities, especially when they interrogate our casual, often contradictory, and even insidious ways of viewing the world.

Remarked Chesnutt, in a letter written early during the composition of *The Marrow of Tradition*, "[i]f I could propose a remedy for existing evils that would cure them over night, I would be a great man. But I am only a small social student who can simply point out the seat of the complaint" (*"To Be an Author"* 156). Despite his self-deprecatory tone, it seems clear that Chesnutt cherished both of these goals for his fiction and saw them as related. In practice, realist writing is limited to "pointing out" social ills, but in its potential realism is capable of spurring radical social transformation—since, he believed, only genuine knowledge of the social world could bring about dramatic change. But genuine knowledge means more than having information: people, it seems, are failing to invest their observations of the world with the proper significance and fullness. Verisimilitude—in the form of deep context, objective presentation—is not a certain conduit to more nuanced viewpoints because the problem is not that people have too little data; it's that people don't *do* the right things with the data they have. Much of Chesnutt's aim in the novel is to construct a text that compels readers to look at things they would just as soon avert their eyes from; this, I would argue, is just as central to his realism as the dense histories he draws.

Yet this aim is tempered by the realization that people can look at what is directly in front of their eyes and still not see it; seeing is less a matter of what enters the eye than a matter of what the brain allows itself to process. Over and over in the novel are scenes in which a character appears to know something that he or she is unwilling to acknowledge. Two of the most prominent are John Delamere's gradual conviction that his grandson Tom is the villain who murdered Polly Ochiltree, which he seems to understand at some level before he admits it to himself, and Olivia Carteret's comprehension of the contents of the envelope left by her late father, which she resists opening because she knows she does not want to see its contents. Delamere enacts the sort of response Chesnutt seems to hope his white readers will achieve: faced with contradictory convictions—that neither Tom nor Sandy could have committed murder—he is sufficiently stirred by the rank injustice of Sandy's impending lynching that he comes to accept the conclusion that is less convenient for him personally, that more deeply shakes the world he has known as white patriarch, but that is more truthful.

For her part subject to a "vague uneasiness" arising from Polly Ochiltree's hints that half of Olivia's inheritance ought, by rights, to have gone to her sister Janet (255), Olivia expends considerable energy trying to discount the evidence in her own mind. The more knowledge Olivia acquires about Janet's legitimacy as an heir, the more vigorously she attempts to discount that knowledge, illustrating the degree to which the uses of knowledge are, for Chesnutt, hostage to their context of reception. Olivia is acutely aware that to acknowledge Janet's legitimacy as her sister and fellow heir would carry a cost—"[t]o have it known that her father married a negress would only be less dreadful than to have it appear that he had committed some terrible crime" (270)—yet the consequences of ignoring her muted awareness, and more generally the legacy of violence and disinheritance bestowed on African Americans, are also shown to be costly to Olivia. The novel dramatizes the anguish she experiences as she struggles with an understanding of the reality of what has been done in her name. She (in common with Chesnutt's Northern white readers) is implicated in these legacies, and a necessary step toward the resolution of racial problems is the acknowledgment of this implication. Simply to acknowledge the facts of what occurred at Wilmington, as Matthew Wilson indicates, was more than many of the novel's readers were willing to do: the bulk of contemporary reviews of *The Marrow of Tradition,* coupled with the disappointing sales of the novel, reveals that it failed to persuade a white readership of its author's "right to enter into discussion in the public sphere with an alternative view of important events" (*Whiteness* 119). Even had it succeeded in this respect, simply for readers to concede the facts of the case would have been insufficient. In *The Marrow of Tradition* Chesnutt insists that these readers also examine their own implication in a legacy of racism, motivated by psychological and even material self-preservation if not by a sympathetic imagination.

He attempts to bring readers to this understanding in three main ways, each of which is affiliated with a realist aesthetic. First is an attempt at understatement in challenging his white audience: in an often-quoted passage from his journal of 1880, he announced his intent "to lead [the reading public] on imperceptibly, unconsciously, step by step to the desired state of feeling" (*Journals* 140). *The Marrow of Tradition* seems meant to adhere to this approach, challenging white readers much less directly and forcefully than it might have under the circumstances. However, the reaction of both Chesnutt's contemporaries (such as William Dean Howells) and recent critics suggests that his approach in the novel was not taken as subtle. Chesnutt seemed genuinely surprised and offended, in the wake of negative reviews of the novel, at the tendency of even sympathetic readers such as Howells to interpret it as unduly "bitter" (*"To Be an Author"* 234).

Second, as I have suggested, he presents the argument to his readers in terms of simple self-interest. The narrative repeatedly suggests that a changeable, even volatile, environment has (ironically enough) been created by the efforts of Carteret and others to regain an unconvincingly idealized past, and it underscores that their desires for the future—a constant reference point in the novel—will not likely be realized in such an environment. The interests of neither Miller nor Carteret are well served by present circumstances. "The South," writes the narrator in an uncharacteristic intrusion, "paid a fearful price for the wrong of negro slavery; in some form or other it will doubtless reap the fruits of this latter iniquity" (241).

Third, and most crucially, Chesnutt's narrator adopts the perspective of his various characters neutrally, and in such a way that even the most villainous of them is furnished with several moments in which his or her interior life is represented in a balanced and even sympathetic manner. For example, the thoughts of the murderous Tom Delamere—though the most unknowable of the novel's characters given his thoroughly performative nature—are narrated with considerable detachment, as when Tom's "sense of security" is ruptured by Carteret's lecture (94). Readers are invited to adopt the perspective of even the solidly evil Captain McBane in a scene in which he attempts to force Tom to sponsor his membership in the elite Clarendon Club (an event which indirectly leads to the race riot). The narrator registers McBane's awareness of Tom's elitism: "McBane was good enough to win money from, or even to lose money to, but not good enough to be recognized as a social equal" (158). In a realist vein, the attempt is not to judge but to understand McBane's position at this moment, yet Chesnutt also realizes that the moment carries emotional resonance: a typical reader's response is likely to be against Tom's snobbishness and therefore—helplessly—in favor of McBane's appeal to Tom, which itself is part of a plan of cynical social climbing that the novel conditions readers to fear. Chesnutt, quite daringly, asks his readers to identify with evil, a position that he possibly could himself identify with as an author who found it necessary, as a political agent and a literary writer, to imagine and write down words like McBane's: "All niggers are alike. . . . A nigger will steal a cent off a dead man's eye" (181). It must have been intensely uncomfortable for Chesnutt to devise and write those words, and no less discomfort is expected of their readers, who must experience, through the act of reading, their own complicity in evil, and thereby—it is hoped—be motivated to excise that evil by enacting political change. Even as readers may resist identifying even momentarily with Tom or McBane, they are pressed to acknowledge that they are not mere spectators.

Critics who have faulted *The Marrow of Tradition* for its supposedly one-dimensional characters fail to recognize the degree to which this evaluation is forced by our unwillingness to assess how much of a Tom Delamere or a Captain McBane resides in us. And we—meaning readers who easily see the injustice of the white supremacists' machinations—reside in them, to a larger extent than may be seen at first. The novel's Southern whites, even deeply racist ones such as Carteret or Belmont, do not believe that black people are genetically inferior or that "Negro domination" threatens whites' well-being. Rather, they fully know—though they do not often allow themselves consciously to acknowledge—that these "beliefs" are *lies.* The horror of the novel is that these characters can act as they do *despite* their submerged awareness of the immorality of their behavior. What is interesting to Chesnutt is the ability to blind oneself to the implications of one's own actions, in the face of evidence (for example, of African Americans' intellectual equality) that is self-condemning.

Though Chesnutt grants that Carteret and his peers are often sincere in their private comments in favor of segregation, he also makes clear that their perspectives, however heartfelt, are rooted in an understanding that is *partial,* and not only partial from a cultural standpoint—partial in terms of self-understanding, as well. Carteret's antiblack editorials, we learn, are written with "entire conviction" (31), and his and others' "revulsion" at the sight of African American authority is "spontaneous" (33). Nonetheless, such statements are consistently accompanied by others like the following: "In serious affairs Carteret desired the approval of his conscience, even if he had to trick that docile organ into acquiescence. This was not difficult to do in politics, for he believed in the divine right of white men and gentlemen, as his ancestors had believed in and died for the divine right of kings" (33–34). Though Carteret's belief system passes every empirical test of sincerity, Chesnutt still seems convinced that there is a "conscience" in each individual, a guide to right behavior that lies deeper than mere political belief. This conviction is central to one of the novel's fundamental tenets: that ultimately no one, white or nonwhite, benefits from racism. *The Marrow of Tradition* unabashedly speaks the language of truth even though it also, in a realist vein, shows truth to be complex, fragmentary, and essentially unknowable except in partial, interested form.

Chesnutt elaborates on this view in a 1904 speech on "The Race Problem," in which he challenges his primarily white audience to see past the propaganda of white supremacist leaders and acknowledge their own instinctive sense that injustice is occurring:

> I think it is safe to assume that you are all here because you realize that there is something wrong about the national attitude toward the Negro, and that as good citizens and as Christian men and women, you are anxious to know the right, in order that you may the more effectively do it. I know, too, that your minds are clouded by a multitude of diverse opinions; nor am I sanguine enough to hope that they are entirely free from prejudice—and by that I mean the influence of ances-

> tral tradition and current opinion. I know that able arguments are presented every day by forceful writers, entirely of your own blood, to convince you that the white race was ordained to overrun and rule the whole earth, and that [ministers and politicians] preach the same doctrine. . . . And yet, in spite of all this diversity of view and forcefulness of argument, I am convinced that you are anxious to know the right, and are groping about in this cloud of conflicting opinions, in search of it. (*Essays and Speeches* 198)

By analyzing the rhetorical gesture of this nonfiction work, one can get a clearer glimpse of what Chesnutt was aiming to accomplish in *The Marrow of Tradition.* Appealing to both his white audience's self-conscious idealism and their rather murkier, less self-conscious sense that "there is something wrong" in contemporary racial discourse, he invites them to align their idealistic and their pragmatic selves and to resist being manipulated by those who serve a racist political agenda, who threaten idealism by endlessly muddying the national discourse about race.

The result, he suggests, will be a clear vision of a complicated situation, one that "involves the painful and difficult problem of race, of blood—which reaches questions of labor, and popular education, and social movement, the distribution of wealth" and cannot be remedied with a quick fix (199). Once a majority of whites come to recognize that "[t]his problem is your problem," he concludes, they will prepare themselves for the necessary work of eradicating racism (201). The job of the novel, likewise, is not to provoke the reader into moral outrage so much as it is to clarify that the work of ending racism is work for both whites and nonwhites. If the ending is capable of producing an outraged response, it will be because the novel's prevailing moral and pragmatic stances have, at last, become consolidated. Racism, in the novel's design, is meant to be understood not as an abstract problem occurring in the distant South but as a problem that Northern whites participate in, and whose consequences they share—something immediate and real.

The observable use of realist technique in *The Marrow of Tradition*—in particular its objectivity of narration—is part and parcel of Chesnutt's activism as a writer; these do not exist in tension but, rather, work together. Charles Duncan cites *The Marrow of Tradition* as a prime example of the way in which Chesnutt's "skillful handling and arrangement of several voices in addition to his own" allow him to explore "issues of racial interaction from varied points of view" (12). The novel's social purpose can largely be explained in terms of Chesnutt's conviction that truthful knowledge, although always tenuous and partial, must ultimately reveal that racism is in almost no one's self-interest; however, because of its tenuous, partial nature, such knowledge can only be achieved discursively, through one's immersion in many different voices. The novel reveals its author's fascination with the contradictory meanings a given text takes on depending on context. The primary example of this, of course, is the editorial by Barber, "a frank and somewhat bold discussion of lynching and its causes" which dares to assert that some accusations of rape by white women against black men are false and instruments of racism (85), and which is used by white supremacists to stir up the race riot. Other examples abound, however: Ellis's verbal protection of his rival, Tom Delamere, which results in his own motives being misinterpreted; Merkell's will, which favors his wife, Julia, but is stolen by Polly Ochiltree in an assault on Julia's rights; and Carteret's instigation of the riot itself, which quickly flares out of his control and eventually jeopardizes the life of his own son.

The effect of Barber's editorial upon its white readers is odd, in that literally it does no more than establish what its readers tacitly acknowledge as truth but nonetheless provokes outrage: "Its great offensiveness lay in its boldness: that a Negro should publish in a newspaper what white people would scarcely acknowledge to themselves in secret was much as though a Russian *moujik* or a German peasant should rush into print to question the divine right of the Lord's Anointed" (243). That is to say, the outrage is a response not to the literal content of the editorial but to the power its author appears to have asserted in presenting these claims to the public. And yet, even in responding to that assertion of power by Barber, the white population of Wellington is responding to somewhat of a fiction: he does not seem willfully to have provoked scandal by positing a "right" to speak plainly to them; the presumption seems entirely to be subjectively understood, imposed upon the editorial by its readers. So what exactly are these readers responding to? Not the editorial's literal content, nor to anything that can be called a rhetorical implication created by Barber's employment of words, but evidently to an implication of the editorial that resides entirely in its readers' unconsciously acknowledged sense of things as they are. That is, they are rioting in response to a document that acts merely as a mirror, one that relates nothing more nor less than the truth of their own actions.

In the 1890s South, an African American speaker of truth like Barber is compelled to be diplomatic and restrained, or suffer the consequences, whereas a white man like McBane may utter vile lies with impunity. Although despicable, McBane is useful to Chesnutt as a relatively unvarnished speaker of an actual sentiment, one with which he and other African Americans had to contend. In a sense, McBane—as a speaker unable to edit his sentiments—is less a threat than the insidious Major Carteret. Although McBane is overtly more violent, the novel suggests that Carteret's strategic approach enables McBane's violence; the latter is a function of the former. Much as the white supremacist "Big Three" (Carteret, Belmont, and McBane) enact a plan to use Barber's editorial in a way that its author would consider abhorrent, Chesnutt finds voices useful even—or especially—when they articulate a position that is diametrically opposed to his political agenda. In this sense, Miller is wrong in claiming that Barber's editorial "could do no good" (277). Like any group of words, to the extent the editorial has power it is capable of doing either good or bad. As an instrument, it is neutral, although readers' uses of it are not. Thus, rather than simply lament the existence of the editorial, Miller's responsibility is to help create a context of reception in which it does its proper work. Far from being a propagandistic attempt to shut off opposing voices, *The Marrow of Tradition* manifestly embraces them as at least potentially useful—if, that is, readers can learn to regard them from an appropriate perspective.

Changing one's vision is no simple matter, but it is the work for which Chesnutt attempts to prepare his readers—always with the awareness that these efforts may be for naught. Repeatedly, the novel illustrates instances in which what appears obvious is, in fact, diametrically at odds with the truth. One example is Polly Ochiltree's suspicion of an affair between Sam Merkell and his housekeeper, Julia, which—although this affair does eventually occur—was at that moment untrue. A more central example is that of Sandy, John Delamere's servant, who is supposedly seen winning a cakewalk and, later, leaving the scene of Ochiltree's murder. Both cause trouble for Sandy, who is cast out from his church in the first instance and jailed (and nearly lynched) in the second. Readers can recognize these outcomes as particularly unjust because they can see, more quickly than characters in the novel, that Tom Delamere in disguise is the real culprit. In order for the novel to do its cultural work, however, the reader's vision must be problematized as well. It is a simple matter to see that Sandy is the victim of an injustice; readers must also ask how many injustices (both intra- and extratextual) they have not so easily recognized.

Tracing what is suggested but unseen is central to the act of reading the novel successfully, and Chesnutt plants numerous hints of an unseen world, the understanding of which is critically important. This technique helps to establish Chesnutt as an adherent, and a contributor, to realism: in common with Howells, James, Wharton, and other acknowledged practitioners, he places great significance on invisible elements of reality, that which is understood without being shown or stated directly. The question for such an author, then, has to do with the social conditions that enable one to function (or not to function) in such a world. A world heavily marked by the unseen and unsaid is deeply politicized, since it depends so greatly upon certain social understandings that are taken for granted. These understandings, need it be remarked, are rooted in exclusivity; one must be a member of the club fully to grasp their presence and import, though of course they also have great influence on those who are not part of the club. Chesnutt is astute in recognizing these elements in the social milieu of Wilmington, North Carolina, and in allowing his readers to notice as many of them as their attentiveness permits them to notice. His efforts are by no means restricted to pointing out the unseen aspects of social existence—many of them, notably Sandy's apparent kinship to Tom Delamere,[8] are left to the reader's imagination (or, more accurately, interpretation). Chesnutt is training his readers to read his book, and—more crucially—the types of social relations his book portrays. The reading act he advocates requires us to be more attentive readers but also, paradoxically, less attentive ones, considering that the ways in which racial divisions (and their putative rationales) are "kept constantly in mind" (56) are part of the problem. Being a better, more productive reader depends on noticing the hidden signifiers that explain how our world works, but for Chesnutt it also seems to depend on getting underneath these hidden signifiers and, in a tenuously idealistic vein, acknowledging common realities that are not contextually dependent, that are simply truthful.

The effect of tracing the theme of "truth" in *The Marrow of Tradition* should not be to cast Chesnutt as naïve or simplistic in his assumptions. How can one know the truth? I believe the answer to this question offered by *The Marrow of Tradition* might be summed up as follows: one *cannot* know the truth definitively, but the work of trying to know it is essential work. Of course, this undoubtedly is work he hopes his readers can learn to become engaged in, too, and the book can be explained as an extended attempt to help readers do just that (as can the most useful criticism that has followed its publication). *The Marrow of Tradition* is resplendent with disruptive moments, such as the novel's ending, which cause the psychological and political barriers to abstract truth to crumble. Such moments, however, primarily cause the characters *within* the novel to lose their blinders; Chesnutt, meanwhile, seems concerned with his readers' own shortsightedness. If truths are linguistically complex and from a practical standpoint unknowable, why bother? The answer that *The Marrow of Tradition* offers to this question reveals the real complexity of the novel.

In the social landscape portrayed in *The Marrow of Tradition,* neither the powerful nor the powerless are at liberty to speak plainly; both must exercise a great, even a troubling, amount of verbal discretion, either in order to maintain power or to avoid annihilation. Only those who have little left to lose, either due to social circumstance (Josh Green and other resisters during the massacre) or due to age (the devastatingly blunt Polly Ochiltree), habitually say what they mean. While the white supremacists' words are often striking in their ugliness, Chesnutt seems greatly interested in ways these words are shaped by political exigencies, and in how else they might be shaped by the properly employed imagination. As Jae H. Roe writes, Chesnutt "calls his reader's attention to the historical record of 'the newspapers,' but immediately subverts the authority of that official history by giving greater authority to the counter-memory of 'the people of Wellington'" (236). Only if "the people" find a way to resist received ways of interpreting racial discourse, and thus to upend political realities in which few of them prosper, can meaningful change be enacted. As Roe persuasively argues, *The Marrow of Tradition* leaves only the possibility of "collective resistance" (242) as a reasonable, proportionate response to the legacy of racial violence Chesnutt portrays. Given what he recognized to be the inability of his readership to rise to the occasion, says Roe, the "real anguish of the novel" arises from Chesnutt's palpable recognition that it must fail in its mission (237). While Roe shows Chesnutt to write from a position of desperate powerlessness, even hopelessness, what he doesn't quite articulate is how much this state of affairs frees Chesnutt to speak plainly, to challenge his readers and harness his urgent vision toward political ends.

In exploring *The Marrow of Tradition,* I have traced its balancing of historical contexts and detailed environments against an emotional and ethical appeal to abstract concepts such as justice.[9] In examining his adeptness at playing objective and subjective methods off of one another, a seemingly ancillary question has been that of Chesnutt's place in the canon of American realism. This is, however, no mere matter of definition or categorization, for classifying (or not classifying) Chesnutt as a realist author begs an important, but often overlooked, question: how does literary realism account for the construction of race? For example, do traditional definitions of realism allow room for useful and productive depictions of race and racism; or must we content ourselves with the highly problematic (yet firmly enshrined as realist) presentations produced by figures like Twain, Tourgée, Cable, and Howells himself?[10] Understanding Chesnutt's achievement, I believe, requires us to reassess what realism is and does, notably (though not exclusively) because he opened up possibilities, merely suggested by his realist contemporaries, for depicting matters of race in narrative.

To articulate realism as Chesnutt seemed to—as nothing more or less than the attempt to use art to refocus individuals' understanding of surrounding realities rather than affording them the luxury of escape—does no injustice to its coherence or usefulness as a concept. In light of this evaluation of *The Marrow of Tradition* and its continuing possibilities for readers, it seems necessary to endorse and extend the ongoing redefinition of realism, one that acts less as a framework to be imposed upon texts than as a concept that arises *from* texts and helps to explain how they work.[11] Insisting on a preexisting framework can lead us dangerously close (from a narrative if not a political standpoint) to the approach of Katherine Glover, who wrote a review of *The Marrow of Tradition* that appeared in the *Atlanta Journal* in 1901. With astoundingly bold ignorance, Glover wrote: "Chesnutt should print his picture with his book in order to allow his readers to know whether he is a white man or a negro. This is said with all seriousness. After reading the work it is impossible to tell. The preponderance of evidence suggests that he is a negro. It really makes a difference, because it is possible to understand how an educated, ambitious, and disgruntled negro could have written the book, but it is not possible to understand how a white man of sound mind in his sober senses could have been guilty of the book upon which Chesnutt places his name" (84). Leaving aside the irony that, were Glover able to examine Chesnutt's photo, she would no doubt have come to the wrong conclusion (since Chesnutt appeared white), and apart from the abject racism of this passage, the problem here is that Glover claims a disturbing inability to interpret a novel in the absence of a framework, some outside machinery that would tell her what to make the words mean. At bottom, she invokes the question of narrative authority: the question of whether Chesnutt is white or black is, for Glover, equivalent to the question of whether he has the authority to say what he has said. How, she wonders, has Chesnutt asserted the right to write a book "that is totally at variance with those on which all that come from this section have been writing" (84)?[12] Glover's response reveals exactly what Chesnutt was getting at in the novel: that the power of words to communicate is not simply a matter of denotation; more significantly, it is a matter of how they may be used in a particular cultural moment—and by whom.

Instead of simply despairing in recognition of this state of affairs, Chesnutt attempts to reawaken his readers to the discursive choices available to them, to reclaim for them a position of active involvement in the making of meaning (without, on the other hand, ceding to them so much authority that they may escape less convenient implications of the text's indictment of racism). Rather like Olivia Carteret in the last pages of the novel, who asks "[w]as there no way to move this woman [Janet]?" (327), he wants to know how he can compel readers to come to the right conclusion about what they have just read. His writing seems designed to compel readers, somehow, to see what they already understood the world to be like but conveniently forgot. *The Marrow of Tradition* suggests repeatedly that every white racist knows the reality that his or her treatment of blacks is unjust, though those who believe they stand to lose out from the observation will consistently—perhaps always—either push this knowledge somewhere down in the unconscious or ignore it. Thus, the effectiveness of realist methods, narrowly defined, is compromised: showing people what injustice looks like can hardly be expected to have a deep effect if people are roundly unwilling to see it for what it is.

The Marrow of Tradition is defined by moments in which characters, especially the representatives of the white power structure, come to an instantaneous recognition of what, Chesnutt suggests, at some level they already knew to be true. Often, these moments occur as a result of violence or other great dissonance, as in the conclusion when Carteret discovers the reason why Miller refuses, this time, to save his son: "In the agony of his own predicament,—in the horror of the situation at Miller's house,—for a moment the veil of race prejudice was rent in twain, and he saw things as they were, in their correct proportions and relations" (321). Reading the novel itself seems to be designed to induce such a sense of dissonance. Yet the troublesome problem of the novel, one that Chesnutt declines to resolve in the open-ended final lines, is how to translate one's understanding of "things . . . in their correct proportions and relations" into action, how to make such moments of revelation count. The narrator describes selfishness as "the most constant of human motives" (239), and for this reason it seems questionable whether knowledge of the truth can ever be relied upon to bring about ethical decisions. After prospective lynching victim Sandy has been proved innocent, and the lynch mob dissipates in chapter 27, the narrator seems nearly at a loss for words that will make sense of the events: "Thus a slight change in the point of view had demonstrated the entire ability of the leading citizens to maintain the dignified and orderly processes of the law whenever they saw fit to do so" (232). At issue is not only the possibility of changing people's behavior by altering their perspective, but also Chesnutt's prospects, as an author, of getting his readers to use the revelations brought about by the novel to some purpose. In either case, people may be moved to change, but only, it seems, if their selfish inclinations cause them to do so. Chesnutt's aim for the novel, then, is equally important for his contemporaries and for readers of the twenty-first century: to instill a degree of self-consciousness, of involvement as a reader with a stake in what's being read, that may make such self-involved, inert readings a little more difficult to sustain.

People are least likely to sustain self-involved, self-interested readings of the world, Chesnutt suggests throughout his writing career, if they retain at least a relative idealism that does not render any semblance of hope foolish.[13] Chesnutt can come across as rather cynical indeed about the prospects for racial progress, as he does in this opening to a 1916 speech titled "A Solution for the Racial Problem":

> Several evenings ago a young man called at my house to talk over the Race Question; an intelligent, eager young man, filled with zeal for social service and the uplift of humanity. With the impatience of youth, he wanted to find an immediate solution for this vexed problem. We discussed various suggested remedies—education, property, the ballot, assimilation, segregation, expatriation—in fact every "'ation" except annihilation, which, historically, has settled some racial problems. When he left, about eleven o'clock, I was glad to see him go, and the Race Problem was no nearer solution, except by about three hours time, than it was when we began. I don't know that we will be any further along with it when I shall have finished, except perhaps by another hour. (*Essays and Speeches* 384)

Here Chesnutt seems gently to mock the "young man," but—importantly—he is not altogether dismissive of the sense of urgency his visitor conveys. In fact, though he is quite understandably frustrated by the lack of practical solutions the dialogue has produced and "glad to see" his visitor leave, Chesnutt has spent three hours discoursing with the young idealist about how to alleviate racial problems, and it seems no stretch to say that, despite its apparent futility, for him *this is the work that needs to be done.* After all, in the absence of black Americans' voices in discourse about their fate, nothing less than "annihilation" looms as the alternative the white community may resort to. One might even surmise, given the incident's placement at the beginning of this speech—a speech in which Chesnutt points out that racial problems are "solved" or "in rapid process of solution" in other Western Hemisphere nations—that Chesnutt describes the visit in order to accentuate his hopefulness amid futility, or at least to counterpoise these two modes of thought in some productive balance.[14] Indeed, whereas Chesnutt begins the speech on a cynical note, the tenor of his remarks becomes increasingly idealistic as he continues, so that near the end he states, "[t]here is but one way to settle the race problem; that is to give the Negro equal rights. It is not difficult; given the will to do so on the part of the white people, it is the simplest thing in the world" (397).

What, then, will produce in white Americans the will to advocate equality for nonwhites (in the face of which the social and economic barriers faced by African Americans must quickly crumble), and in black Americans the will to sustain hope in the face of virtually no evidence that any results will accrue? It is this question that Chesnutt ponders as the author of *The Marrow of Tradition,* though nowhere more clearly or deeply than in the novel's striking and controversial ending. I have been suggesting that how closely Chesnutt adheres to something like "reality" is the wrong question to be asking, even in the context of considering him as a realist author, given that such an approach to realism begs the question of whose reality is being spoken of. The question Chesnutt faced as a realist, rather, is this: how might realities be portrayed in a manner that produces an appropriate and proportionate reaction to them? Lorraine Hansberry once asserted of her play *A Raisin in the Sun* that "[i]f we ever destroy the image of the black people who supposedly do find these things tolerable in America, then the much-touted 'guilt' which allegedly haunts most middle-class white Americans with regard to the Negro question really would become unendurable" (196). Essentially, she is asking what it will take to move readers and viewers beyond a rather passive emotional reaction to her play and toward the actions that such emotions would seem to demand. Chesnutt asks a similar question with the ending to *The Marrow of Tradition.* The final chapter, "The Sisters," is almost unavoidably seen as manipulative, and critics who wish to defend it seemingly must defend its manipulative nature, which in turn would seem to jeopardize the novel's status as a realist text.

The narrative perspective of the novel's penultimate chapter, interestingly, is that of Major Carteret, and the final chapter's perspective is that of Olivia Carteret. How can these characters, whose beliefs and words have been thoroughly saturated by racist ideology and momentary self-interest, learn to see the world differently—or can they? These are not questions to which Chesnutt seems willing to provide a definitive response. Because the Carterets serve as stand-ins for Chesnutt's primarily white readers, their capacity to be changed is equivalent to these readers' capacity to extend their understanding and use of the novel into the extraliterary world; both are unresolved at the novel's end, which provides both promising and dispiriting evidence. At issue is agents' (here I mean both the Carterets and the novel's readers) ability to do just what Chesnutt has done, that is, involve oneself in the discourse of another. Major Carteret enters the scene of the Millers' grief sensing that "[t]here was some mystery here which he could not fathom unaided" (320). Although his awareness, when it comes, of what he has done causes him to see things "in their correct proportions and relations," his resignedness to the "pure, elemental justice" of Miller's refusal is problematic (321).

Carteret, though shaken, seems likely to remain unmoved in the long term from his supremacist position. As Wilson writes, "Carteret's unracialized vision here is characterized as momentary" (*Whiteness* 138). While overtaken by "a certain involuntary admiration for a man who held in his hands the power of life and death, and could use it, with strict justice, to avenge his own wrongs" (*Marrow* 321), he is still firmly situated in the rhetoric of Western justice and power. Miller has won this round, we can surmise, but Carteret's recognition of his humanity—which recognition has always informed his views, if silently—will not equip him with any certainty to change his behavior. Passive acknowledgment of African Americans' humanity is not enough; Chesnutt asks more of his white readers.

Although Olivia's appeal to the Millers is rooted not in a concept of justice but in self-interest (as are all actions portrayed in this novel; Chesnutt is up front in asserting that this impulse governs all human behavior, and that self-interest, properly seen, is in conflict with racism), it is somewhat more positively constructed. In asking herself "[w]as there no way to move this woman?" (327), Olivia implicitly learns that the very immovable nature by which she had heretofore defined her world—the supposedly unshakable ideology that allowed her to function up to then—is a problem, and not just a problem for others; it is now, as it has always been (though less visibly), an impediment to her own self-definition and her material and immaterial pursuits. A prerequisite to change is talk, and so it is significant that the welled-up feelings of both sisters, Olivia and Janet, must come out in order for the bare possibility of progress to surface. The thrust of this outpouring of feeling is not that it will allow the sisters to become close once more: Janet makes it abundantly clear that "I have but one word for you,—one last word,—and then I hope never to see your face again!" (328). Rather, it is the last in a series of disruptive moments in which the novel explores what is necessary for a change in position to take place. Is Olivia's emotional appeal, ultimately, hypocritical? Assuming that Dodie is saved, will she continue to acknowledge Janet as her sister as she promises to do? These are matters of interpretation; that is, of response. The answers lie not in any conclusion Chesnutt can provide to us, but in the nature of the world as readers continually make it.

Critics such as Roe and Wilson have emphasized the undercurrent of despair in *The Marrow of Tradition,* an element that seems to undercut the hopefulness of the novel's last line: "There's time enough, but none to spare" (329). Readings that find the ending optimistic, writes Wilson, are "contradicted by the events of Wilmington" (*Whiteness* 139); Roe similarly contends that the novel questions, rather than endorses, "the uplifting effect of Miller's actions upon the Carterets [and] the power of writing itself" (238). Yet the novel argues dramatically that no one can be sure of what the future will bring, and its narrative strategies are predicated on readers' ability to do—someday—what they have not yet shown the capacity to do. Given that the final chapter seems designed to evoke a flood of emotions even within the most hardened cynic, two categories of response seem possible: to regard the evocation of emotion as the novel's stopping point, its essential essence (whether in celebration or contempt), or to locate ways to use those emotions as an impetus toward change. Simply put, energy is created by the ending of *The Marrow of Tradition* and must be expended; how it is expended is a question of whether or not a particular reader is willing to be changed. Those who are not, I contend, are compelled instead to adapt their conception of what the novel *is*—to assert that the novel has fallen short rather than its readership. Though Chesnutt, I presume, knew very well that many of his readers would misconstrue the novel in reaction to their feeling that it asks too much of them, he also seems to have recognized that a novel that asked less could never match his aspirations as a realist writer.

4

The Colonel's Dream

Reconsidering a Radical Text

As a cultural and economic analysis in literary form, *The Colonel's Dream* merits serious study alongside realist and naturalist works by writers like Wharton, Dreiser, and Norris. It also warrants attention as a precursor to calls for African American resistance voiced by writers like Du Bois, Wright, and Malcolm X. In saying this, I am conscious of being out of step with the critical consensus both of Chesnutt's day and among recent scholars. Even those who take *The Colonel's Dream* seriously tend to damn it with faint praise.[1] The 1905 novel, which relates the unsuccessful attempt of Colonel French, a former Confederate officer turned Northern businessman, to reform the Southern economy through the infusion of capital and a classical-liberal emphasis on hard work and enterprise, effectively ended Chesnutt's writing career. Apparently demoralized by the novel's lack of commercial success, he published only a handful of stories during the remainder of his career.[2] William L. Andrews writes, "Chesnutt seems to have viewed *The Colonel's Dream* as his last chance to get it all said in one book, so to speak, before going on to other literary topics" (*Literary Career* 222). The impulse to "get it all said in one book" is useful in understanding Chesnutt's narrative decisions: rather than a departure, *The Colonel's Dream* is in many ways the logical extension of what the author had been attempting in his previous novels.

The Colonel's Dream explores some of the same terrain as *The Marrow of*

Tradition, taking place once again amid white Southerners' fears of "nigger domination" (73) and demonstrating that these fears cause them to act not only brutally but, from the perspective of rational self-interest, stupidly. Rather than representing the consequences of oppression as explosively as he had at the end of *The Marrow of Tradition,* however, Chesnutt now subjects them to a studied, carefully paced analysis. The slow, unchanging quality of the town of Clarendon provides the author opportunities to document the myriad ways in which both whites and blacks have been burdened by the adherence of the former to a racist ideology, which in turn is cynically exploited by robber barons like Bill Fetters, the villain of the novel. Into this environment Chesnutt inserts the would-be catalyst Henry French, a Confederate colonel who has in the decades since the war become a wealthy Northern capitalist. Initially returning to Clarendon for the health benefits of its warm climate, French becomes enamored of the town's Southern charm, which for him is suffused with warm nostalgic feelings, and at the same time outraged by its lethargy and inefficiency. Declaring his intent to extend his stay and "wake them up," French undertakes to reform Clarendon by building a cotton mill and hiring laborers for "decent hours and decent wages" (120), thus reforming a system in which white and black men remain out of work while women and children spend sixteen-hour days laboring for low wages in the cotton mills of adjoining towns (115).

Like the editors of a local newspaper, the *Anglo-Saxon,* French assumes that the South's "vast undeveloped resources needed only the fructifying flow of abundant capital" in order to pull the region out of its feudal state (86), and like them he does not connect its economic problems to its enduring racist legacy. At first he finds reform as easy to spark as he had anticipated. Even the relatively modest act of buying and restoring his former home causes signs of a thriving economy to be seen. Before long, however, French's ambitious efforts are thwarted by local opposition. Not only does he face the active opposition of Fetters, whose firm control over the town is threatened by French's efforts, but local whites' hostility is provoked by his qualified disavowal of "the deep and distinct color line" (156). Motivated slightly, if at all, by egalitarian principles, French intends—if only on the basis of sound business—to hire African American workers on an equal basis to whites and to fund black students' education in "an industrial school or some similar institution" (161). Even these limited reforms become the "thin entering wedge" that undermines his popularity in Clarendon and dooms his chances of success (191). Although French rightly considers the antagonism of Fetters his most difficult obstacle, it is not his enemy's economic prowess but Fetters's ability to stoke the town's enduring racism—something French never regarded as his battle—that ultimately defeats him. Fetters's agents effectively blame French for the violent acts of an African American convict, Bud Johnson, who was freed from de facto slavery with French's assistance. Yet the final straw in demoralizing Colonel French is, as far as readers are told, not directly related to the battle with Fetters. An anonymous "committee" unearths the grave of his African American servant Peter to send a racist message, finally breaking French's will and sending him back to New York, his reform work in shambles.

Critics have traditionally, and correctly, seen in French's discouragement a hint of Chesnutt's own disillusionment as a writer. In *The Colonel's Dream,* Chesnutt pushes his faith in realism to its limits. By sacrificing much of the unity that marks the earlier novels, *The Colonel's Dream* takes both Chesnutt's narrative technique and his political analysis farther than he has taken them before, minimizing the degree to which he shapes reality so that it is palatable to white audiences. In doing so, he once again questions—both formally and thematically—whether or not realism can achieve the result he has hoped for with his writing career.[3] In *The Marrow of Tradition,* Chesnutt had brought his outrage at the brutal stupidity of white supremacy, and the ostrichlike acquiescence to it by more liberal whites, to the fore; however, the novel's apparently wide-open ending mitigates this outrage, if not the analysis behind it, by concluding the narrative on a tone of hope. *The Colonel's Dream,* in contrast, demonstrates that the elusive hope expressed in *The Marrow of Tradition* is, after all, delusional. It is the culmination of Chesnutt's efforts to reform realism, and its disavowal of almost any narrative devices meant to motivate or inspire readers renders it his most honest work.

The inferiority of *The Colonel's Dream* is usually argued on two bases. First, the novel is (along with other of Chesnutt's writings) seen as didactic: the generally sympathetic Frances Richardson Keller, for example, writes that it "leans more heavily toward the presentation of a thesis" than Chesnutt's better works (194). As I hope to show, and as critics such as Dean McWilliams have also argued (166), the "thesis" of *The Colonel's Dream* is less obvious or uniform than it has been taken to be, although it is true that Chesnutt does orient the novel around some of his most strongly felt beliefs. Secondly, *The Colonel's Dream* has been regarded as lacking in unity. Andrews, though largely neutral on the novel's aesthetic merits, articulates what a New Critic would find lacking in the novel, writing that in order "to construct a novel that would be widely read despite its distressing sociological thesis, Chesnutt leaned even more heavily on the props of the popular southern romance and the stage melodrama," leading to "a strange hybrid indeed" (*Literary Career* 223).

Gary Scharnhorst, on the other hand, finds a payoff in this presumed flaw, describing *The Colonel's Dream* as "a remarkably modern, multilayered experiment . . . that satirically rewrites many of the standard literary formulas popular around the turn of the century before the story implodes and collapses in the final pages" (271). Pointing out ways in which the novel parodically employs elements of temperance novels, Uncle Remus–style tales, hidden-treasure stories like *Tom Sawyer,* and other genres, Scharnhorst describes the novel as a unique, if limited, achievement for its time: "More than any other turn-of-the-century novel, *The Colonel's Dream* disrupts the familiar patterns of popular fiction and disdains the comforts of a happy ending" (280). However, Scharnhorst's assessment appears, from available evidence, still to be in the minority.[4]

Another, rarely stated, reason *The Colonel's Dream* may lack critical attention is that its main characters are white. Andrews notes that "the pendulum of authorial interest swings almost totally within the confines of white experience, between a white hero and heroine, between a white protagonist and antagonist. There are only two noticeable black faces among the supporting cast in the story, and these two figures provide more symbolic than realistic racial portraits" (*Literary Career* 223). Like Hurston's *Seraph on the Suwanee* (1948) and Wright's *Savage Holiday* (1954), *The Colonel's Dream* has perhaps seemed a relatively minor work from an author considered to be preoccupied with issues of race; at any rate, these three novels have received little critical attention compared to their authors' other works. In common with *Seraph on the Suwanee* and *Savage Holiday,* however, *The Colonel's Dream* cannot accurately be said to evade issues of race.[5] In common with his earlier works, in this novel Chesnutt describes racism as a problem for all citizens, regardless of racial identity; to the extent that whites have disproportionate power in the society, it is especially their problem (though, of course, the burden of the problem in real terms falls most heavily upon African Americans and other nonwhites).[6] Though Chesnutt had, in his earlier works, felt a duty to replace stereotypical characterizations of African Americans with fuller and more positive ones, in *The Colonel's Dream* his primary purpose is to analyze the root causes of racism; this leads him to questions of power, especially economic power, and that was, of course, the nearly exclusive province of white Americans. Critics must be careful of assuming that the absence of black characters equates to the absence of "race" or of a productive racial analysis.[7]

Considered as an example of literary realism, *The Colonel's Dream* appears to tend in contradictory directions. The novel's establishment of distinct villains and heroes works against its realism, although, as we will see, the boundary between hero and villain is more problematic than it may initially appear. From a contemporary perspective, many sequences can come across as inordinately contrived. Though Chesnutt was willing to shun an unrealistically happy ending, instead documenting the slow, wholesale defeat of French's reform efforts in Clarendon, other plot lines are effectively wrapped up; whether things end well or badly, Chesnutt seems unwilling to leave many loose ends. A sympathetic minor character, Ben Dudley, is rescued from an anticipated life of poverty and stasis when a deus ex machina in the form of a letter arrives to inform him that his invention of a new cotton gin will make him rich. This does not occur, however, before the object of his affection, Graciella Treadwell, has conceded her devotion to him, demonstrating her virtue by accepting his proposal of marriage before he gains wealth, not after. In an especially implausible coincidence, the Treadwells discover that Fetters owes them money—exactly one day before the twenty-year statute of limitations on the debt has run out (253). The debt and its repayment, however, are only incidental to the overall plot, one of several loose threads that might be taken as Chesnutt's lack of artistry but, from my perspective, tend to redeem him as someone who recognized that the world is not as unified as most novels.

In several respects, *The Colonel's Dream* seems an almost ideal specimen of both realism (as a genre) and realistic prose. In the vein of a reform novel, it incorporates raw data (such as an accurate enumeration of some of the most oppressive laws of Southern states) into a compelling story, in recognition that even the "enlightened few" do not realize the nature of the situation in the South (228). Many of the novel's dramatic pyrotechnics, in fact, seem intended to make the otherwise dry reform-oriented material palatable to a reading audience, and Chesnutt integrates these elements rather well—producing a narrative that aptly demonstrates the impact of political issues on private lives.[8] With apparent accuracy, the novel documents racialized discourse of the late nineteenth century (much of which evokes Civil Rights opponents' discourse into the late twentieth century). The rampant foreshadowing of his other novels is more restricted here, most often subtly underlining the interconnectedness of events rather than providing an artificial flair to the narrative. Chesnutt also seems interested in playing with his readers' expectations as novel readers, bending what initially seem like standard romantic elements out of their usual shape, with the effect being a novel that provokes self-consciousness of its adherence (and non-adherence) to literary conventions. For example, French's engagement to Laura Treadwell, the embodiment of female aristocratic virtue, seems a foregone conclusion by chapter 10; when a complication develops in the form of seventeen-year-old Graciella's romantic interest in the colonel, it seems like the baldest contrivance. As it's meant to: the trivial complication is quickly dismissed, and when French's eventual engagement to Laura is, after all, ended in chapter 27, the reasons for the breakup, and the emotions and dialogue surrounding it, hold up compared to other realist works of the period.

While the novel's characters do at times carry heavily symbolic functions—French's son Phil, in particular, as the last in the ancestral line, carries the same significance as Dodie Carteret does in *The Marrow of Tradition*—in spite of these functions most characters are fairly well developed and exist as more than contrivances. Although Phil dies, and his death (of course) serves a function in the plot, it does not carry the heavy-handed symbolism that Dodie's brushes with death, and the death of the Millers' (curiously unnamed) child, do in *The Marrow of Tradition.* Whereas the Miller child dies directly, and Dodie's life is threatened indirectly, as a consequence of the Wellington race riot that is central to the plot of *Marrow,* Phil's death upon being hit by a railcar is, in comparison, incidental. The later novel's deaths are important primarily in how they are interpreted: French's enemy Fetters claims that Phil's death is "a judgment on" French (268) and the disposition of the body of Peter, who also dies in attempting to save the boy, becomes subject to dispute. Furthermore, Chesnutt refrains from investing Phil's death with the religious overtones that Harriet Beecher Stowe imposes (as Jane Tompkins has argued, to great rhetorical effect) upon Little Eva's death in *Uncle Tom's Cabin.* The movement from *The Marrow of Tradition,* in which a child's death is in itself rendered heavily symbolic, to *The Colonel's Dream,* in which things are significant not as they are but as they are interpreted, represents a progression in Chesnutt's surety as a novelist, one he had been working toward for some time.

As a consequence of Chesnutt's growing pessimism, and of his apparently heightened intent to document troubling realities without attempting to finesse his readers' response to them, *The Colonel's Dream* is his least tightly structured, symmetrical novel, a fact that has led to its remaining ignored. As we have already seen, events that in Chesnutt's previous efforts would have been tightly interwoven remain loosely connected at best, worth mentioning in the same book only because they happen to fall within the year of Henry French's life that the novel documents. Perhaps, at last for Chesnutt, the events are not capable of being connected in any meaningful way; perhaps all data do not eventually form a coherent system (whereas his earlier works' coherence suggests his faith in a moral order). Most notably, one finds disturbingly little connection between French's ideals, his means of enacting them, and the results that accrue. This is not to suggest that there is no cause/effect relationship among these factors, but that the shape that forms when they are connected is not symmetrical but strikingly ugly: the causes and effects we see in the novel cannot reassure us of a meaningful social world, but must lead us to a sense of this world's inherent ugliness and, from an ethical standpoint, its lack of meaning.

The specter of meaninglessness leads, as it has in each of Chesnutt's novels, to the question of interpretation. *The Colonel's Dream* represents the logical extension of Chesnutt's career to that point in that it blends a rigorous social analysis—a consideration of social conditions as they are—with a more self-conscious contemplation of the act of interpretation itself. For Chesnutt, a situation never exists except through interpretation, and interpretation is, at bottom, a matter of people's uses of language. As in each of Chesnutt's novels, talk is a form of action—in fact, it is the most important form since it is prerequisite to, and shapes, action. The reaction of many of Clarendon's whites against Colonel French is not, in the main, described as spontaneous or visceral; instead, we learn that various white townspeople (admittedly, in the conspicuous absence of blacks' voices, given the heavily segregated nature of the South) feel differently about the colonel's reforms, and debate them behind closed doors. Only gradually does the ferment of feeling against French build up as "a great deal of intemperate talk" comes to a head and leads to disastrous consequences (271). (For all its gradualism, the eventual failure of French's reforms seems like a foregone conclusion, equally certain at the beginning of his plan as at the end.) The gradual, surprisingly controlled nature of the movement against the colonel reinforces our sense that the bigotry and conservatism of Clarendon's white citizens are not innate (as Chesnutt rarely saw such unhealthy feelings as innate) but the result of a carefully enacted conspiracy by Fetters against an essentially political antagonist.

As in both *The House Behind the Cedars* and *The Marrow of Tradition*, few major events occur without having been the subject of substantial discourse and deliberation beforehand. In *The Colonel's Dream* the ugliness of the whites' actions is not really a matter of their running out of its instigators' control, as was the case in *The Marrow of Tradition*. Fetters shows a surer political hand than either Carteret or McBane, combining the former's shrewdness with the latter's malevolence. Fetters's control over the town can be explained in terms offered by 1930s historian Horace Mann Bond, who describes the manipulation of Alabama's postwar economic and political landscape by cold-eyed financiers: "Without sentiment, without emotion, those who sought profit from an exploitation of Alabama's natural resources turned other men's prejudices and attitudes to their own account, and did so with skill and a ruthless acumen" (qtd. in Zinn 202). As Chesnutt has argued before, racism, though devastating in its own right, is fundamentally an exercise of power—of someone else's power, since few, if any, of its adherents ultimately profit by it.

In *The Colonel's Dream*, unlike his previous novels, we encounter an individual, Fetters, who actually does profit from the South's recalcitrant racism. Whereas white supremacists like George Tryon in *The House Behind the Cedars* and Philip Carteret in *The Marrow of Tradition* suffer at least to some extent in consequence of their actions, in Fetters Chesnutt portrays for the first time a character who is capable of negotiating racist discourses to his own benefit. Somewhat unexpectedly, Fetters—the "petty boss of a Southern backwoods county" whose acumen French reflexively discounts (133)—is a much more astute strategist than the successful New York businessman, French. Certainly, this conclusion flies in the face of French's conception of himself and of his antagonist, whom he initially imagines as "a tall, long-haired, red-faced, truculent individual, in a slouch hat and a frock coat, with a loud voice and a dictatorial manner, the typical Southerner of melodrama"—not the unremarkable-looking businessman he actually encounters (222–23). In contrast, French's most noteworthy attribute, in business and in life, is his impulsiveness: readers are informed more than once that "[f]rom impulse to action was, for the colonel's temperament, an easy step" (106). Perhaps this should not be surprising given that we are introduced to French in the midst of a large financial gamble, apparently the unavoidable consequence of remaining in the textile industry imprudently long, which will either make him rich or bring him to the edge of ruin. French and Company win, and the reader may be lulled (as apparently the colonel is, himself) into thinking that he is wise rather than lucky. At least, French's guiding assumption is that, as an experienced businessman with an accumulation of wealth, he can control his environment—and Chesnutt, who slyly tips the scales in French's favor by remarking that he *looks like* a "man of well-balanced character" (3), seems to write with the expectation that most readers will assume the same.

Upon closer examination, French is less different from Fetters than he may appear. Both are, after their own fashions, exemplary capitalists, and while their antagonism in the novel superficially represents a debate about the definition of proper capitalism, ultimately both are defined by an economic system that is blind to its consequences and unbending to its adherents' ethical ideals. To the extent that French differs from Fetters, the differences may not be what we are led to expect. The evidence suggests that Fetters is a more astute businessman than French: while French has received a windfall through economic speculation, Fetters makes *sure* he will profit by luring others into dangerous speculations (52). Whereas Fetters appears to be the ultimate adult, having shed any possible idealism to the point that all that remains is a terrible, pragmatic core, French's impulsiveness is so central to his character that he ends up seeming childlike. Although Fetters has "not forgotten" his childhood embarrassment at French's hands, he believably claims that his motivations are not revenge but power and profit (225–26). French, in contrast, lives childishly in the moment, so that the long-forgotten youthful battle suddenly looms large in his consciousness. His adolescent son Phil's maturity serves as a contrast to French's underlying immaturity. Phil's one act of impulsiveness, chasing a black cat, is described as uncharacteristic—even "the wisest of men sometimes forget" caution, notes the narrator (257)—and leads to his death only because Colonel French, not for the first time, has been neglectfully absorbed in his own thoughts.[9]

French's childlike, impulsive spirit can be read more than one way. From a romantic, Blakean perspective it is part of what makes him an attractive character, and by reading the novel strictly from such a perspective one can see the purely sentimental, if didactic, work it has sometimes been taken to be. Not only does the novel seem to valorize childhood, but it exposes the effects of ruthless capitalism in terms that evoke, if less poetically, *Songs of Experience:* "In the open doorways, through which the flies swarmed in and out, grown men, some old, some still in the prime of life, were lounging, pipe in mouth, while old women pottered about the yards, or pushed back their sunbonnets to stare vacantly at the advancing buggy. Dirty babies were tumbling about the cabins. There was a lean and listless yellow dog or two for every baby; and several slatternly black women were washing clothes on the shady sides of the houses. A general air of shiftlessness and squalor pervaded the settlement. There was no sign of joyous childhood or of happy youth" (113). At the same time that he attempts to use realistic details to pull at readers' heartstrings, however, Chesnutt interrogates the efficacy of the romantic mode of thinking, which after all has caused the romantic idealist French himself to fail to recognize the effects of his actions.[10] All of French's efforts to reform Clarendon and the South are a direct result of his spontaneous, romantic outlook; though he expects to profit by them, he is more certain of profit if he ignores his ideals and invests his money outside of the community in which he was raised. As a way of thinking that is not directly defined by (though it may be in sync with) capitalism, such an outlook is crucial in Chesnutt's analysis, but also crucially doomed to failure. For French's romanticism, and the way in which it reinforces his individualistic sense of detachment from others, causes him to be both a socially responsible agent and a monster.

The portrayal of Colonel French as an overgrown child reveals two very troubling aspects of his character. First, he is shown to be not a dynamic character (as he may appear) but a static one. Virtually every characteristic that drives French as a reformer is, at one point or another, connected by the narrative to an aspect of his childhood. Likewise, the colonel does not substantially change from the beginning of the novel to its end. He mainly *reacts* to new (or newly revealed) developments according to clearly established patterns; in his personality and ethics, he remains an unreconstructed Southern white man. French's childish nature also is revealed in his propensity to abandon others when it suits him.[11] He left Clarendon a hero but has not returned to it for decades (though the prodigal son seems to expect a warm welcome, the resumption of things as they were, and gratitude at his interventions when he does return). Once in Clarendon, he callously neglects his Northern friends, especially Mrs. Jerviss, to whom he was practically engaged before his departure; when he spies Jerviss during a brief trip to New York on business, he guiltily hides, and "felt safer when the lady was well out of sight" (179). Finally, he abandons both his fiancée, Laura Treadwell, and his reform efforts in Clarendon—as much, it appears, out of self-pity as due to his understanding that he has failed. When his final promised reform, a new hospital, is squelched because the building burns down, "he was hardly sorry" to escape his commitment (291).[12] Given his incapacity to alter his own outlook, French's attempts to reform Clarendon seem more like acts of aggression than of benevolence.

That he portrays such a character with indulgent neutrality rather than contempt illustrates that Chesnutt is after realism here, not propaganda: he wishes his readers to understand his characters, not condemn them. As McWilliams argues, French rightly should be regarded as "not simply victim but also nemesis" (167). But what nature of nemesis is he? At the heart of the novel's evaluation of romantic idealism is its internal debate regarding aristocracy as an alternative to capitalism. For French, no debate is necessary: aristocracy and capitalism can both be employed at once; his inability to see an inherent conflict between these modes of thought is what renders him blind to the significance of much of what is going on around him, and ultimately is what leads to his failure. If forced to choose between the aristocratic and the capitalistic modes, French would certainly choose aristocracy. Ernestine Williams Pickens argues that "Chesnutt believed that the loss of aristocratic values was at least, in part, a loss of a moral force in the community" (99); whether or not she is correct regarding Chesnutt's belief, certainly this statement summarizes Colonel French's philosophy. As Pickens points out, Fetters is portrayed as "riffraff, who has no lineage, no breeding, and no character" (99); for French, and probably for many of the novel's readers, these qualities define him more strongly than his malicious acts do.[13] To be sure, French's aristocratic, romantic idealism causes him to act in ways that Fetters's more pure capitalism does not. He chooses to invest his considerable capital in Clarendon, even though he knows he could get more from his money elsewhere, because he believes (as does Chesnutt, apparently) in a localized economy. He proudly, and bravely, insists on his right to hire whomever he wishes, promoting a black man to the position of foreman of the masons.

If Chesnutt seems to approve of some consequences of the colonel's aristocratic worldview, however, he also points out that "most things evil [are] the perversion of good" (192). French's charitable and reformist acts, rooted as they are in his sense of aristocracy, rest too heavily on their *personal* nature. He assumes, for example, that Clarendon's magistrate must be justified in making virtual slaves out of criminals until a known quantity, his beloved former servant Peter, is arrested. He decides not to intervene in the brutal beating of a black laborer only because he does not realize the victim is Bud Johnson, upon whose behalf Laura Treadwell has asked him to prevail. Even when the citizens of Clarendon directly benefit from French's actions—such as an African American barber's profit in selling the old French estate back to the colonel—his aristocratic worldview is depicted as a problem, not a solution:

> In principle the colonel was an ardent democrat; he believed in the rights of man, and extended the doctrine to all who bore the human form. But in feeling he was an equally pronounced aristocrat. A servant's rights he would have defended to the last ditch; familiarity he would have resented with equal positiveness. Something of this ancestral feeling stirred within him now. While Nichols's position in reference to the house was, in principle, equally as correct as the colonel's own, and superior in point of time—since impressions, like photographs, are apt to grow dim with age—the barber's display of sentiment only jarred the colonel's sensibilities and strengthened his desire [to buy back the house]. (81)

In short, French's reforms at best are motivated by his sense of aristocratic entitlement, and if those fortunate enough to know him personally may benefit from his actions (though often they do not, either), Chesnutt shows that such an idiosyncratic, personalized, and self-indulgent approach is no basis for meaningful reform.

Any effective reform will have to be systematic, and thus French's devotion to the system of capitalism might seem to carry more potential. Up to a point, the novel could be read as a paean to the virtues of capitalism. The colonel's ire, and his reformist plans, are initially raised in response not to Fetters's nefarious actions but to the slothfulness and inefficiency he repeatedly encounters when doing business in the South. For French, such problems are not merely economic but reflect a deeper malady of personality and even of morality. The novel, which generally takes on French's point of view although it is narrated in the third person, is full of seemingly approving descriptions of trickle-down economics (88–89) and what might today be called Reaganesque rhetoric: "Perhaps not one of them had ever quite realised the awful handicap of excuses under which they laboured. Effort was paralysed where failure was so easily explained" (108). French's commitment to free enterprise is so great that he is unwilling to provide charity to his impoverished former slave Peter, insisting instead on finding "something for Peter to do, so that he would be able to pay him a wage" (71)—never mind the years of wageless labor Peter has already provided. As an ethically neutral system of values, capitalism, French believes, offers an antidote to racism. He understands slavery to have been anathema to his free-enterprise values: he knows he "had prospered because, having no Peters to work for him, he had been compelled to work for himself," unlike those who remained in the South (29–30). And he sees that whites like John McLean reflexively scapegoat African Americans for the economic problems facing the South (72), whereas from French's perspective, an infusion of capitalist spirit ought to cleanse the region of its unhealthy, dead-end attitudes and bring about both economic and moral prosperity.

On the other hand, it is difficult to miss Chesnutt's disappointment in capitalism's consistent failure to live up to its promise. Though Chesnutt, throughout his career, continued to argue against racism on the basis of rational self-interest—consistently claiming that whites are hurt by it as well as non-whites—*The Colonel's Dream* is in the end fueled more by its indictment of capitalism's harmful nature than by its support of the free-enterprise system. Whereas the narrator remarks that "[c]ommunities, like men, must either grow or decay, advance or decline; they could not stand still" (118), the novel cautions readers about uncontrolled growth, anticipating John Steinbeck's description of an economic "monster": "When the monster stops growing, it dies. It can't stay one size" (44). *The Colonel's Dream* is not an argument against reform efforts per se, but it does demonstrate that reforms such as the colonel's, which take on problems only within the current system, are ultimately counterproductive. The system is thoroughly sick, its laws "clearly designed to profit the strong at the expense of the weak" (228). Furthermore, it is the lust for money, not (as in *The Marrow of Tradition*) abject prejudice, that prevents people from seeing things "in their true light," as Ben Dudley realizes when he finds that his uncle has wasted his life searching for lost gold (275). In his attempt to locate the heart of society's illness, Chesnutt finds the pursuit of economic gain to lie underneath people's bigotry and other expressions of misanthropy; underneath the shell of racial prejudice, in his analysis, is economic calculation. Or miscalculation: if the enslavement of other humans ever made economic sense, it surely no longer does, Chesnutt shows, and so those who refuse to relinquish their racist beliefs are merely perpetuating their own impoverishment.

In assessing aristocracy and capitalism, then, Chesnutt implies that neither approach to social life works from an ethical standpoint. Reminiscent of *The House Behind the Cedars*, *The Colonel's Dream* employs a romantic (aristocratic) critique of capitalism but also a realist (pragmatically capitalistic) critique of the aristocracy. Aristocracy (even if it were not severely limited as an ethical instrument by its inherent elitism) is ineffectual and, as the narrator notes, has basically reached the point of extinction: "There had been a time when these old aristocrats could speak, and the earth trembled, but that day was over" (225). Capitalism, while it certainly remains a powerful agent of change, is amoral at best and in practice proves destructive to any ethical ideals. Despite his idealism, French's economic mindset causes him fatally to misunderstand the nature of the events in which he is embroiled. In one revealing scene, he is dead certain (and dead wrong) that he can use money to persuade Fetters to release Bud Johnson, not realizing that the power relations symbolized by Johnson's confinement are much deeper than one transaction can account for (224). As a free-market capitalist, French stupidly regards events in isolation; his limitation is that of abstraction, a problem repeatedly referenced in the narrative.[14] In contrast, as one who frankly uses money (and any other available means) to gain power, Fetters understands his world more completely, though he acts with less of a moral compass. In a capitalist system, it seems, one can see clearly or behave ethically, but not both. Although Chesnutt himself was a successful and apparently committed capitalist, as a novelist he was yet more committed to a realistic understanding of events, one which French roundly fails to achieve. *The Colonel's Dream* tends to locate more ills than benefits in capitalism, creating a space for later writers to address the question he does not: if not capitalism, what else?[15]

The lack of a plausible answer to this question causes Chesnutt to show bleakness where once he would have found hope. Although he has two old enemies, the Southern aristocracy and the African American population, find common cause—both "the Negroes [and] the old master class" have likewise been pushed into "political obscurity" by the resurgence of skilled and populous poor whites (264)—he conspicuously does not locate in this development new possibilities of reform; both groups seem simply fated to remain powerless in the new South. Something that presumably ought to be uplifting—the formulation of new connections and alliances between differently situated people, more or less what Chesnutt previously sought to achieve through the writing of fiction—instead tends to deaden optimism. Such connections seem now more a matter of advertising (upon which French has built his business in the North) than of art. Similarly, Chesnutt now seems discouraged by forms of behavior that might under other circumstances be regarded as inspiring—such as an individual's strict adherence to ethical ideals. French's commitment to his ideals, in fact, helps prevent him from recognizing the implications of his decisions in human terms. When Fetters offers to free Bud Johnson if French will drop several lawsuits he has filed against him, the colonel "[does] not hesitate a moment," preferring to hold onto his ideals rather than accept an immediate, compromised gain (231). However, he personally suffers no loss at all in making this decision; it is Johnson who remains in Fetters's custody, in which he is literally tortured, not French. Though readers may admire French's fidelity to his ideals, it is difficult to escape the point that he has not even momentarily *considered* the cost of his decision for Johnson. For Chesnutt, ideals are virtually useless if they remain purely abstract and are not enacted in historical and human terms; this shortcoming of the colonel's is a key to his eventual failure.

The passage in which French refuses to compromise with Fetters does represent a potentially important step, though. The narrator states that French "had risen now to higher game; nothing less than the system would satisfy him" (231). Prior to this point, French has not regarded himself as a wholesale reformer so much as a tinkerer; he assumes that the Southern economy, as he finds it typified in Clarendon, is corrupted by lethargy but basically sound, and that reforming it to his and the community's mutual advantage will be a relatively simple matter. Only at this point, relatively late in the novel, does French truly realize that the hyper-capitalistic ideology, with its strongly (and cynically) racist overtones, is both pervasive and rotten to the core. His new determination to push toward systemic, not incremental, reform is a development of which Chesnutt generally approves. But what is the nature of the "system" that Colonel French has set his sights on? As it turns out, French's conception of the system he is attacking is strictly bounded by his understanding of reason in a traditional, Western capitalist sense; that is, the novel shows him to be unaware of how completely his reform impulse is circumscribed by his subscription to a particular construction of "reason." To the end, "even in his dreams the colonel's sober mind did not stray beyond the bounds of reason and experience," the narrator informs us. "That all men would ever be equal he did not even dream; there would always be the strong and the weak, the wise and the foolish. But that each man, in his little life in this our little world might be able to make the most of himself, was an ideal which even the colonel's waking hours would not have repudiated" (280–81). And, although French has garnered in himself the will to change Clarendon dramatically, his rationalist appeal to permanent, stable ideals renders his vision vague to the point of impotence: he reflects, nebulously and in passive voice, that "[a] new body of thought must be built up, in which stress must be laid upon the eternal verities, in the light of which difficulties which now seemed insurmountable would be gradually overcome" (247).

Significantly, the colonel's thought process is—much more than he is aware—shaped by his subscription to racial hierarchies: for example, he defends his late servant by stating that "[o]ld Peter's skin was black, but his heart was white as any man's! . . . on the judgment day, many a white man shall be black, and many a black man white" (262). Clearly, he is willing to consider new social permutations *within* the familiar categories his construction of reason allows for, but is not able to think past these "rational" boundaries. Although, for his part, Chesnutt might be seen as sharing his protagonist's rationalist assumptions, the author signals that he means to critique, not endorse, French's perspective by demonstrating the degree to which it is enmeshed in the thought and language of monetary exchange, which is repeatedly exposed in the novel as a false, indeed counterproductive, impetus for reform. The colonel assumes that "[t]he love of money might be the root of all evil, but its control was certainly a means of great good," and in so reflecting he "glow[s] with the consciousness of this beneficent power to scatter happiness" (211). The narrator's assessment here drips with irony, and throughout the novel Chesnutt clearly demonstrates that French is absolutely wrong in his faith in money's "beneficent power." Although French may *feel* benevolent toward African Americans, his feelings are analyzed as worthless given his deep investment (literally and figuratively) in an economy that actually continues to enslave them. Thus, it is shocking—but thematically appropriate—that French finds himself, early in the novel, literally buying Peter at an auction:[16] despite the abolition of slavery with the Thirteenth Amendment, the Southern penal system has fluidly adapted, providing landowners with indentured labor by rounding up black men on trumped-up "vagrancy" charges and then "selling" them to the highest bidder in exchange for the payment of their court-imposed fines.[17]

French is not, as he has sometimes been taken to be, Chesnutt's role model for whites. Rather, French's character is much like the "fool" as described by Mikhail Bakhtin: a character who "does not understand this world, does not acknowledge its poetic, scholarly, or otherwise lofty and significant labels" (402). In this regard, Chesnutt's protagonist is influenced by the author's friend and correspondent Albion Tourgée, whose *A Fool's Errand* is a major inspiration for *The Colonel's Dream* (Andrews, *Literary Career* 254). In his foreword to *A Fool's Errand,* Tourgée defines the "fool" in a way that anticipates Bakhtin: "He differs from his fellow-mortals chiefly in this, that he sees or believes what they do not, and consequently undertakes what they never attempt" (5). Tourgée's fool, Comfort Servosse, is (like Henry French) "the most sincere of mortals" (5), naïve, moralistic, and (for better or worse) blithely unaware of the political undercurrents that exist at the roots of the society in which he operates.

Such a character's denseness about the world, Bakhtin writes, "in the novel is always polemical: it interacts dialogically with an intelligence (a lofty pseudo intelligence) with which it polemicizes and whose mask it tears away" (403). Similarly, French's basic stupidity about what he is undertaking, while ultimately the subject of Chesnutt's scorn, is useful in that it reveals the hidden workings of what are taken to be natural, inevitable elements of Southern life:

it enables Chesnutt's analysis of racism and its relationship to capitalism. An interesting facet of French's portrayal is that, in contrast to the marginal and/or naïve characters who are usually ascribed that role, French is a culturally and economically privileged fool: he occupies a central role in his society, but the problem is that the society doesn't know what to make of itself. Being a fool is no longer, in this post-Reconstruction world, an outsider's vocation, but fundamentally a part of American selfhood: any attempt to make sense of the mores of such a world is destined to achieve absurdity. Like Bakhtin's fool, French is best seen not as a role model but as a device for compelling readers to view their world differently, to become unsettled. Before he can ask his readers to act differently, Chesnutt prods them to *see* differently, which is what American literary realism always attempts.

Some recent critics have concluded that *The Colonel's Dream* ends on a note of hopelessness. The novel's reflective conclusion—"White men go their way, and black men theirs, and no one knows the outcome. But there are those who hope, and those who pray, that this condition will pass, that some day our whole land will be truly free, and the strong will cheerfully help to bear the burdens of the weak, and Justice, the seed, and Peace, the flower, of liberty, will prevail throughout all our borders" (294)[18]—is taken by these critics to place the novel's actual, intended message of hopelessness in relief. McWilliams, for example, argues that Chesnutt parts ways with the novel's optimistic narrator in the end, demonstrating that the narrator's "Christian consolation is unconvincing" (179). Chesnutt's earlier novels reveal him to be unwilling to relinquish hope as long as it is barely possible to retain it, so if indeed he has abandoned it at last, it is a significant move for him.

On the other hand, it might be more productive for readers not to assume that Chesnutt has abandoned hope altogether in the face of a dismal social and political situation, but that he now places his hopes, however small they have become, elsewhere—outside of the white community and its established institutions. Certainly, the novel locates few possibilities in reform within the current system—the inevitable failure of such reform is its central theme—but that is emphatically not to say that Chesnutt has resigned himself, or believes his readers should become resigned, to the state of things as they are. In writing this novel, he is neither content nor complacent. As Pickens writes, in Chesnutt's view "the South needs a moral revolution more than it needs economic or educational reform" (118). Or—absent the likelihood of a "moral" revolution—more simply put, a revolution is needed.

Given Colonel French's well-intentioned but disastrous attempt at reform, does the novel put forward any more positively construed solutions to the physical, mental, and economic violence against African Americans it portrays? Perhaps not, but *The Colonel's Dream* does, at least, come close to sanctioning violent resistance by armed blacks, something Chesnutt had seemed to denounce in *The Marrow of Tradition*. Bud Johnson's secret war against the Fetters gang does not end well, since Johnson is captured (after his identity is reluctantly reported by French) and ultimately lynched. Still, his shooting of Fetters's son Barclay and of his overseer Haines is more consequential than French's slow, elaborate, and expensive plan to build a cotton mill. Both gestures are shown to be, in the end, useless and even destructive, and if Chesnutt does not risk proposing that Johnson's violence is justifiable, at least he shows that French's actions are equally vain.

This vein of thought remains merely suggestive in the novel, but it does indicate that Chesnutt was mindful of realities and solutions toward which he could no more than gesture. *The Colonel's Dream* represents Chesnutt's most conspicuous intent to achieve a thorough realism, one that would prefer to be unaesthetic rather than be untruthful if such a choice is necessary. Yet the truths the novel speaks are not, as they may seem to be, those of white liberalism. Implicitly, Chesnutt places the impetus for reform on African Americans, even if the ethical burden by rights should fall on whites, the oppressor class which continues to hold almost all power.[19] As someone who has found in Chesnutt's previous novels an effort to nudge along the white reader who is almost there, who is capable of responsibly reading the novel in a way that actually acknowledges one's implication, and changes one's vision, in the case of *The Colonel's Dream* I must recognize that Chesnutt does not reach out to that reader any longer. As Matthew Wilson writes, "in representing the contradictions of a racial 'liberal,' Chesnutt is putting the last nail in the coffin of his career, because even racial liberals like William Dean Howells and George Washington Cable were unable to extricate themselves from the historical horizon of American racism" (*Whiteness* 162). On the other hand, the novel does not (and in 1905 could not) speak the language of African American resistance. But in demonstrating the inefficacy and hypocrisy of any reform attempts imaginable in the present system, Chesnutt attempts to remove the oxygen from the atmosphere of polite reform efforts, creating a vacuum which arguably only a future movement of black self-determination could fill.[20]

Ironically, in his only published novel focused primarily on white characters, Chesnutt has finally forsaken his appeals to a white audience; he is no longer willing to meet a white readership halfway, and what few suggestions of political possibility inhabit the novel are found in its (admittedly highly limited) representations of black agency. If the increasingly impotent aristocracy represents in Chesnutt's conception the past, then the disempowered African American community represents America's future, however uncertain. In making these narrative choices, Chesnutt has finally achieved the degree of realism to which his career has long pointed. However, that achievement comes with a cost; by putting the finishing touches on his craft, he self-consciously draws his career to a close, one that he would not successfully reverse. In *The House Behind the Cedars* and *The Marrow of Tradition* the conspicuous departures from a deeply historicized realism, and the gaps left open by the narrative, leave room for interpretation and response, and therefore room for the majority-white audience to change. Change, however, this audience by and large did not. *The Colonel's Dream* is less dialogic—much less open-ended, leaving little wiggle room for a careful reader. It depicts a world of events whose outcomes are highly determined by a deeply corrupted cultural economy and shows that the only possible response to such a world is not deconstruction, but destruction. Careful reading brings us closer to the finality of his conclusions, not toward the novel's continuing sense of possibility as it has in Chesnutt's earlier works. Although he attempted, unsuccessfully, to pick up a fiction-writing career a decade and a half later, *The Colonel's Dream* represents an end to Chesnutt's career in more than one respect.

5

"The Category of Surreptitious Things"

Paul Marchand, F.M.C. and *The Quarry*

Accounts of Charles W. Chesnutt's writing career typically have taken the shape of a rather steep bell curve: after an apprenticeship of several years practicing the craft and achieving occasional publication, his stock quickly rose with two successful short-story collections and then, just as quickly, dropped as the author's novels failed to attract the popularity of his stories, leading him to abandon fiction writing and resign himself to the business of legal stenography and local political work.

This standard narrative of Chesnutt's life is complicated by the fact that he never entirely stopped writing fiction after the failure of *The Colonel's Dream* in 1905. Numerous critics have attributed Chesnutt's relative silence after 1905 to his disillusionment, reinforced by the public's apathetic response to *The Colonel's Dream*, with fiction writing as a form of political advocacy.[1] In the late 1990s, however, the appearance of two previously unpublished novels by Chesnutt—*Paul Marchand, F.M.C.* (c. 1921) and *The Quarry* (c. 1928)—forced critics to reassess the author's late career. These 1920s novels do not, precisely speaking, represent a return to optimism. Although Chesnutt appears to have believed that the "New Negro" movement, or Harlem Renaissance, represented a change in artistic sensibilities from which he and other African American artists might benefit, the novels themselves reveal an enduring pessimism about how the questions of representation and identity raised in his earlier novels might now be answered. Perhaps encouraged, as William L. Andrews suggests, by film projects based on his previous novels (*Literary Career* 265), or by the serial republication of *The House Behind the Cedars* in 1921–1922, Chesnutt (wrongly) thought that a new work might reach an audience, but there is no expression of confidence that his audience would respond rightly to the issues he would raise.

It seemed clear to Chesnutt that there was now an expanded audience for "books by and about colored people" (*Essays and Speeches* 514). In his address upon receiving the NAACP's Spingarn Medal in 1928, he rather defensively explained, in retrospect, that "I had to sell my books chiefly to white readers. There were few colored book buyers" (514). Matters seemed to be changing, so that (as he claimed with undue optimism in the 1926 essay "The Negro in Art: How Shall He Be Portrayed?") "[t]he difficulty of finding a publisher for books by Negro authors has largely disappeared" (*Essays and Speeches* 491). Nonetheless, the audience consuming African Americans' fiction continued to be predominantly white.[2] Such a situation was both full of possibility and fraught with risk from Chesnutt's perspective. Black writers had the opportunity to gain a hearing, but the conditions of that hearing were, as they had always been, stacked against African Americans due to the endurance of racist assumptions and stereotypical tastes. Despite the artistic recognition gained by some, there was little evidence that in the larger culture blacks would be able to control their destinies to a greater extent than before.

Like a number of others among the older generation of Harlem Renaissance writers, notably including W. E. B. Du Bois, Chesnutt's response to this state of affairs smacks of conservatism. He admonishes younger black writers to create idealized black characters—"[i]f there are no super-Negroes, make some," he inveighs in "The Negro in Art" (*Essays and Speeches* 492)—and in the famous 1931 essay "Post-Bellum—Pre-Harlem" he decries the tendency toward "brilliantly written" novels in which, nonetheless, "there is not a single decent character" (547). Based on such statements as these, it would be easy to conclude that Chesnutt endorsed an approach in which African American characters would be represented as exclusively virtuous, strong of character, and politically moderate—the better to placate mainstream white sensibilities. That conclusion would be only partially correct, leaving out the degree to which creating politically effective characters and texts remained a vexing problem in Chesnutt's mind. Though the expansion of publication opportunities for African Americans opened up new possibilities, making the resumption of a novel-writing career seem worthwhile, it did not, for Chesnutt, answer the aesthetic and technical questions he faced as a politically oriented writer. It merely raised the stakes.

True, in "The Negro in Art," Chesnutt impels African American writers to produce positive black characters: "Why does not some colored writer build a story around a Negro oil millionaire, and the difficulty he or she has in keeping any of his or her money? A Pullman porter who performs wonderful feats in the detection of crime has great possibilities. The Negro visionary who would change the world over night and bridge the gap between races in a decade would make an effective character in fiction" (*Essays and Speeches* 493). *Paul Marchand, F.M.C.* and *The Quarry* basically follow this formula, presenting the least morally compromised, strongest African American characters of any of his novels. Granted, then, that at this stage in his career Chesnutt is interested in representing strong black characters, the remaining question has to do with *how* to represent such characters. Far from being African American supermen, the protagonists of these two novels—Paul Marchand and Donald Glover—are complex figures, both because they face difficult moral choices (and face them with due difficulty) and because they are unable to break out of the confines of an oppressive society.

Realism has never demanded the strict avoidance of exemplary characters; what it demands is the treatment of such characters, along with everyone else, as part of a complicated social milieu. In the decisions that shape their existence—or rather, given their limited agency, contribute to its shape—neither Marchand nor Glover ever is able to act with moral certainty. The last line of *The Quarry*—"I'm not at all sure that you didn't make the wise choice" (286)—underscores the muddled moral landscape found in both novels. Such a landscape, from Chesnutt's perspective, demands *more* realism, not less. In his 1920s nonfiction, Chesnutt describes his aesthetic philosophy in more detail than he has before, and the aesthetic he defends is that of realism. In "The Negro in Art," he clarifies that his admonition to create positive black characters is meant to serve, not to trump, realism: "The colored writer, generally speaking, has not yet passed the point of thinking of himself first as a Negro, burdened with the responsibility of defending and uplifting his race. Such a frame of mind, however praiseworthy from a moral standpoint, is bad for art. Tell your story, and if it is on a vital subject, well told, with an outcome that commends itself to right-thinking people, it will, if interesting, be an effective brief for whatever cause it incidentally may postulate" (*Essays and Speeches* 492–93). In the acceptance speech for the Spingarn Medal, Chesnutt clarifies his view that realism is fundamental. Increasingly, he says, African Americans are writing fiction, and in turn the whites who write about black life, while they may not "write the Negro up[,] at least seek to tell the truth about the conditions in which he lives, and the truth is in the Negro's favor" (514). Telling a truthful story is inherently a progressive act, although it is complicated, as Chesnutt demonstrates in his fiction, to say what telling a truthful story actually means.

As Matthew Wilson has cogently suggested, playing off a reference to Rousseau's *Émile* that appears in *Paul Marchand, F.M.C.*, these novels are "in some way about the consequences of education, about a 'cynical' educational experiment set in a system of racial oppression" (*Whiteness* 191). Both are epistemologically oriented novels, asking the question: how does one *know* something? Does knowledge arise through historical circumstances, through tradition, through science? Or is it a matter of communication in which descriptive language is capable of relaying information reliably? Chesnutt explores all these ways of knowing—historical, traditional, scientific, and linguistic—as he once again takes on the issue of what, if anything, race might mean. For the characters in *Paul Marchand, F.M.C.* and *The Quarry*, the vexed question of the protagonist's race is central, a linchpin that, once answered, informs them of everything else they need to know. But Chesnutt asks his readers to reconsider: what does this knowledge really tell us?

A hallmark of Chesnutt's thought, as recorded in both his fiction and nonfiction, is that race is overly weighted. African Americans' status, he believed, "might be considerably promoted if other people did not have [race] so constantly in mind" (*Essays and Speeches* 566). Since race did not seem likely to mean *less* anytime soon, however, he attempts to complicate its meaning, showing that the data used to support racialist assumptions are so haphazard that a political, not a scientific, explanation supports them—and, once untangled, the politics may favor other interests than supposed. As we saw in chapter 1, at the beginning of his career Chesnutt hinted at the racial ambiguity that potentially marks *any* individual's existence; but, unwilling to let his readers in on the joke, he left the themes of miscegenation and passing submerged. In the 1920s novels, Chesnutt explores the themes in a more overt manner but the question he poses is similar: what would happen if the mooring provided by racial difference, upon which people rely not only to substantiate a particular type of hierarchy but to enable *meaning* more generally, were swept out from under us?

The Best Revenge: *Paul Marchand, F.M.C.*

Chesnutt's fiction can seem manipulative, and unrealistic, because of his propensity to create unlikely situations that he thought would elucidate the true nature of race relations in the United States. As I have been arguing, from the perspective of contemporary literary theory, the occasional departures from probable, known realities cannot simply be dismissed as a lack of realism; the absurd racial landscape with which he struggled often required, in response, a warping of the probabilities of time and space to instill in readers a sense of what he recognized to be true. Like a convex lens that bends light in order to project an accurate image onto film, Chesnutt's fiction manipulates the events it portrays into a truthful whole, due not to a lack of faithfulness to the realities he hoped to capture, or to a less-than-sharp vision, but in recognition that successful realism must put readers into a situation where they can comprehend realities that ordinarily would escape them. His technique is to condense and select, but with the underlying purpose of arranging a more complete, and often a more troubling, picture. Always, the effort is to train the reader to see historical realities more accurately—which means seeing them not in isolation, but properly contextualized. The fiction does not shirk from the historical and personal realities it attempts to portray; rather, it is unrelenting in insisting that readers recognize these realities for what they are. Realism, as Chesnutt's novels suggest, is not a basis *from* which narratives can be constructed; on the contrary, narratives must do considerable work before realism (which for Chesnutt means an appropriate and proportionate response to reality) can be achieved.

Thus, in *Paul Marchand, F.M.C.* Chesnutt employs a somewhat implausible set of occurrences in the 1820s to comment on the realities that "any thoughtful, observant person who reads the newspapers" would observe in the 1920s (127). The novel tells the story of Marchand, a prosperous "free man of color" in New Orleans who is tormented by the Beaurepas family, five white Creole cousins, until he is revealed to be both white and the heir to the Beaurepas estate. The premise is both inventive and odd, and there is no indication that Chesnutt adapted the specifics of Marchand's situation from any historical record. Yet, as Robert E. Fleming has written, the novel's "bizarre and outdated plot, involving duels with swords, babies switched at birth, mistaken identities, and large inheritances, allows Chesnutt the freedom to fictionalize views on race and racism that he had not previously expressed in his published fiction" (364). Chesnutt seems to have sensed that to get at the deeper realities of racial life in America would require him to depart from strict fidelity to established facts. As he states in the foreword to *Paul Marchand, F.M.C.*, "[i]f there was not a Paul Marchand case in New Orleans, there might well have been, for all the elements of such a drama were present" (xxxvii). To put it another way, if someone like Paul Marchand did not exist, he would have to be invented.

In chapter 17, "Paul's Dilemma," the narrator risks "some repetition" to sum up the back story, the history of racial hierarchy in New Orleans that makes Paul Marchand's story, if not likely as played out in the life of one individual, in some sense inevitable. Writes Chesnutt, "any merit which this story may have as a social study must depend upon a reasonably accurate knowledge of the conditions which surrounded those who figured in it" (127). Chesnutt's priorities, as indicated in this passage, must be kept in mind: the narrative of Paul Marchand enables Chesnutt's real target, an understanding of the historical circumstances Paul embodies—not the reverse. *Paul Marchand, F.M.C.*, then, tells two stories. If we take one of them, the life history of the individual Paul Marchand, to be central, then the backdrop of New Orleans's history and social strata simply puts the implausibility of the story into relief. But it should be clear that Chesnutt's real mark is this apparent "backdrop" itself. If the events of the novel had been more plausible, ordinary ones, then they presumably could have occurred in any context; but the events of Paul Marchand's life could have transpired only under certain cultural circumstances. This is no attempt at a "universal" story.

At the same time, Chesnutt clearly meant for his readers to connect the 1820s setting to modern life. The novel's conspicuous employment of the "local color" genre which peaked in the 1890s might make it seem like a throwback, but as Dean McWilliams argues, "despite these gestures toward an earlier movement and an earlier style, *Paul Marchand, F.M.C.* is, in many ways, Chesnutt's most modern work" (183). In the foreword to the novel, Chesnutt is at pains to stipulate that "the student of sociology . . . may discover some interesting parallels between social conditions in that earlier generation and those in our own" (xxxvii–xxxviii). He describes the setting of the novel as one of overarching change:

> From 1812 to 1821 the population had nearly doubled. The Mississippi swarmed with steamboats, laden with cotton and sugar from the upriver districts, destined for shipment to Europe or the North. The old city walls had been torn down, the moat filled up and converted into boulevards. From a sleepy, slow, but picturesque provincial French town, with a Spanish veneer, the Crescent City had been swept into the current of American life, and pulsed and throbbed with the energy of the giant young nation of the West.
>
> Nevertheless, these changes were in many respects as yet merely superficial. The great heart of the community,—the thoughts, the feelings, the customs, the prejudices, the religion of the people,—remained substantially unchanged. The current was swifter, but the water was the same. (1–2)

The setting is useful in allowing Chesnutt to explore the conflicts inherent in an environment of great change but also of great conservatism—an environment, in short, that much resembles the American 1920s. One quickly is reminded of the Harlem Renaissance, a moment when the work of black artists, the contribution of African Americans to American culture, seemed valued as never before. Was this change superficial, or did it have the potential to alter social realities? What might come of such an environment? These are the questions Chesnutt asks of his 1920s audience, and while his ultimate answer offers little optimism, it does at least map out the responsibility of readers to create genuine, not superficial, change. It attempts to train its readers to read with a sense of investment, not passiveness, while also recognizing, once again, that this may be too much to ask.

How to read is, as often in Chesnutt's novels, the core question. In the vein of the realist novel, *Paul Marchand, F.M.C.* is amply stocked with sensory evidence of various sorts, but the narrative makes clear that this evidence has no import unless one knows how to interpret it. In *The Interpretation of Cultures,* Clifford Geertz (following Gilbert Ryle) defends the necessity of "thick description" in the social sciences by referring to three boys "rapidly contracting the eyelids of their right eyes." One boy has an "involuntary twitch," the second is winking as a "conspiratorial signal to a friend," and the third is "parodying someone else's, as he takes it, laughable attempt at winking" (6). Three events that look identical are, due to the boys' various motivations, in reality altogether different things, which is why none of the events can be understood without contextual knowledge. As in the case of the winking boys described by Geertz, in *Paul Marchand, F.M.C.* what is visible means both everything and nothing—everything in the sense that, without such visible signifiers, no meaning would be possible; nothing, in that without contextual information that is, as it were, invisible, these signifiers cannot do their work, cannot signify anything. Visible objects do not, upon examination, produce meaning; properly described, they are locales in which meanings that are produced elsewhere—by the social relations that are the novel's actual focus—periodically surface.

When Paul is publicly struck on the cheek by Hector Beaurepas, a blow which as a quadroon he knows he cannot return, his pain extends well beyond the physical injury itself or even the immediate symbolic significance that the blow carries. By it, Paul is reminded of a whole network of social contingencies that permeate his and others' lives and are constantly present, but which he normally is only too happy to forget: "[H]e could have remained in New Orleans indefinitely, to his financial profit, had it not been for the conditions under which he, like others of his kind, were obliged to live, of which his treatment by Hector Beaurepas on the street in front of the cathedral was an illustration, although an aggravated one, and for which his sojourn in France had entirely unfitted him. No white man had ever struck him before; perhaps none would ever strike him again; but that it could be done, and he could not resent it, were gall and wormwood to him" (15). The blow is damaging to Paul not primarily for the physical pain it causes, nor the public shame experienced in the moment itself, but because it reminds him that "it could be done"—that the moments of apparent tranquility in which Paul is *not* actually struck in the face are nothing more than a veneer covering over a hierarchical social landscape underlain by the constant threat, and sometimes the reality, of violence. As the above passage suggests, being part of a society does not necessarily cause one to see it more sharply. The effect of socialization is, instead, to lull the society's participants into a kind of forgetfulness—not the potentially dangerous sort that causes Paul temporarily to forget that "the path which he must walk, in his intercourse with white men, was a straight and narrow one" (20), but a state of mind in which such rules are constantly kept in mind yet only rarely acknowledged consciously.

Had Paul not gone to France to receive his formal education, his recognition of the real import of Hector's blow would have been muted. Having spent time in an egalitarian society, he has become "unfitted" to see the act with a native's resignation, as simply the way things are. His "colored friends," the narrator indicates, "were philosophical enough to recognize the existence of facts as they were, and conform to them as the price of life and some degree of comfort" (22). Such detachment, it must be said, would not necessarily give Paul a more accurate vision; Chesnutt suggests that Paul's psychological investment in the event, his inability *not* to take it personally, aids rather than detracts from his understanding. As both an insider and an outsider, Paul can see the true nature of social "conditions" more completely than most, though of course his vision does not allow him to do anything about them.[3] Needless to say, Paul's socially constructed status as a "quadroon"—one who is neither white nor black—serves as an analogue for the mixed status that the novel explores in various ways. As Wilson notes, "cultural hybridity gives him a wide range of sympathy and understanding," although "it does not blunt Marchand's sense of abiding outrage" (*Whiteness* 194).

Paul Marchand, F.M.C. is about the interpretation of documentary evidence, often in literal terms—the evidence provided by documents. The most obvious example is the will left by Pierre Beaurepas, which according to legal logic ought to answer the questions raised by the narrative definitively but in reality, of course, does not. In fact, documents of various sorts permeate the novel, beginning with the absent document that certifies the freedom of Zabet Philosophe, the former Beaurepas slave: "Indeed, her immunity from slavery had lasted so long that her free papers were never asked for—no more than one would have looked for the charter of the city or the title deeds of the Cabildo" (5). Despite Zabet's status as a New Orleans institution whose position seems unquestionable in a sense, the absence of her free papers renders her vulnerable, as Paul demonstrates when he threatens to return her to slavery if she does not identify which of the Beaurepas men is her son. In the society both Paul Marchand's 1820s peers and Chesnutt's 1920s readers inhabit, absence can speak just as loudly as presence. The "lawful thing," as the narrator notes in an unrelated passage, is to assume a black person without free papers is a slave (44). Having free papers, then, would afford Zabet a degree of protection, but Chesnutt's real target is the underlying system that invests these or other sorts of documents with meaning, a system that Chesnutt associates—at increasingly deeper levels—with the law, economics, and violence.

Legally, Zabet's status is clear: having no free papers, she is equivalent to a slave. The question remains, however, whether or not anyone will assert her status and reclaim her into slavery, as Paul threatens to do. The answer to that question is, in a sense, a matter of economics: Zabet produces capital in the form of information for her former master, Pierre Beaurepas (for whom she acts as a sort of undercover agent), and so there is no reason for him to assert her formal status as a slave. (Paul, for reasons of his own that might or might not be read in similarly economic terms, has little interest in claiming Zabet as his slave upon inheriting the Beaurepas estate, that is, once she divulges the information he seeks.) Once the economic implications of a given moment are recognized, the threat of violence is never very far away, as seen when Zabet hesitates to sell out her son and Paul commands her to "take your choice—the slave gang, the whip, the pistol, or the sword" (95). All this is to say that, for Chesnutt, the legal fictions by which a society is shaped are explained by somewhat more amorphous economic exchanges, and in turn the economic order is undergirded by the constantly present, only occasionally overt, threat of violence. A shorthand term for the interplay of legal, economic, and violent explanations for social behavior is power.

Paul Marchand, F.M.C., then, shows discourse to be an employment of power, but this insight does not answer the interpretive questions the novel raises; it makes them exponentially more complex. No position, including silence, is an ethically pure one: no matter what, one enacts choices that have consequences. Silence can be as devastating as any words, as Paul's wife, Julie, comes to learn. During the two weeks that Paul contemplates his new future as a rich white man, Julie is left in the dark: "[H]e had not slept at home, spending his days at his office and his nights at the house he had inherited." The reader, however, is assured that Paul "had written several times to Julie, brief notes, to say that he was busy, and that he would be for a few days at his father's house, and that she must not worry about his absence" (133). The impact of this incidental passage comes mainly from what is not said. The reader can hardly help but reflect on the weakness of this gesture by Paul to his wife, considering her full awareness that "[i]f he so chose, [she and their children] must accept the inevitable": their marriage is now legally void, and he is not bound by law or conventional morality to provide any longer for his family (131). She is entirely vulnerable, and Paul's behavior following the announcement of his inheritance is not at all reassuring; without these contextual realities being kept in mind, the "brief notes" Paul sends to her cannot be read rightly—in fact, taken by themselves, they do not really mean anything at all.

To read the letters requires a fleshed-out knowledge of the events that preceded them, and in this sense they are an emblem of the entire novel. A reading of Paul's notes, or of the novel, can be authorized only by the historical circumstances that created the text, and yet, somewhat paradoxically, the text itself points toward nothing more than those same circumstances that produced it. It has no purpose or meaning, in and of itself, but—given a properly self-conscious reading—has the potential to deepen one's understanding of, one's enmeshment in, the historical circumstances of its creation.[4] In other words, the novel *Paul Marchand, F.M.C.* does not, in the end, rearrange documentable historical circumstances to create something new, but articulates those circumstances in a manner calculated to help them speak with full force, to inhabit the mind of the reader. It is much more fundamentally a work of realism than a work of unfettered imagination.

Any rhetorical agency Paul has unavoidably implicates him in a cultural history of violence and economic oppression. Paul understands less well than Chesnutt appears to the power relationships that have created, and whose very logic is undermined by, his uncertain racial status. Understandably, Paul's most fervent wish is to cut through the discursive Gordian knot, the confusion of narratives that places him in an untenable position. His frustration is visible when he takes solace in his journal, writing in "large letters, heavily underscored" (22)—he wishes to communicate clearly and forcefully, to abandon a survival based on constant negotiation and strategy and simply rely on the power of his words and the abstract justice they speak. Part of Paul's problem, however, is his desire for abstraction, his adherence (in the words of Michel Foucault) to "a whole tradition that allows us to imagine that knowledge can exist only where the power relations are suspended and that knowledge can develop only outside its injunctions, its demands and its interests" (27). As Foucault suggests, one is mistaken in the attempt to opt out of the game of power, as pernicious as its effects may be, because such an opting-out is impossible. For Foucault, no form of knowledge can exist outside of power structures—all knowledge is "power-knowledge"—and so it is a question not of being inside or outside of power relations, of being a subject "who is or is not free in relation to the power system," but of the type of knowledge, and of agency, one will produce in such a system (27).

According to Chesnutt's analysis, the only way to be an ethical agent is, paradoxically, to take part in the very forms of discourse that imprison oneself and others. He presents this analysis in literal terms in chapter 6, "In the Calabozo" (the New Orleans city jail), in which Paul—imprisoned at the behest of his Beaurepas rivals—obtains valuable information as a result of his insider/outsider status. Jailed ostensibly for entering the "quadroon ball" in an attempt to protect his sister-in-law, Paul overhears a group of prisoners who have unfairly been jailed as slaves plotting an insurrection. Were Paul not, at this moment, literally an outlaw—had he remained an established, respectable member of the culture—he would not have overheard the plotting and would have no opportunity to prevent it; on the other hand, were he in league with the plotters, then there would be no question of alerting the authorities. Under the unusual circumstances, however, Paul—neither entirely inside nor entirely outside of either narrative framework, established authority and rebellion (or, correspondingly, white and black)—has a privileged insight. That insight, however, by no means solves his problems; it only makes the ethical question he faces more complicated and more urgent. Should he use this newfound information to his own advantage by exposing the plot, or should he remain silent and allow the plotters to harm their and his common enemies?

Paul initially identifies with the plotters, hatching the revenge scheme he will later repudiate: "If he could make [the white men] change place with himself, or with the two degraded Negroes in the adjoining cell, he would do it with a holy joy" (63). On the other hand, Paul reflects, his inside knowledge of the plot might easily be converted into capital: if he reveals it to the authorities, he may be spared a prison term (64). Ultimately, he resists this temptation as well, and does nothing to stop or aid the planned insurrection. But how to interpret this decision, and the thought process that leads to it, is a matter of perspective. Did Paul's newfound identification with other African Americans influence him to withhold his knowledge of the plot from the authorities, or was his failure to act really just an exhibition of passiveness, the inability to make a decision? The answer is not clear. Although these two explanations of his behavior are functionally equivalent, having the same ultimate consequences, it seems from Chesnutt's perspective that the distinction matters. Like Geertz's winking boys, two actions that look the same are, seen in context, very different.

The dilemma anticipates the climactic decision Paul faces at the end of the novel: to abandon his family and assume a new identity as a white man or to retain his identity as a "free man of color"? To the extent Paul is motivated by his own identification with the African American community represented by his wife and children, his decision to relinquish the Beaurepas estate seems honorable, but to the extent it is merely a result of his passivity it is disappointing. Has Paul placed his stake with one community in an essentially political battle, dirtied his hands by taking a side despite serious reservations, or has he sought to attain a purist position and evade a political stance altogether? This paradox suggests something of Chesnutt's response to the younger Harlem Renaissance writers. In demanding (as Langston Hughes and others forcefully did) that their paramount responsibility was an aesthetic one, did these writers evade politics, or did they take a principled and challenging political stand? In producing artworks that could be appreciated from the perspective of an elitist white sensibility, and in repudiating the call for art as "propaganda" voiced by Du Bois, did they replicate the white aesthetic and its underlying politics—producing works that, at least to an extent, looked like that of white writers—or did this apparent aesthetic resemblance belie underlying differences that must be understood contextually?[5] Chesnutt's seemingly conservative response to younger black writers' "brilliant" but immoral fiction, in my view, is more engaged with such questions than it may immediately seem. Though the novel blurs the line, showing that Paul's motive cannot definitely be determined one way or the other, it does present an ethical means of viewing such decisions that takes account of, rather than attempting to operate outside of, political and cultural contexts; and it suggests that such a pragmatic application of ethics is crucial to one's vision.

Paul is part of the power system against which he wishes to rebel, whether he likes it or not. The two scenes described above, in which he threatens Zabet to gain information and in which he withholds information about an insurrection plot, amply illustrate this point. In both cases, Paul declines to publicize the harmful information he possesses, but this scrupulousness of his does not exempt him from implication in the power structures of slaveholding New Orleans because withholding information, remaining silent, is every bit as much an employment of power as releasing it. This is not from Chesnutt's perspective to say that all choices are morally equivalent, but that all morally responsible choices are exercises, not evasions, of power.

By the same token, abstract principles such as "justice" carry weight only insofar as they may be applied practically. The novel's plot is both simple in its pull on readers' sense of justice and complex in asking: what *is* justice? Even as he attempted, as a realist, to discover and express the truths he faced as a light-skinned African American, Chesnutt aspires to a universal sense of justice that he contends is unattainable. It is as if he believes that striving for justice, even as one knows the effort to be fruitless, is the quality of human life that makes it capable of reform.

The concept of justice that Chesnutt imagines in *Paul Marchand, F.M.C.* evokes that of twentieth-century philosopher John Rawls, who in *A Theory of Justice* imagines a realm in which "persons accept in advance a principle of equal liberty and they do this without a knowledge of their more particular ends" (31).

In other words, justice is defined by asking a hypothetical question: what world would you find acceptable if you had no assurance of your particular place in it?[6] In the world in which they believe themselves to live, the "white" Beaurepas cousins have every assurance of continued privilege, and are in no way threatened by the inequities they help to enshrine daily. In the world Chesnutt has created through his reversal-of-fortune plot, that assurance is pulled out from beneath them, and the cousins must adapt their thinking accordingly. In the novel's last pages, Paul announces that not only has he been revealed to be white, but one of the cousins is "of quadroon birth" and thus is unlawfully "exercising the rights and privileges of a well-born white man" (142). Knowing full well what their answer will be, he offers them a choice: "[s]hall I or shall I not" name the quadroon?[7] In unison, the cousins ask that Marchand keep the secret to himself, illustrating Chesnutt's—and Rawls's—point: "justice" seems very different depending on one's social position, one's point of view. This observation does not, however, make the concept of "justice" a relative one; more precisely, it reveals that the abstract concept, though real, is always just beyond our reach. The proper response to such a situation is not to abandon the pursuit of justice, but gradually to strip away the layers of separation between people that enable injustice to prevail so often, though even this more limited goal may, Chesnutt seems to realize, be unreasonably idealistic.

The problem with Rawls's theory is that such a concept of justice is unavoidably imaginary. It has little force in the world in which we live, simply because the experiment Rawls envisions can only be thought about, never enacted. And, given the importance of perspective in determining what justice is, it is unreasonable to expect that our thoughts are any more unbiased in his experiment than they are in real life. Rawls, in essence, is asking us to abandon perspective even as his experiment reveals forcefully just how much perspective really matters in the world we construct. Chesnutt, I think, implicitly recognizes this problem and strives to portray a world in which admittedly perspective *does* matter, it does influence our choices, and yet in which people's actions are not *entirely* circumscribed by perspective; there is at least a relative possibility of abstracting moral choices from one's particular situation.

Chesnutt's enabling assumption in writing *Paul Marchand, F.M.C.* is that thought cannot be abstracted from the larger cultural interchanges in which it is employed. The novel relies heavily on three modes of thought that are often at odds with one another: a deterministic mode, in which actions are almost entirely determined by one's circumstances and social relations are merely the fruit of endless calculations (some more rational than others) of self-interest; a romantic mode, in which individuals really do make sacrifices in the name of abstractions like love and honor; and what might be called a eugenic mode, in which how one behaves is a function of one's genetic makeup, or "blood." The cleverness of the novel is Chesnutt's balancing of these modes in explaining particular exhibitions of behavior, and especially his upending of the most likely or typical explanation of the decisions one makes. For example, the Beaurepas cousins often believe (or at least assert) themselves to be acting honorably when the reader sees that they are desperately, and depravedly, clinging to their privilege as rich whites. On the other hand, Paul Marchand, once he becomes Paul Beaurepas, is fully expected by his peers to make the "rational" move and abandon his wife and children, whereas Chesnutt leads the reader to expect (correctly, but not without a certain tension) that he will act honorably, though at a loss of some social status.

Clearly, for Chesnutt, simply to behave in predictable, culturally "appropriate" ways is an abdication of ethical responsibility; on the other hand, he argues that it is not possible to think about ethics outside of culture. The question is, can concepts such as "honor" or "love" be even relatively unyoked from the ideological circumstances that seem to have produced them—can the "honor" of which Paul speaks, when dealing with the profligate cousins who now depend on his beneficence, be abstracted from the injuries he has suffered in hypocritical protection of the Beaurepas' "honor"?

The answer, Chesnutt seems to conclude, hinges on two factors: Paul's choice and his ability to give cultural force to that choice. If he chooses to act as though honor, properly understood, demands him to defy convention and remain loyal to his family, then such an employment of language, and such a changing of material realities as language can create, are possible, though never easy. It is a speech act, and (in the words of J. Hillis Miller) "[l]ike all speech acts [it] is a historical happening . . . not a description but an act of language that works to divide the sheep from the goats, those who have eyes and see from those who do not, though there is no certain way to decide which of those groups you are in" (*Hawthorne* 125). As such, Paul's invoking of "honor," and our understanding of it, depend on numerous factors including his sincerity, his capacity to act according to the lofty ideals he has expressed, and the force that term and concept have in a particular community. It seems possible to conclude, at least provisionally, that when Paul asserts that abandoning Julie, though it would cause him no social opprobrium, "would seem the depth of dishonor" (138), he means it, and can make the sentiment count—that, though it costs him everything else, his peculiar circumstance has empowered him to change what "honor" can mean in his environment.[8] The novel represents Chesnutt's ongoing work to make the use of an abstract term like "honor" more complicated while not depriving it altogether of its force.

The identity "Paul Marchand" is, similarly, a matter that must be regarded with due complexity. Is Paul Marchand quite simply a different person once he has become Paul Beaurepas? Legally, he certainly is. In his rather more Cartesian mindset, Paul retains his identity regardless of the name he assumes or the legal circumstances that determine what he can and cannot do, so that the insults perpetrated upon "Paul Marchand, free man of color" must, in the name of honor, be avenged by "Paul Beaurepas." He flatly rejects Henri Beaurepas's argument that "[t]he acts of which you complain were directed against a certain *soi-disant* quadroon, who, in his turn, no longer exists" (103)—Paul *knows* that the acts were perpetrated on his body and psyche: "[I]t was this same cheek that tingled with the blow. It was these ears which burned with the offensive epithet" (103). So insistent is he that his identity has not changed that he spurns the name Beaurepas and the attendant privileges and removes his family to France. He rejects his cousins' unsophisticated claim that identity is no more than a legal fiction; and yet Chesnutt's own perspective, while it likewise rejects the Beaurepas cousins' sophistry, is more complex than Paul's. What *does* make Paul continue to be Paul given such a dramatic reversal of fortune, he wonders.[9]

Paul's body, the one thing besides his memory that clearly links his old life to the new one that has been placed in his hands, is treated by Chesnutt as a signifier, much like the letters h-o-n-o-r. It may stand for two different, even incompatible, things without violating the codes by which we all understand our world, and the only way to avoid the troubling slipperiness that seems to follow is to make a choice: Paul *wills* himself to remain as he was, or at least to assert that his present self is continuous with his past self, while recognizing that he will not benefit, but may suffer materially, in making this choice.[10] For Paul, this may seem like a simple matter: *not* choosing integrity of identity would lead to chaos. Chesnutt, in my view, sees the matter somewhat differently: the conventional legal fictions favored by the Beaurepas cousins offer relative *stability,* not chaos—you are either black or white, Marchand or Beaurepas—whereas Paul, in electing to remain Marchand, has chosen for himself a life of complication, of alertness, of anxiety. It is, for Chesnutt, clearly a worthwhile choice, one that requires ongoing maintenance and self-consciousness. Integrity, the novel demonstrates, is never simple.

The question of eugenics, of "blood," is trickier in that Chesnutt's own investment in something like an ideology of eugenics is subject to debate. He occasionally seems to buy into the eugenicist belief that heredity, or blood, predicts behavior, as can be seen in the narrator's reflections on the difference between Paul and the "average quadroon" (60). But more frequently his approach is to undermine the eugenicist logic that otherwise threatens to bind him into some uncomfortable assumptions. Unavoidably, as a realist, Chesnutt assumes that physical characteristics *tell,* but how and what they tell is always subject to interpretation. The hand of Joséphine Morales, for example, "showed, as clearly as a human hand could show, that none of her ancestors had ever done any work" (45). Clearly, the evidence of her hand reveals something, marking Joséphine correctly as a member of the upper class, but what's revealed is a matter not of genetics but of cultural history, the product of a lifetime (and, indeed, the legacy of generations) of leisure.

For comparison's sake, *Paul Marchand, F.M.C.* should be read alongside Mark Twain's *Pudd'nhead Wilson,* a clear inspiration which—while sympathetic to the plight of African Americans generally and light-skinned blacks in particular—is disturbing, even ugly, in its implications, as a bare plot outline reveals.[11] Tom, born to a black mother but perceived as white, is self-centered and boorish while his likely half-brother,[12] Chambers, a white man known to the community as a black man, behaves angelically despite (or perhaps as a result of) his position of servitude. When their "real" identities are revealed by Wilson's detective work, Chambers takes his rightful role as a white slave owner while Tom's perfidy is punished as he is cast into slavery. Twain's apparent intent was to illustrate that environment determines behavior; nonetheless, the implications of his plot are disturbing in their inability to challenge established categories of identity and social hierarchy: the person with "one drop" of black blood is evil and deserves to be enslaved, while his white brother is pure of both blood and motive. *Paul Marchand, F.M.C.* attempts a similar experiment to Twain's, but Chesnutt wisely avoids implicating his narrative so obviously in racist ideologies that he and Twain alike would repudiate. For Twain, identity—though it is created by environment, not by blood—is by no means a matter of choice. It is something passively accepted, not actively taken on, and therefore has no real moral consequences. Chesnutt clearly feels very differently.

Perhaps the simplest way to express the concept of racial identity as it emerges in *Paul Marchand, F.M.C.* is that race (as a form of cultural evidence) is in at least some sense meaningful, but that racial discourse is deceitful in that it fails to express what the actual meaning of race is. The theme of masks that permeates much of the novel provides a useful key. In chapter 5, "The Quadroon Ball," Paul enters the ball to rescue his wife's sister, Lizette, despite the fact that, as a male of mixed race, his presence there is illegal. As it happens, the ball is a masquerade, and so Paul dons a mask so that his identity will not be suspected. Chesnutt, however, demolishes this unrealistic contrivance. Neither Paul nor anyone else at the ball is effectively masked in any genuine sense, since the masks cover only a small part of the face. Other contextual information—such as the uncovered portion of the face, the clothing one wears, one's voice and signature movements—easily reveals the identity of the masked individuals:

> [I]n one corner, in vivacious conversation with a well-known merchant with whom he had dealings, he recognized, under her mask, the sprightly Madame Claudine, the fashionable quadroon *modiste* of the Rue Carondelet, the full battery of whose sparkling eyes and full-blown charms, set off by one of the famous gowns of her own make with which she clothed the *élégantes* of New Orleans, was in active operation. . . . [H]e recognized, with the keen memory of hatred, the voice of the gentleman who was addressing the duke [Henri Beaurepas]. . . . [Lizette] was masked, but he could not have mistaken her anywhere. He had seen the stuff of which her gown was made; he himself had made her a Christmas present of the necklace she wore, and she walked with a seductive grace that bordered unconsciously upon wantonness. (55–56)

Masks, as we see here, hardly disguise an individual. Rather, they are cultural constructs of a sort: by common consent, the participants in the ball implicitly agree to pretend that masks truly obscure one's identity. Even as he participates in the acts of recognition, and of interpretation, that make a culture, reading "wantonness" into the walk of his sister-in-law, Paul rather stupidly fails to recognize that wearing a mask is a figurative, not a literal, covering of one's identity. If the pretense were not useful, or if other pretenses were deemed more useful, it would be abandoned, as we see when Henri Beaurepas recognizes Paul and, upset that Paul has "broken caste," arranges to have him beaten and jailed (58–59).

Chapter 5 envisions a world of masquerade, in which people's identities are known but, by common consent, not acknowledged in deference to an assumed public identity, a mask. The masked-ball setting is suggestive of a carnival atmosphere as articulated by Bakhtin, in which the rules of society are temporarily relaxed, but in *Paul Marchand, F.M.C.* the masquerade environment actually reflects and intensifies tendencies in the larger culture. People, Chesnutt suggests metaphorically, willfully misinterpret appearances according to certain conventional patterns. It is no great leap to suggest that pretending to know *less* than you actually do is one of the things that enables the conduct of social life. Were the masks to be removed, the novel implies that the result would not be some ideal world in which people are known for their "true selves." What's underneath the mask is not identity in some idealistic sense, but *cultural* identity, that is, one's position in a social hierarchy that only rarely takes explicit, visible shape but is implicitly recognized by all. As Henri's betrayal of Paul reveals, unmasking a person does not free him or her. To expose Paul as a colored man is not to reveal his "true" identity but to place him in relationship to tacitly acknowledged, but politely overlooked, webs of power.

That being so, the metaphorical masks in *Paul Marchand, F.M.C.* do cause real damage. Seeing beneath the mask—glimpsing the social relations that create personhood within a culture and, especially important, noting the interconnectedness between one person and another—can be, as Chesnutt suggests in a scene late in the novel, a radical act. In chapter 16, Paul must come to terms at last with his decision not to reveal the insurrection plot he overheard during his incarceration. The prisoners have escaped and headed to the site of their arrest, the Trois Pigeons plantation, which ironically has become in the interim (as part of the Beaurepas estate) Paul's property. Initially, Paul's sympathies seem uncomplicated to him: as the owner of the plantation he must take sides against the insurrectionists, and if "they want revenge . . . they shall have it, on the wrong side of their faces" (122). But, in an important moment, Paul comes face to face with one of the escapees, who has taken Joséphine Morales as a hostage, and his perspective shifts somewhat:

> Here for the first time, in an emergency, Paul's quadroon training pushed itself to the front. The ordinary white man at such a juncture would have seen nothing but a white woman, in the grasp of a black brute. Paul Beaurepas—for the moment Paul Marchand—saw, beyond the evil countenance of the man who faced him, the long night of crime which had produced this fruit—the midnight foray in the forest, the slave coffle, the middle passage, the years of toil beneath the lash, the steady process of inbrutement which the careless endowment of white blood had intensified by just so much vigor and energy as the blood of the master had brought with it. He must save the woman, but he pitied, even while he condemned, the ravisher. (123)

In this stunning scene, Paul completes his journey to become something Chesnutt saw as integral to a culture's survival: a realist author. He sees the prisoner's actions with their due complexity, in the full context of not only the crimes the man has committed that particular day, but a whole network of crimes perpetrated in the name of American civilization—the middle passage, enslavement "beneath the lash," racial violence—which make that act comprehensible.[13] It is a brilliant and daring thing to have said. To comprehend an act of lawlessness in its full context, a context that includes not only the act itself but a whole history of economic oppression and brutality, is to risk excusing the crime, for it is difficult to condemn an act one understands so completely. As the narrator remarks, Paul's "pity was nearly his undoing": understanding the prisoner's actions in context threatens to paralyze him from stopping those actions, and his momentary hesitation nearly allows the prisoner's accomplice to brain him with an ax (124).[14]

One might object, nonetheless, that Paul's recognition of the cultural history of a particular moment has no consequences; despite his "pity" for the prisoner, his priority remains the same, to protect his estate. (Paul kills the accomplice, but the prisoner who had captured Joséphine escapes into the underbrush.) Chesnutt's point seems to be that, while Paul's battle with the insurrectionists *looks the same* as it would have if he had never achieved a moment of understanding, it *is* morally different, even if the difference is, in the short term at least, invisible. His response, at long last, to his "quadroon training" is significant not because it changes everything, but because it has the potential to change something: it does not save him from the murky ethics of a violent culture, but potentially—if tenuously—does make it more difficult for Paul to reenact the sorts of hierarchies by which he formerly has been oppressed. Ironically, Paul must learn to embrace his "quadroon training" (even though it has recently been revealed that he is not a quadroon at all) in order to move closer to his implicit goal, which is to make racial identity mean *less.*

Significantly, although Chesnutt clearly viewed race as socially constructed, he also associates Paul's ethical breakthrough with his newfound identification with the mixed-race caste (represented by the mulatto prisoner) whose ranks he has recently left. It is true enough, as Wilson remarks, that "in finding out that he is biologically white . . . he has become what he hates" (*Whiteness* 195).[15] But it is equally true that, in another sense, "becom[ing] what he hates"—adopting the quadroon identity that formerly he had regarded with contempt—is an important step forward for Paul. It is all the more significant because Paul genuinely adopts this identity only when he no longer has to; only once his public identity has become coded as "white" does Paul manage to subvert the logic of racial identity in a meaningful way.

Chesnutt's point is that race is socially constructed, but that is decidedly *not* to say that it is without meaning or value; perhaps in some ideal world, race would be meaningless, but in the world the novel's characters inhabit the trick is not to deny the significance of race but to craft that significance, within the limits of one's powers, in more useful ways. And doing that requires not the erasure of racial difference but an upending of how racial differences are coded and valued. As McWilliams astutely observes, in *Paul Marchand, F.M.C.* and *The Quarry*, "[a]ssimilation . . . does not mean blacks becoming white as much as it does whites becoming black" (224). Blackness, in other words, is less a fact of identity than it is a sort of perspective. Chesnutt means to help his white readers see reality in a way that more closely approximates how African Americans see it. But the purpose of such an enterprise is not solely to understand oppression from the victim's perspective (which Chesnutt would have regarded as ultimately impossible) but to reap the benefits of a more complicated, complete picture—to see beyond and through the masks that white authority demands one wears. "Becoming black" means, in the end, not a shift in identity but a shift in vision that Chesnutt, like Toni Morrison after him, associates with the properly employed imagination: in Morrison's words, "imagining is not merely looking or looking at; nor is it taking oneself intact into the other. It is, for the purposes of the work, *becoming*" (4).

Like Paul Marchand in the New Orleans city prison, the Calabozo, Chesnutt faced bothersome narrative choices in resuming his novelist's career, none of which must have seemed entirely promising. He could indulge in revenge fantasies against those who spurned him, but while that might satisfy his (and some of his readers') imagination, it would be ultimately evasive of the realities that underlay his particular situation. Or he could renounce such fantasies and, in the vein of realism, work with (and within) the materials at hand. That approach must have appeared to Chesnutt more viable, yet it also presented challenging problems. Paul Marchand is only partially a role model in this regard. For Paul, moving his family to France costs his antagonists nothing; nor is it catastrophic by any means for the Marchands, who have sufficient means to support such a move. It is essentially an attempt to opt out of the social exchanges by which he had previously chosen to live; upon examination, his departure is not so much a triumph as it is a giving-up. Chesnutt, in contrast, was similarly tempted to leave for a more egalitarian society in Europe, but (as Matthew Wilson concludes) "[r]ather than give up the struggle, Chesnutt, unlike Marchand, stubbornly remained in Cleveland and tried, once again, to undermine American racism through fiction" (Introduction xxxi). Such an enterprise required, as he saw, not escape but realism.

The remaining question—would his enterprise find success?—was one that Chesnutt knew he could not answer within the pages of a novel; in a very real sense, the publication venture he initiated in his sixties is itself part of the text which calls for response. With *Paul Marchand, F.M.C.,* Chesnutt signals his interest in the theme of resurrection: the idea that one can be, as Paul was, rendered irrelevant in the circumstances and the interpretation of one's own life and yet come back. It is, among other things, a revenge fantasy in which the protagonist has a rare opportunity to pay back his antagonists in kind. Yet, like many realist works, the novel is more importantly a story of renunciation, of holding back from what one would wish to do in favor of what one must do. From the start, Chesnutt holds back from the impulse to paint glorious pictures of revenge against the instruments of racism—though he does indulge, quite effectively, in one sustained scene of comeuppance, the duel scene of chapter 14. By the end of the novel he has taught his hero to renounce such visions as well, finding them unproductive despite their emotional appeal. Rather than living well at the expense of his cousins, Paul Marchand disavows the inheritance his erstwhile father has left him: "The slaves belonging to the estate I shall manumit—that much of my prerogative as heir I shall exercise. I wish I could wipe out the system as easily—I consider it the sum of all villainies. The remainder of the property, in its entirety, I shall relinquish. I cannot hold it upon the conditions, expressed or implied, which M. Pierre Beaurepas has made. . . . I shall not even assume the family name—I would not bear the name of a man who would treat his son as M. Pierre Beaurepas has treated me" (140). Though Marchand speaks of his decision as a matter of "my own starved honor," retaining honor in this case means that he will not pretend that a solution has occurred when it has not, the real problem being—as he now realizes—not the treatment of himself but the hierarchical system that causes many to face such treatment. Neither he nor Chesnutt will partake of a "solution" to the plot that gratifies sympathetic readers while leaving social realities intact.

A story of resurrection and of renunciation, the novel provides a glimpse into Chesnutt's own self-conception as a writer during this period of his life. Quite openly, he hoped to experience a resurrection of his stalled career, and so his failure to do so has typically been read as a sad commentary, that of an author who outlived his reputation. But if we superimpose a different narrative upon Chesnutt's late career, other conclusions become possible. It seems equally valid to suppose that the novel represents not only a failed attempt at resurrection, but a renunciation of success at any cost. As Arnold Rampersad has suggested, the rejection of *Paul Marchand, F.M.C.* by publishers may be attributable to its challenging vision, not to its outdated tendencies: "White editors and publishers uneasy with his disquieting perspective on race . . . perhaps saw a relatively easy way out, and took it—they rejected the book." Much as Paul Marchand deprives himself of material success in defense of the choices that, for him, comprise an identity, Chesnutt refuses to turn his back on a career of challenging readers, with increasing force, to account for their enmeshment in deeply problematic ways of knowing.

Knowledge as Choice: The Education of Donald Glover

If *Paul Marchand, F.M.C.* with its 1820s setting seems like a backward glance, Chesnutt's final novel, *The Quarry*, is preoccupied with newness. Angus and Grace Seaton, the first of two sets of adoptive parents for the novel's protagonist, Donald Glover, arrive at Columbus City Hospital at the beginning of a new century in "a small red two-cylinder automobile, one of the earliest models developed" (3). The hospital, we learn, is "furnished with the latest and most approved equipment" (3). New discourses and sciences are in the air, including psychotherapy, "then in its infancy" (4), and the emerging "science of babiculture" (11): the methodological rearing of children to best advantage by their prosperous parents (who are sure to take advantage of the new development called Pasteurization, then also "in its infancy" [13]). The dance emulated by infant Donald, the "epileptic terpsichorean orgy" known as the Charleston (13), anticipates the dangerous-seeming jazz of the '20s.

The Quarry considers the fate of Donald, a white infant mistakenly taken to be part black, who is rejected by his adoptive white parents, the Seatons, and raised by a prosperous black couple, the Glovers, at a moment when the consequences of both decisions seem less certain than a nineteenth-century outlook would predict. The brave new world depicted in the novel is, unsurprisingly, also a world of experimentation. Donald's second adoptive mother, Mrs. Glover, in a successful effort to provide an education for Donald "conduct[s] experiments and devise[s] several formulas" for hairdressing products, eventually "establish[ing] a laboratory in her own home." The impetus for her experiment is, ultimately, economic: African Americans, the narrator explains, found the selling of such products "a promising way of escape from economic disaster" (95). Though the Glovers are not near "economic disaster," they realize they cannot procure the education they desire for Donald on Dr. Glover's income; hence Mrs. Glover's enterprise. The experiment is not necessarily tainted by its economic motivation, although her endeavor's success in the marketplace links Mrs. Glover yet more strongly to Angus Seaton, whose well-timed invention (at the beginning of the automotive age) of a type of carburetor has rendered him wealthy. As someone who often made clear his determination both to change the world through his writing and to make a living at it, Chesnutt must have felt tolerant of his characters' mixing of economic and idealistic motives, though he also recognized the difficulty of achieving success in both realms.

The education that Mrs. Glover's laboratory procures for Donald is itself described as an experiment: his mentor at "Bethany College," Professor Dean, tells him that the "school is a laboratory in which, in time, a great many hoary prejudices face extinction" (100).[16] Education, in this novel, is the means for achieving enlightenment; yet by no means is the ideal education construed by Chesnutt as an impartial seeking-after of knowledge. Chesnutt clearly approves, for example, of Mrs. Glover's efforts to educate Donald, which are consistently founded on her belief that he can become a "new Moses" for the African American people. For example, she sends him to an integrated Southern college rather than to a New England school out of concern that "the obvious advantages of being white, in a community where race lines were less tightly drawn than in the South, might pull him away from the Negro" (96). Herself an adherent to what today would be called Afrocentrism—she "had convinced herself, with small evidence at the time upon which to base her belief, that somewhere buried in the sands of Africa were the remains of ancient civilizations which the Negro or Negroid natives had founded" (62)—she strives to get Donald not the best education available in some abstract sense (a dubious abstraction, from Chesnutt's perspective), but an education that will prove most efficacious at molding Donald into a leader for his race.[17]

For Chesnutt the novel (meaning *The Quarry* specifically but also the novel as a genre) is itself a grand experiment, or more precisely a laboratory in which ideas might be combined in new ways, under realistic but controlled circumstances, and the results of the combination recorded. Chesnutt seems to describe his own undertaking with this novel in the words of Dr. Freeman, the head of the City Hospital, who suggests that the Seatons raise Donald as a white boy: "It would be a psychological experiment of rare interest, and, if he turned out well, might shake some prevalent theories and prejudices" (23).[18] As a realist, Chesnutt treats ideas in the novel from a somewhat scientific perspective, tracing the effects that personalities and ideas have when mixed together in particular ways. The combination, examined in isolation, may or may not be typical of what's found outside the laboratory, in nature or in the social landscape—even at several hundred pages, how could it be anything other than partial?—but at least it is plausible, and if the experiment is a success it will prove informative about some aspect of the outer life it attempts to represent.

Chesnutt also calls into question the nature of such a scientific approach itself, demonstrating that such an approach is inherently biased. On one hand, the inevitability of bias calls into question the legitimacy of Chesnutt's, or anyone's, literary experiment, especially if he is considered as a practitioner of realism, a writer interested in empirical truths. But with that problem arises potential: Chesnutt's strongest model in *The Quarry* for a successful life seems to be that of the person who achieves a balanced pursuit of both empirical truth (which comes from observation) and idealistic truth (which precedes observation). Donald Glover, who eventually publishes a treatise discounting reason in favor of imagination, is at best a qualified role model in this regard. Donald's own mentor, Professor Dean, more closely approximates the approach Chesnutt seems to advocate. Dean, who believes "in a just and benevolent God—in spite of reason and experience" (100–101), seems less an object of satire than a model of the balance one must achieve, that to which a proper education leads. There is, no doubt, a fine line between motivated truth of the sort Chesnutt both seeks and models in *The Quarry* and outright bias; it is this line that the novel seeks to articulate.

The main point to be taken here is that Chesnutt's realism, which (as has often been observed of realism) is specifically connected to the novel genre, attempts a mix of empirical accuracy and considered, not to say biased, *use* of accurate data toward a specific end. Much like Hamlin Garland's concept of realism, defined as "the truthful statement of an individual impression corrected by reference to the fact" (152), Chesnutt's realism, as *The Quarry* clarifies, is a motivated employment of accurate observation, "situated knowledges" as the historian of science Donna Haraway terms them. Writes Haraway, "[s]ituated knowledges require that the object of knowledge be pictured as an actor and agent, not a screen or a ground or a resource, never finally as slave to the master that closes off the dialectic in his unique agency and authorship of 'objective' knowledge" (198). Drawing from Haraway's insight, I argue that Chesnutt's work is best read as an exploration of how knowledge is *used,* not merely what knowledge *is;* though reading his novels as statements of belief yields some insight, it can easily (and often has been) overdone.

The matter of Chesnutt's personally held conservatism or his radicalism (both of which have been delineated by critics) is ultimately less important than how narratives that create the meaning of race in his works *open up* or *close off* new possibilities of understanding for readers. Fiction, not quite science, this form of realism relies equally on empirical observation and on faith—faith that the act of shaping those data one observes is, itself, a morally productive endeavor. In realism, as Chesnutt appeared to regard it, the seemingly opposite impulses of empiricism and belief not only commingle; they become indistinguishable from one another.

The danger of such an approach, as Chesnutt well recognized, is that a scientific approach founded on faith has created the exact problem that subjects Donald Glover and others to misery. One person's faith is another person's bane; situated knowledges can produce a Donald Glover, who seems capable of cutting away old habits of interpretation and helping his peers to see the world anew, but have also brought the eugenics movement, propelled forward by Darwin's cousin Francis Galton in the 1880s and invested with great currency in the early decades of the twentieth century.[19] "Galton proclaimed that racial differences were biological and that they determined not only exterior physical features but also innate, inherent moral and intellectual characteristics"; his theories "placed a new emphasis on heredity as a determining factor in deciding one's moral character, intellectual potential, and physical health" (Smith 42–43). Chesnutt grapples with the biased assumptions and methodology of the eugenics movement throughout *The Quarry;* in particular, his concept of motivated knowledge requires him to grapple with the reality that Galton and other eugenicists practice just that: their science is a mingling of ostensible empiricism and dubious faith, producing results that seem scientific but also push toward an obviously preconceived conclusion.

His disinclination to write a novel that boils down to a scientific argument, as we will see, disallows the possibility of refuting scientific racists directly. His commitment to realism, to allowing truths to speak for themselves, prevented him from discoursing freely about what the available evidence *means,* although in small, subtle gestures Chesnutt suggests that he does not buy into eugenicist principles. The eugenics movement is "science" politically applied, and in this it resembles, in structure if not in content, Chesnutt's practice of realism, which assumes that empirical truths, applied with a practical focus, cannot help but have practical implications.

Chesnutt's awareness of the problem here—that applied knowledge may produce healthy (antiracist, possibly Afrocentric) or unhealthy (eugenicist) biases—is visible in the way in which he takes on the problem of eugenics in *The Quarry.* Though Chesnutt's flirtation with something like a eugenicist approach has often been remarked upon, available evidence suggests that he saw scientific racism as merely ignorant. In *The Quarry,* Mrs. Glover successfully attacks a book claiming to prove black and mulatto inferiority "by the time-worn arguments of failure and inadequacy and achievement" (62), much as (McWilliams points out) Chesnutt once succeeded in having William Hannibal Thomas's specious *The American Negro* removed from circulation (*The Quarry* 288 n. 1 to chapter 9). It is clear to the reader of *The Quarry* that Chesnutt's faith, like Mrs. Glover's, is in "breeding" in the educational sense, not the scientific one. Donald, who is raised not by his biological parents but by two successive sets of adoptive parents, seems to be a success due to environment; his genetic makeup, Chesnutt appears to argue, is irrelevant.

Or is it? Chesnutt's attack on the eugenics movement is not unequivocal; he does not attempt to claim that *no* evidence suggests a hereditary basis for one's personal qualities or even behavior. Rather, his quarrel is with the application—the interpretation—of data that any neutral observer, or one from either perspective, could accept as accurate. It's even true that, at some level, racism and the racial pride of someone like Mrs. Glover can look like the same thing[20]—though it's critical to stipulate that, for Chesnutt, despite this appearance they *are not* the same thing. Like Southern whites, Mrs. Glover insists on using the term "Negro" rather than the conventionally more polite term "colored" (88)—again, accentuating that a given datum can be used very differently by people with different intents.[21] Chesnutt himself flirts with seemingly eugenicist assumptions: his narrator describes, for example, how "the competition of whites, *often of greater energy or enterprise,* who no longer scorned these humble pursuits, had cut into the Negro barber's white patronage disastrously" (95; emphasis added). The question is, if Chesnutt observed that some white businesspeople demonstrated "greater energy or enterprise" than their black competitors, what can he *do* with these observed data? Is it a matter of circumstances, which may change, or of genetic heritage, which cannot change except by the distillation of one race by another?

If Chesnutt's apparent attitude toward the nature-or-nurture question advanced by the eugenics movement could be summarized in a sentence, that sentence might be: the eugenicists' claims are correct, except when they aren't. Given the evidence represented by Chesnutt's various comments on biology and on what might be called racial determinism, if not outright eugenics, what interpretation of this evidence will prove most truthful—or, we might hazard to say, absent some clear conception of "truth," what interpretation proves the most productive for readers of his works? I believe that, while he was genuinely troubled by blacks' relatively slow social progress compared to that of whites, and by Galton's and others' attempts to provide a scientific explanation for this discrepancy, Chesnutt saw the issue as fundamentally a political, not a scientific, one. Though he is clearly aware of the eugenicists' argument, he endorses "the scientists of our day" who maintain "that there is no essential difference in races, any apparent variation being merely a matter of development" (63). Importantly, this does not lead Chesnutt to categorically deny the impact of heredity claimed by Galton and his ilk; it's not that science yields no answers, it's that the answers it yields are equivocal, and have political stakes.

As a result of this observation, he carefully structures much of the evidence in *The Quarry*—the evidence the novel's characters (and readers) are most preoccupied with, that of the source of Donald Glover's personal qualities—to support either a hereditary or an environmental explanation. The effect is that no claim made by either eugenicists or their opponents is uncomplicated; all claims are matters of interpretation. For example, the person initially believed to be Glover's biological father, a mulatto named Will Johnson, is described both as one who came from "a good family and had a good education" and as a gambler and cocaine user (28). If Johnson's sister is to be believed, he is even a descendant of Thomas Jefferson (31). The more we inquire into one's genealogy, it seems, the more things become not clarified but muddled. So, is Glover's exceptionalism—or, for that matter, the "sickly" nature of the Seatons' biological children (90)—a result of his blood? His own education and strivings? The evidence, in short, is indeterminate, and Chesnutt's point seems to be that, given the complexity of the evidence involved in claims about heredity, one can support virtually any claim one wishes.

In fact, he is quite clear about this. Like Professor Dean, Chesnutt appears to regard the debate about whether or not African Americans are equal to whites intellectually as "beside the question" (100): trying to prove one conclusion or the other is largely a waste of time since the central issue is one not of the rightness of white supremacists' claims but of their ability to enact a particular vision. Scientific racism is not what its adherents claim it to be—a matter of justice, or of social planning, or of nurturing innate talents—abstract concepts all; it is a matter of power, which properly understood is never abstract. As the narrator explains, "[t]he question could never be settled in the abstract. It was easy to find Negroes who were intellectually the superiors of many white men, but as to the mass, it could never be proven except by a test under equal conditions" (100). Further, such a test will never occur, in part because it would be too risky for those who hold power. For example, the "state legislature, foreseeing danger to the purity and prestige of the dominant race by this vicious example of social equality in their very midst," bans the experiment of integrated education conducted at Bethany College (101).

The central theme of *The Quarry* is that evidence will always be employed as a function of power. Writes Chesnutt, in an incidental passage, "[n]aturally a light-hearted people and fond of travel and change of scenery, [African American association members] spent far more than they could afford on long journeys in special cars to distant points, to attend conventions from many of which one could discover no gain except 'a good time.' The same might be said of the whites, but they were, presumably, better able to afford it" (180). Whites, in other words, have the cultural capital to do what most people enjoy—such as travel and have "a good time"—without these data being taken to represent pernicious "natural" qualities. Ultimately, *The Quarry* does not argue for a suspension of habits of interpretation, but their expansion to include whites' behavior as well as blacks'.[22]

If science is a matter not only of empiricism but also of interpretation, and therefore at some level a matter of choice, or even of faith, then why not make good choices?—which seems, as Chesnutt presents them in this novel, to mean something like *publicly defensible choices.* Chesnutt reveals the science of eugenics to be thoroughly politicized, yet he makes a virtue out of a politicized scientific approach by exploring results such as race pride: if heredity is deemed important, why not celebrate the achievement of Alexandre Dumas, whose African ancestry Chesnutt implicitly supports in attacking its deniers, or even Robert Browning, about whose putative African heritage Chesnutt seems more suspicious—but whose willingness to publicly embrace such a possible heritage he clearly admires (42–43)? If it's a problem that the African American community *needs* these European ancestors, it's a political problem which time seems destined to overcome, and the "New Negro" movement seems a promising start (34).

At its heart, *The Quarry* is yet another novel about interpretation: how can available data best be put to use? Although it touches on scientific debates of its day, as we have seen, the evidence supplied by the novel is social and cultural, indicating that, for Chesnutt, prospective answers to questions of race and the "color line" must be tested not by science but in the realm of human experience, the realm of the realist novel. Chesnutt does not directly evaluate the nature of the scientific argument propounded by Galton and his ilk; what he does is to explore the various ways in which such an argument, and the evidence used to prop it up, might be employed in the social world. That the eugenicists' argument carries force, rightly or wrongly, is simply a fact; rather than attempt to argue the facts away or demonstrate their falsity, Chesnutt's tactic is to experiment, through his characters, with different possible responses to the argument from various perspectives. *The Quarry,* at the outset, seems to validate the argument against eugenics, but by the last chapters the emphasis, and the evidence supplied by Chesnutt, seem to favor the idea that genetics (a) determine ability and behavior, and (b) apply not only to individuals, but to familial "lines" and possibly to ethnic groups and races. Importantly, though, even as the evidence employed by Chesnutt seems, at one level, inevitably to support his subscription to something like eugenicist belief, the intricacy of the novel increases exponentially. If Chesnutt wrote himself into a corner where he could not help seeming to advocate an argument that demonstrably worked against his political intent, he makes this tendency something other than final by investing the narrative with increasing layers of complexity, making the last third of *The Quarry* difficult indeed to interpret satisfactorily.

When I first read *The Quarry,* I was intrigued (as I still am) by Chesnutt's clever signification on contemporary ideas about racial determinism. That intrigue metamorphosed into outrage and pain, however, as I witnessed how the novel handles Donald Glover's discovery that he is, in fact, genetically all-white. I knew from previous criticism that Glover would make this discovery; how, I wondered, would Chesnutt handle the revelation itself, which is deferred until late in the novel? Well before chapter 28, when the discovery takes place, it becomes apparent that Chesnutt is in a tight spot: the "Moses of his people," cast as the brightest star of his race, will be revealed as not "of his people" in the first place, implying, to some readers at least, that only a "pure" white man could attain the intellectual heights that Chesnutt has associated with the seemingly superhuman Glover. Chesnutt has, by this point, increasingly flirted with an endorsement of eugenicist thought, as when in chapter 23 he articulates an ugly sentiment in disavowing folk wisdom about railroad porters: "There was a prevailing superstition among colored people that the Pullman porters were made up of supermen whom race prejudice had condemned to menial servitude. Donald had not found it so. Most of them were stodgy, middle-aged black men, and though poorly paid, their work as porters was, as a rule, at just about the level of their intelligence. The dining room waiters, on the other hand, were mostly mulattoes, and many of them were students earning the money to put them through college or professional school" (197).

In case there is any ambiguity about where Chesnutt stands, the story of Glover's racial heritage seems to clinch the author's own ideas about racial hierarchy and heredity. We learn from Dr. Freeman, the former head of the hospital from which Glover was adopted, that

> [h]is father was Reverend Sinclair Marvin, who had been a Congregational minister. The history of this old and prolific New England family is quoted by writers on sociology, crime, and heredity as conclusive proof of certain theories. It seems that back in colonial times a certain young gentleman of this family, whose grandparents had come over on the *Mayflower*, had a passing amour, while yet unmarried, with a feeble-minded maid at an inn where he put up one night. This meeting proved fertile and the girl bore a child. Careful records were kept and verified, showing that every generation of the descendants of this child produced thieves, prostitutes, murderers, forgers, drug addicts, and drunkards. The workhouses, asylums and jails of New England swarmed with them. Female virtue was almost unknown among them, and most of their children were illegitimate. (258–59)

Reading this passage, quite frankly, made me angry. The inclusion of the "passing amour," which serves no purpose in the plot (the "feeble-minded maid" is, contrary to what one might guess from the above passage, not Donald's ancestor[23]), seems especially to be a cheap shot, included apparently only to hammer home the inescapability of eugenicist principles. After I was angry, however, I started to think. (It is not incidental, I'd argue, that the effect of Chesnutt's narrative is to induce anger and then thought.) Why *would* Chesnutt have included the reference to the "feeble-minded maid"? What purpose does it serve? If Chesnutt's previous writings provide any kind of guide, he was disinclined to introduce loose ends unless they serve some subtle purpose, and as a craftsman he was certainly capable of avoiding such a conspicuous one if he wished to do so.

The reference to the child of the heir and the maid is interesting in that it calls to mind the child that Mamie Wilson, the scheming young woman to whom young Donald lost his virginity, claimed to have conceived in chapter 10. Neither of these children's existence is independently verified; perhaps neither exists. It seems significant that the narratives that tend to support eugenicist belief are generally filtered through characters' perspectives, supporting the ideology that most favors a given character's place in life. Glover, for example, has adequate psychological reasons to assume that the Pullman porters are as stupid as they seem to him; otherwise, how could he hold onto his self-concept as the savior of his race, a role that requires him to act and feel superior to most members of that race? He has apparently forgotten, or has chosen to ignore, just how close he once came to becoming stuck in the position of "a waiter or porter" himself (79). Similarly, it seems reasonable to infer that Dr. Freeman, who first articulates eugenicist principles in the novel, tells the story of the two New England families, that of the Brahmin and that of the "feeble-minded maid," to support his personal beliefs with a kind of "evidence"; in fact, the story seems to serve no other purpose—the question is, is Chesnutt employing it to that purpose as well? What other possibilities are available? Perhaps the point behind the story is that, with all these references to illegitimate children, a scientific explanation of character based on genetics is simply untenable because laboratory conditions do not pertain: who really knows where ones bloodline has meandered along the way?[24]

Recognizing that people tend selectively to notice data that reinforce their preconceptions, Chesnutt attempts to remind his readers of factors that, if acknowledged, might make ethical choices more complicated. Take, for example, the decision Glover faces in chapter 27: should he marry the wealthy and aristocratic Lady Blanche or his first love, a black woman named Bertha Lawrence? As Chesnutt has done more than once before, the choice of which woman to marry represents which life this young man will pursue: either he will join the aristocracy and leave his troubles behind him or he will continue to identify as a black man, with all the political baggage that represents. In marrying Lady Blanche, he will leave behind the racial heritage that his mother has made a life's work of instilling in him. His attempt to find a rhetorical solution to the choice—"if he should properly stress Lady Blanche's West Indian origin it might be easy to convince her that he was not abandoning the cause of their people" (252)—he recognizes as a lost cause; it must be one or the other.

It would be easy to overlook an important implication of this decision: *either* role that Donald might assume is, in a critical sense, a false one. "He had thought himself loyal to his race, but how far did that loyalty go, and was it consistent with the life of a wealthy Englishman?" (247). If being "black" only tenuously fits Glover's lived experience, on the other hand he is certainly not to the manor born. Choosing marriage to Lady Blanche might solve some problems for Donald—he reflects that "he could find it easy to love a rich and affectionate wife" (247–48)—but it is no more an answer to the questions raised by Donald's ambiguous past than marrying Bertha is. Neither choice confirms a past identity that has remained obscure; instead, to make either choice is for Donald to *adopt* an identity, to commit himself to a particular version of the future. While either decision would, of course, have implications on a past—a history—that informs the present and future, Chesnutt's point seems to be that Donald's history can only be known to himself and to others as it is interpreted, and interpretation is, to a large degree, a function of choice.

According to Alfred Habegger, the availability of choices is integral to realist literature: "Realism never tells us what is to be done, but it assumes, fundamentally, that choice, regardless of the difficulties, exists" (111). And, as McWilliams has argued, *The Quarry* extends this principle to its central motif, the meaning of race: in the novel, he says, "[r]acial identity is a social construct not a biological given. Environment is only part of the story, however, for there is also choice. At some point one must choose what attitude one assumes toward one's experience and those with whom one has shared it" (220). Of course, Chesnutt never claims that decisions concerning one's identity are absolutely free or that they exist outside of limiting historical contexts. As McWilliams implies, choice is just one factor among others in determining racial identity. A thorough examination of such choices as the novel's characters face may, in fact, lead to the conclusion that choices exist only theoretically, given the degree to which they are circumscribed by circumstance. Cynthia A. Callahan, for example, writes that "[t]he 'choice' that the Seatons face [upon determining that Donald is of mixed race] exists only in theory. The social mores of the time center around the one-drop rule, which clearly demands that anyone with any degree of African ancestry be categorized as black. The smallest percentage of black blood perceived in Donald is enough to taint Mrs. Seaton's own heritage (as she has always passed herself off as Donald's biological mother), threaten the family's current social status, and result in Donald's being socially 'demoted' to the status of African American" (323).

In this, Callahan is absolutely correct. Yet it seems important to Chesnutt that however theoretical they may be, such choices as the Seatons face are regarded as real and as having cultural force. The Seatons have been placed by their author in a curious position: apparently bound by cultural imperatives that are larger than they are, they nonetheless sense (and act as if) they are in the teeth of a moral quandary, one which Mr. Seaton continues to stew about until the novel's end. Logically, this makes no sense: if the Seatons are, in fact, bound by circumstance, then as individuals they have no guilt. But Chesnutt's point does not seem to be that the Seatons' feelings are illogical. He instead suggests that their qualms are perfectly understandable: they reveal a disjunction between contemporary ethics and a principled position on race. Their feelings of moral uncertainty reveal something they cannot quite intellectualize: that the social structure as it exists is fundamentally unjust. The rupture between *felt* morality (the terrain of the romanticist) and a deterministic environment (naturalistic territory) is at the core of the novel. If people were perceived as free to act according to their hearts' dictates, or conversely if they were assumed to be mere tools of their environment, the novel simply would not work.

Instead, the novel presumes a world that is largely fixed by convention—as a quick perusal of available evidence will easily show—but also constantly made and remade by individuals' choices. As we saw in the case of *The House Behind the Cedars,* Chesnutt describes a world in which concepts such as racial identity become stabilized not due to any inherent quality but through endless repetition; they are no more or less fixed than the particular words used to describe them. As McWilliams notes regarding *Paul Marchand, F.M.C.,* it is a world in which "the same stupid mistakes are repeated generation after generation" (207). But it is fundamentally important to notice that, in such a world, a swift change in direction is always plausible, if difficult to enact.

Having made this point, Chesnutt is unwilling to spell out in precise terms what direction racial policy should take, or how individuals should respond to racial problems. Although Donald writes a master's thesis outlining "a simple, clear, rational, and humane solution of this vexed question" (178), the novel conspicuously fails to lay out what that solution might be.[25] It would have been uncharacteristic as well as foolhardy for Chesnutt to spell out an ideal solution to the knotty problem of racial prejudice in his novel—he seems more interested in clearing a space in which future solutions may be developed than in resolving the issue himself—but his silence about Donald's proposal suggests another point as well. Donald's solution is apparently a purely theoretical one, and therefore, for Chesnutt, hardly worth the paper it is written upon. As Donald himself points out to Amelia Parker, his white girlfriend at Columbia University, the problem is not really a theoretical one: "Professor Boaz[26] may postulate and demonstrate that by way of race I am as good as you . . . but, except in theory, few other white people feel that way" (127). In other words, racism can be understood intellectually to a degree, but it does not withstand theoretical analysis, or at least not the sort of abstract philosophical analysis in which Donald seems prone to engage. Despite some predictable patterns, it can be understood only as it is enacted, which is ad hoc. To convince whites "in theory" that racism is misguided seems not to dispel their deeper-seated prejudices; in their visible aversion to darker-skinned blacks, they "acknowledged in practice what they rigorously denied in theory" (189). And because racism is the kind of problem that is not susceptible to abstract reasoning, but only to a form of understanding that is responsive to what Bakhtin calls "living discourse,"[27] Chesnutt places his faith where he always has: in the realist novel.

Notes

Introduction

1. Stephen P. Knadler states, "[t]he critical obsession with naming either Dr. Miller or Josh Green as the novel's hero shows a failure to understand the novel's radical deconstruction of whiteness as a rhetorical performance" (441).

2. In the famous review in which he lamented the "bitter" tone of *The Marrow of Tradition,* William Dean Howells defended Chesnutt against the charge, still made today, that he subordinated a realist aesthetic to political ends: "[H]e does not paint the blacks all good, or the whites all bad. He paints them as slavery made them on both sides, and if in the very end he gives the moral victory to the blacks . . . it cannot be said that either his aesthetics or ethics are false" ("Psychological" 83).

3. Chesnutt also uses the phrase in the story "The Sheriff's Children," in which the narrator describes a moment of moral clarity in which "all the acts of one's life stand out, in the clear light of truth, in their correct proportions and relations" (*Collected Stories* 147). The formulation appears to show the influence of Howells's *The Rise of Silas Lapham,* in which the Reverend Sewell remarks that "novelists might be the greatest help to us if they painted life as it is, and human feelings in their true proportion and relation" (162).

4. After the Civil War, Rohrbach indicates that "readers restricted their humanitarian interests to their own class and race issues" (116), and realist writers—motivated by the literary marketplace—let the antiracist dimension of realism fade

from view. Thus her book is an attempt to fill in the hidden influence of slave narratives and other abolitionist texts on realism.

5. In addition to the work by Boeckmann discussed here, see discussions of Chesnutt's fiction in Bert Bender's *Descent of Love: Darwin and the Theory of Sexual Selection in American Fiction, 1871–1926* (1996), Brook Thomas's *American Literary Realism and the Failed Promise of Contract* (1997), Michael A. Elliott's *The Culture Concept: Writing and Difference in the Age of Realism* (2002), Sämi Ludwig's *Pragmatist Realism: The Cognitive Paradigm in American Realist Texts* (2002), Kathleen Pfeiffer's *Race Passing and American Individualism* (2003), and Henry B. Wonham's *Playing the Races: Ethnic Caricature and American Literary Realism* (2004).

6. For additional insight on this point, see the letters of 1890 in which he accuses white author H. S. Edwards of plagiarizing his story "How Dadsy Came Through" (*"To Be an Author"* 57–64). Edwards's reply that both he and Chesnutt must have borrowed the story from an African American folktale that was essentially in the public domain (*"To Be an Author"* 63 n. 2) was clearly unsatisfactory to Chesnutt, who nonetheless dropped the charge when it became clear that neither his influential correspondent George Washington Cable nor the publisher of Edwards's story, Richard Watson Gilder, would support him.

7. Although Chesnutt in this case was speaking to a largely black audience, he did not hesitate to challenge whites with similar comments. See, for example, the 1904 speech "The Race Problem," in which he bluntly tells a mainly white audience that African Americans would not need to be informed about the injustices faced by—or the progress made by—their race, for "[t]hese things they know, better than you could. . . . They view their people as a whole," and thus their vision is not limited by stereotypical images of blacks as waiters, bootblacks, and criminals (*Essays and Speeches* 197).

8. See Wilson, *Whiteness* 16–17.

9. See Thomas 156–63 for further discussion of Chesnutt's response to *An Imperative Duty* in *The House Behind the Cedars.*

10. William L. Andrews has voiced a similar charge: "[T]he greatest erosion of verisimilitude in *The Marrow of Tradition* arises from the readiness with which Chesnutt could classify his characters under sociopolitical genera and species" (*Literary Career* 202).

11. McElrath adapts this idea from the arguments of scholar SallyAnn Ferguson, who has accused Chesnutt of subscribing to "the principle of unitary racial development" ("Rena Walden" 204) and correspondingly of flattering whites' racist beliefs about racial qualities at the expense of any genuine recognition of black people's realities. Ferguson sees Chesnutt as prone to voicing, in both fictional and nonfictional writings, "racial propaganda" (204) in favor of the whitening of the race through amalgamation.

12. Specifically, McElrath writes: "[J]ustice would reign in life-as-it-ought-to-be as pictured in *The Marrow of Tradition:* the humiliation of Major Carteret and

his wife is a splendid manifestation of the way life *should*—but did not—run its course in Wilmington, N.C." (101).

13. My discussion of "Rena Walden" is based on two typescripts written at approximately the time that Gilder had rejected the story, which are housed in the Chesnutt Collection of Fisk University. The Fisk typescripts of "Rena" are hand-edited drafts; we do not have a polished copy of the sort that Chesnutt would have submitted to *Century* magazine.

14. Morris is summarizing Georg Lukács's approving take on the fiction of Stendhal and Balzac.

15. As further demonstrated in an 1891 letter to Houghton Mifflin declaring his willingness to consider any omissions except "Rena Walden" from a proposed book of short stories (*"To Be an Author"* 76), Chesnutt was more interested in achieving a reasonably uncompromised voice than he was in publication for its own sake, or for financial remuneration.

16. See, for example, Barthes, "Reality Effect" and "Myth Today"; Miller, "Fiction of Realism"; and Jameson, "Realist Floor-Plan."

17. On Chesnutt, see Ames, and Andrews, "Representation of Slavery" as well as the works cited in note 5, above; on Harper, see Ammons, *Conflicting Stories* 20–33, and Warren, *Strangers* 110–11, 131–34; on Hopkins and Dunbar-Nelson, see Ammons, *Conflicting Stories* 59–71, 77–85; on Du Bois and Johnson, see Warren, "Troubled Black Humanity"; on Johnson also see Boeckmann 174–204. For a discussion of realism in the works of later African American writers and artists, see Morgan.

Chapter 1

1. Frances Richardson Keller suggests the possibility of a seventh unpublished novel, a work of around 1928 referenced in correspondence between Chesnutt and James Weldon Johnson (194 n. 63). See also Chesnutt's submission letter for an unnamed novel composed around 1930 (*Exemplary* 274).

2. *Evelyn's Husband* is listed as "about 1900" in the Chesnutt Collection at Fisk University; however, Chesnutt's correspondence indicates that he was working on it, and later submitted it, in 1903 (Andrews, *Literary Career* 130–31). Chesnutt occasionally reworked and submitted works for publication long after their original composition, and in terms of style and technique *Evelyn's Husband* seems comparable to his earliest attempts at a novel, the 1890s texts *Mandy Oxendine* and *A Business Career.* Matthew Wilson, on the other hand, believes that *Evelyn's Husband* logically follows *The Marrow of Tradition* in Chesnutt's progression as a novelist (*Whiteness* 20–21, 42).

3. In fairness, Wilson points out that to read Chesnutt's early novels as romances is not to conclude that they are evasive of social realities, or merely flattering of their audience's preconceptions. He situates his argument in the context of recent developments in criticism that "see that popular fiction also performs the function

of constructing cultural common sense, that the writers of romance and their audiences are actively rather than passively linked, that writers actively collaborate with their audiences to create fictions that shift, however marginally, the cultural imaginary" (24).

4. Andrews treats Chesnutt's then-unpublished late novels, *Paul Marchand, F.M.C.* and *The Quarry,* in slightly more detail, though he is not much more enamored of their quality. To Andrews they represent Chesnutt's propensity for the "problem story" (265) or "thesis novel" (269), which he finds to have failed when unleavened by more traditionally artistic qualities, as the novels that achieved publication more often exhibited in his view. Andrews does regard *The Quarry* as a work that "can be read with interest and profit by the student of Chesnutt's literary career" due to its autobiographical tones (271). I am aware of only a few brief mentions of *A Business Career, The Rainbow Chasers,* or *Evelyn's Husband* in scholarship published between Andrews's 1980 study and Matthew Wilson's excellent *Whiteness in the Novels of Charles W. Chesnutt* (2004), which is discussed in this chapter. They appear in a chronology in the 2002 Library of America edition of Chesnutt's works, in Wilson's introduction to *Paul Marchand, F.M.C.* (vii) and his essay "Who Has the Right to Say?" (33 n. 4), and in the introduction to *An Exemplary Citizen: Letters of Charles W. Chesnutt, 1906–1932,* ed. Jesse S. Crisler, Robert C. Leitz, III, and Joseph R. McElrath, Jr. (xxiii).

5. Consistent with his philosophy that the truth is generally accessible to all, depending only on one's ability to recognize it, Chesnutt frequently couches the idea of dimly acknowledged truths in terms of familial resemblance, as in *A Business Career* when Truscott learns Stella's true identity, accounting for "a certain likeness that he had observed but had never been able to identify" (209). The use of physical family characteristics as a metaphor for an unacknowledged world of significance points to the submerged themes of heredity and race that will be explored later in this chapter.

6. In other ways as well, Chesnutt suggests but declines to pursue a thrilling tale: for example, he leads the reader to believe that a dramatic chase scene, the pursuit of Truscott's unscrupulous accountant Ross, is about to occur, but forsakes the chase: Truscott learns that Ross, the novel's only real villain, has escaped to "a certain South American country with which at that time the United States had no treaty of extradition" (170). Sensationalism is trumped by legal minutiae.

7. Perhaps what Chesnutt renounces is not daydreaming per se, but revenge fantasies. He frequently uses the device of articulating, but then renouncing, a revenge motive for his most sympathetic characters; notably, *The Marrow of Tradition* and *Paul Marchand, F.M.C.* hinge thematically as well as technically on this maneuver, first attempted in *A Business Career.* Of course, in the later two novels, the question of revenge is explicitly connected to the theme of race relations; the development of this theme in *A Business Career* is one reason to suspect that this novel is less disconnected from Chesnutt's racially oriented fiction than it might appear.

8. Similarly, Wilson argues that Stella "inhabits the professional world without giving up her essential femininity, [and] thus represents a compromise in a gender debate in the white world, a realistic figure in a romantic novel" (*Whiteness* 31).

9. Unless otherwise noted, references to *The Rainbow Chasers* are to the 188-page typescript, heavily hand-edited, labeled Copy 1 and cased in File 15 of Box 8 in the Charles W. Chesnutt Collection of Fisk University, although it should be noted that this version pieces together portions of typescripts that clearly were written at various times. Files 16–20 of Box 8 in the collection contain additional manuscript and typescript fragments from the novel-in-progress. Although Chesnutt submitted *The Rainbow Chasers* to Houghton Mifflin, a fully intact manuscript version is not known to be available.

10. The various manuscript fragments, in fact, offer a lovely window into Chesnutt's composition process, suggesting a hypergraphic personality who, apparently constantly, scribbled prose onto the margins of concert programs and the backs of advertising letters and cardboard boxes—accounting, among other things, for his completion of six novels in a few years' time—honing these fragments as he worked them into various successive drafts of the novel at hand.

11. The satire of science in the novel is evidence that Chesnutt ultimately rejected eugenicist principles; Quilliams's adherence to the belief that heredity will out is shown to be a product of his unquestioning faith in science (141).

12. Chesnutt's comments on interpretation are far from innocent of their own questionable assumptions. As he does throughout his career, in *Evelyn's Husband* he reveals his ambivalent adherence to the idea of hereditary types, as shown in an incidental passage in which a "young Greek of the degenerate modern type which seeks our shores, to black our shoes" contemplates a classical Greek sculpture (55). Chesnutt (who almost always filters bigoted sentiments through some other character's perspective than the narrator's) recounts Evelyn's thoughts on the discrepancy between "the beauty of the old Grecians" and the contemporary immigrants "who bear their name and mutilate their ancient speech" (55). Even as he relates these thoughts of Evelyn's, however, Chesnutt implies at least some awareness that the novel's democratic appeal is enabled only by the denigration of a designated other, introduced expressly for that purpose.

13. Wrote Howells, "Realism is nothing more and nothing less than the truthful treatment of material, and Jane Austen was the first and the last of the English novelists to treat material with entire truthfulness" ("Palacio Valdéz" 96–97).

14. These developments might have been borrowed from the last several chapters of Harold Frederic's *The Damnation of Theron Ware* (1896), in which the protagonist acts rashly (and with devastating consequences) based on similarly wrong assumptions about a woman's trip to New York accompanied by an older man.

15. Wilson identifies an evident source text for *Evelyn's Husband:* naturalist author Frank Norris's 1898 novel *Moran of the Lady Letty,* which likewise moves from an upper-class setting to the high seas, where the male protagonist is able to

get "back into contact with his primitive man" (*Whiteness* 37), a response (as Wilson convincingly reads it) to anxieties about "beleaguered masculinity" in the 1890s (38).

16. In a bizarre passage, Manson imagines—without apparently recognizing that his scenario is dead-on—what would happen if Cushing happened to be on the island: "If, to help him carry out some dark scheme of revenge, he let me live, he would try to conceal his identity. He would never have the manliness to confess the wrong he had done me. His conscience would have made him a coward; he would be afraid to face even a poor, blind, helpless castaway whom he had wronged. But he could not have deceived me. An unerring intuition would have taught me the truth, and I should have been on my guard. But I shudder to think of the situation—I should have been so entirely at his mercy!" (197). This seems like cheap irony on Chesnutt's part, and it is, but it is also evidence of the self-referential nature of this part of the novel.

17. Self-consciously, Chesnutt's narrator acknowledges that "[p]erhaps never before in the history of mankind had quite the same situation existed" (238).

18. Chesnutt complicates this question in an important way by introducing, though vaguely, the variable of race: using free indirect discourse to represent Cushing's position, the narrator states that "his race, his civilization, his training, all constrained him" from simply killing Manson while on the island (177).

19. Of course, a literary text populated exclusively by whites is no less a text about race than any other, a point I take up in chapter 4, which considers *The Colonel's Dream.*

20. Chesnutt's employment of dialect has been defended by critics; for example, Dean McWilliams analyzes Chesnutt's short stories in which "linguistic interaction . . . produces a situation where the two languages and value systems stand as equals" (74). McWilliams makes an ample case for his claim, but George's speech as represented in *The Rainbow Chasers,* in my estimation, does not withstand a similar analysis.

21. Wilson comes close to making this point, noting that a comment by Quilliams about Julia—"Justly or unjustly, the sins of the father *are* visited upon the children" (147)—closely mirrors a line used to describe Rena in *The House Behind the Cedars.* Writes Wilson, "[m]ixed-race characters must pay socially for the sexual sins of their fathers; they are always marked by their difference. Conversely, the daughter of an embezzler and cop killer, while marginalized, labors under a handicap that is not insuperable" (*Whiteness* 33). Of course, in Chesnutt's vision, the distinction between an acknowledged mixed-race character such as Rena and a putatively "white" character like Julia is merely that of one's respective cultural position; without consciousness of race, race does not exist.

22. Though Howells means to treat Olney as a morally scrupulous pragmatist, not a cunning manipulator, he is clearly aware that the advantage gained with newfound knowledge places his character in an ethical predicament. Olney's hopes of marrying Rhoda are enhanced by the death of her aunt (since it decreases the chances of her secret being more widely revealed) and by Bloomingdale, his main

rival, not being given the chance to demonstrate his open-mindedness. Though Olney forbears to play his hand by helping along either of these occurrences, the narrative makes clear that he is, in each case, tempted to do so (202, 218–19).

23. Furthermore, Chesnutt implies at the end of *Evelyn's Husband* that racial identity is contingent on arbitrary factors such as time and place. As Wilson points out, the doctor who restores Manson's sight in Brazil "would be considered black in the United States, as if Chesnutt were rewriting the conclusion of *The Marrow of Tradition,* in which the African American Dr. Miller is invited to operate on a white child" (*Whiteness* 42).

Chapter 2

1. Among others, Reginald Watson argues that "Chesnutt seems to rely on traditional Southern images in order to critique, not support, the black stereotypes that were normally associated with such literature" (53), but notes that "there is some mixture of opinion about whether Chesnutt was truly successful in creating realistic mulatto characters" (54); Charles Duncan similarly concludes that the novel's "plot derives from, but ultimately revises, an established genre, in this case that of the tragic mulatto fiction" (13); and Darryl Hattenhauer likewise disputes that Chesnutt's treatment of mulatto characters is stereotypical (43). Among critics who are more suspicious of Chesnutt's use of the genre, Trudier Harris finds blackness in the novel to be "a source of entertainment and the butt of jokes—from Chesnutt as well as from the characters he creates" (227); SallyAnn H. Ferguson contends that "the novelist almost always portrays 'genuine Negroes' in stereotypical terms" ("Chesnutt's Genuine Blacks" 436); Cathy Boeckmann claims that "[t]he two mulatto protagonists are incapable of being read as anything but white and superior; moreover, they are read as signs of white racial perfection" (157).

2. In *Modernism and the Harlem Renaissance,* Baker reads Chesnutt's story collection *The Conjure Woman* as an example of mastery of form (41–47).

3. Charles Hackenberry, the editor of the 1997 edition of *Mandy Oxendine,* dates the completion of the manuscript at early 1897 at the very latest, though he believes it was probably finished earlier and that Chesnutt may have had a draft "as early as 1889" (xv).

4. Though Mandy seems least plausible as a suspect, a review of her thoughts on Utley's death shows only that she watched Utley and her protector struggle, that the protector left a prostrate Utley, and that Mandy, upon leaving the scene herself, sensed that "a mortal blow had been struck" (82). It remains just possible that Mandy, though she seems later to believe that "her hand had not struck the fatal blow" (85), put the finishing touch upon the beaten Utley.

5. John Edgar Wideman makes a similar point regarding another Chesnutt text, the short story "A Deep Sleeper": "In effect, the writer can profit from the diversity among his readers rather than be limited by it. Chesnutt took full advantage of this possibility by playing to multiple audiences, designing his 'A Deep Sleeper'

in layers, layers corresponding to the conflicting versions of reality perceived by blacks and whites" (66).

6. In *Charles W. Chesnutt and the Fictions of Race,* Dean McWilliams also explores a deconstructive reading of *Mandy Oxendine,* uncovering ways in which "Chesnutt complicates and overturns the conventional oppositions" between black and white, male and female, and so forth (126). However, in my view McWilliams could have gone even farther in showing how thoroughly inadequate Chesnutt finds these oppositions to be. For example, McWilliams points out that "it is the mulatto couple who act nobly, while the aristocrat and the minister act immorally" (126), but does not probe beyond this relatively simple reversal into Chesnutt's reconsideration of what terms like "acting nobly" really mean.

7. The novel frequently spoofs sentimental or romantic forms of narrative, as in its dry quotation of a "beautiful and brilliant" couplet sent by Mandy to Tom: "If you love me like I love you, / No nife can kutt our love in 2" (30).

8. Rena Walden's straightforward reply to a similar question in *The House Behind the Cedars*—"Yes, ma'am, I am colored" (161)—is more positively constructed.

9. Regarding John Warwick, the narrator states, "[m]ore liberally endowed than Rena with imagination, and not without a vein of sentiment, he had nevertheless a practical side that outweighed them both. . . . Warwick's imagination, however, enabled him to put himself in touch with her mood and recognize its bearing upon her conduct. He would have preferred her taking the practical point of view" (53–54). Tryon, according to the narrator, is "a man of too much imagination not to be able to put himself, in some measure at least, in [Rena's] place," but these thoughts do not cause him to reconsider his belief that he, not she, has been wronged (97).

10. As Brook Thomas points out, this is essentially Edward Olney's argument in Howells's *An Imperative Duty,* a perspective that Chesnutt critiques in *The House Behind the Cedars* (159).

11. As Boeckmann indicates, Rena's predicament is inflected by both race and gender: "[A]s a woman she cannot maintain the power to control her story. . . . Because of Rena's gender, her racial identity depends on the mind-set and attitudes of others" (165–66). Chesnutt also arguably scapegoats his female characters, suggesting it is Rena and especially Molly who maintain intraracial boundaries, for example by excluding Frank Fowler from a party because he "was black, and would not harmonize with the rest of the company" (145).

12. Unfortunately, in my view, the comparison is usually implied to be a backhanded compliment for Chesnutt. A notable exception is Russell Ames's essay of 1953, "Social Realism in Charles W. Chesnutt," which praises Chesnutt's objectivity—"which is apparent to Negro observers but not to whites" (151)—and contrasts it to Faulkner's "decadent" and shallow portrayal of race relations (152).

13. In a journal entry from 1875, when he was teaching school as a teenager in North Carolina, a frustrated Chesnutt writes, "I believe I'll leave here and pass anyhow, for I am as white as any of them" (*Journals* 78). As Dean McWilliams points

out, nowhere else in his journals does Chesnutt appear to consider passing as an option for himself (25).

14. Throughout his career, Chesnutt insisted that most whites are disadvantaged by racism, though of course less severely and directly than African Americans are. For example, the South has remained in a "semi-barbarous condition" due to its stubborn adherence to principles of slavery (*Essays and Speeches* 196), and Southern whites have inflicted moral as well as material self-harm in their "dealings with the negro" (*Exemplary* 196).

15. Given this attitude, *The Colonel's Dream* represents a change in Chesnutt's thinking: with great regret, he concludes that the white-dominated South indeed can and will resist social and cultural change even at the expense of its own prosperity. White Southerners, he demonstrates in the later novel, have engaged in a faulty analysis; they have come to treat racial identity not as a means to the end of power, but as an end in itself, and the consequence is economic self-annihilation.

16. Evidence that Chesnutt is critical of, and distances himself from, Warwick's capitalist stance is pointed out by Darryl Hattenhauer: the novel shows Warwick to have achieved his wealth indirectly through the exploitation of his late wife's slaves, and by no means through his own efforts or abilities; furthermore, Hattenhauer remarks, he attempts to marry Rena to Tryon for the sake of a business connection. "Warwick's passing endorses racial equality insofar as it depicts blacks who can do what whites do. But it does not endorse them for their success at imitating the dominant culture" (40).

17. Chesnutt privately tended to characterize his identity in terms of liminality, as in a well-known journal entry of 1881 in which he complains that he is "neither fish[,] flesh, nor fowl—neither 'nigger', poor white, nor 'buckrah'" (*Journals* 157). When he first proposed publishing a book, in 1891, he identified it as "the first contribution by an American with acknowledged African descent to purely imaginative literature," but asked that his biracial identity remain unadvertised lest it interfere with the book's commercial or critical reception ("*To Be an Author*" 125). In the following years, however, he increasingly (if ambivalently) embraced an African American identity: in an 1896 letter he writes "I am really seven-eighths white, but I have never denied the other, and would be quite willing for the colored people to have any credit that could derive from anything I might accomplish" (89).

18. John seems implicitly to recognize this, and wishes he could "argue the question in a general way," with reference to abstract principles (54–55); unable to do that, he simply deflects the question, which to him seems "a merely academic speculation with which Warwick did not trouble himself" (55).

19. In this, he seems reminiscent of a writer whose career he almost certainly was unaware of: Harriet Wilson, who in *Our Nig* directly "appeal[s] to [her] colored brethren universally for patronage, hoping they will not condemn this attempt of their sister to be erudite" (Preface, n.p.). The failure of Wilson's literary/financial venture, as well as her being vaulted to canonical or near-canonical status in the 1980s upon Henry Louis Gates's rediscovery of her manuscript, should be a re-

minder of the quite serious risks and possibilities involved in the enterprise of serious writing—that which challenges its readership—particularly for an African American writer.

20. In considering Chesnutt's writing career, Matthew Wilson uses *Uncle Tom's Cabin* as a cautionary model of "how the reception of an anti-racist work can transfer it into support for racism" ("Who Has the Right" 26). Wilson characterizes Chesnutt as a writer who, while initially failing to recognize the nature of the problem as he modeled his career after those of Stowe and Tourgée, soon came to understand "the power of the national imaginary to transform arguments against racism into arguments in support of racism," but nonetheless avoided co-optation only at the expense of literary success, as his work ended up "subsumed into the larger project of cultural amnesia" (32). In partial dissent to Wilson, I do see Chesnutt's attentiveness to this problem, and more broadly to the necessity of training readers (as far as possible) to minimize such grave misreadings, as central to his writings. I think, however, that his great achievement was to risk (and for years of his life to experience) failure while recognizing that the very arguments of the racists, considered from the proper angle, could likewise (given a rightly motivated audience) be converted into arguments against racism. In his boldness, he is reminiscent of a very different writer, Zora Neale Hurston, although without a legal stenography career like Chesnutt's to fall back on, Hurston clearly shouldered a heavier personal burden in her obscurity.

Chapter 3

1. Similarly, William L. Andrews writes that "[r]eading *The Marrow of Tradition* in the contexts of its creator's career and the larger social and literary milieu leaves one finally with an appreciation of how ambitious in form and purpose Chesnutt's second novel was" (*Literary Career* 207).

2. Chesnutt describes the same eventuality in *The Colonel's Dream,* though in this case he represents it directly, as an occurrence rather than a legal possibility (109). Yet another such reference appears in *The Quarry* (197–200).

3. For example, the African American lawyer Watson finds that his so-called "friends" among the town's whites are unwilling to warn him of the impending riot: "When the race cry is started in this neck of the woods, friendship, religion, humanity, reason, all shrivel up like dry leaves in a raging furnace" (280). William Miller learns a similar lesson when a tradesman with whom he has done business hostilely interrogates him at gunpoint (288). As Watson articulates, theoretically unracialized elements of life such as "friendship" and "reason" are, in reality, superficial in turn-of-the-century Southern discourse compared to underlying notions of racial hierarchy, a fact that the "riot" makes apparent.

4. One might compare a similar theme in James Weldon Johnson's 1912 novel *The Autobiography of an Ex-Colored Man,* in which the narrator remarks,

> the difficulty of the problem [of race] is not so much due to the facts presented, as to the hypothesis assumed for its solution. In this it is similar to the problem of the Solar System. By a complex, confusing, and almost contradictory mathematical process, by the use of zigzags instead of straight lines, the earth can be proven to be the center of things celestial; but by an operation so simple that it can be comprehended by a schoolboy, its position can be verified among the other worlds which revolve around the sun, and its movements harmonized with the laws of the universe. So, when the white race assumes as a hypothesis that it is the main object of creation, and that all things else are merely subsidiary to its well being, sophism, subterfuge, perversion of conscience, arrogance, injustice, oppression, cruelty, sacrifice of human blood, all are required to maintain the position, and its dealings with other races become indeed a problem, a problem which, if based on a hypothesis of common humanity, could be solved by the simple rules of justice. (78)

Eric Sundquist, in discussing Chesnutt's short fiction in *To Wake the Nations,* makes reference to the same passage by Johnson, though with a somewhat different intent (375).

5. As Frederick Douglass stated in his July Fourth oration of 1852, "where all is plain there is nothing to be argued. What point in the anti-slave creed would you have me argue? On what branch of the subject do the people of this country need light? Must I undertake to prove that the slave is a man? That point is conceded already. Nobody doubts it" (190).

6. Chesnutt seems to suspect that, the more fully a white person's sense of self has been defined by slave owning, the more deeply ingrained one's ideology will be—that is, the more a racist ideology will appear to be actual belief and not a mere temporary positioning. Consider, for example, his story "The Passing of Grandison," in which Colonel Owens appears genuinely to believe in Grandison's loyalty and contentment. Without such a conviction—that blacks know themselves to be better off under slavery—he cannot function as a slaveholder, and he is so unshakable in his belief that Grandison easily fools him and escapes. The colonel's son, Dick, on the other hand has no such conviction; he is under no illusion that slaves are content in their present condition. As a result, his complicity as a slaveholder is, if anything, even more chilling.

7. One character, Dr. Price, seems to believe that Burns's acquiescence is a matter of economics as well as convenience: "[T]here was a large fee at stake, and Dr. Burns was not likely to prove too obdurate" (69).

8. As Eric J. Sundquist notes, "there is more than a hint that there may be a blood relationship between them" (*To Wake* 432). Most plausibly, John Delamere is Sandy's father or grandfather, although the absence of any acknowledged father for Tom, or of any mention of a father's absence, and the puzzling event described by

old Delamere in which Sandy prevented the ostensible kidnapping of his "young mistress" (i.e., Tom's mother) and the infant Tom by "black Sally" (207), coupled with the resemblance between Tom and Sandy (who is about twenty years older), could be taken to suggest that Sandy is Tom's father. These are clues for a mystery that, at best, is alluded to in the novel; of course, readers are not always predisposed to pay attention to such clues when the mystery itself remains beneath the surface. Recognizing that these clues about Tom's origins add up to *something* depends on awareness of social context (such as the widespread practice of miscegenation, the very act that Barber's editorial significantly fails to deny), and of textual referents, such as the recognition of Twain's *The Tragedy of Pudd'nhead Wilson* as a source text, one upon which Chesnutt is signifying in one of several senses defined by Henry Louis Gates, Jr.: "[r]epetition of a form and then inversion of the same," a form of revision meant "to create a new narrative space for representing the recurring referent of Afro-American literature, the so-called Black Experience" (104, 111).

9. For an enlightening discussion of how Chesnutt negotiates an appeal to abstract, universalized "justice" and an acute awareness of historical conditions, see Hardwig, "Who Owns the Whip?: Chesnutt, Tourgée, and Reconstruction Justice," esp. pages 6–7 and 10–17.

10. In his introduction to *American Realism: New Essays,* Eric J. Sundquist draws attention to the problem in somewhat similar terms with the following example: "[W]hat outrageous claims must be made about Twain's *Pudd'nhead Wilson* (1894) in order to include it in more classical or traditional definitions of realism?" (5).

11. Writes Amy Kaplan, "[i]f, as successive generations of literary critics have asserted, realism repeatedly fails in its claims to represent American society, then the realistic enterprise must be redefined to ask *what* realistic novels do accomplish and *how* they work as a cultural practice" (8). Her book *The Social Construction of American Realism* thus is part of a movement, described by Fredric Jameson, away from "old fashioned 'interpretation,' which still asks the text what it *means,* and [toward] the newer kinds of analysis which . . . ask how it *works*" (*Political Unconscious* 108).

12. Tellingly, Glover seems especially anxious that the author of *The Marrow of Tradition* may be white: an African American's authorship "may in these days be overlooked" without disrupting available narrative frameworks; but the possibility that a white author wrote the novel is harder to reconcile with available narratives, and can only be addressed, Glover contends, "with contempt" (84).

13. For Chesnutt, hope and faith that the future will eventually alleviate racial conflict is not naïveté, but a political act, especially considering that Southern racists often predicted the inevitable self-destruction of the supposedly inferior African American population. This is clear, for example, in his forceful response to a 1906 novel by John C. Reed advancing the latter thesis: contrary to Reed, states Chesnutt, "I think the Negroes of this country are making very great progress, under great

disadvantages, and that a very large part of the ninety-five per cent. whom Mr. Reed so uncharitably condemns to extinction, will win out in the struggle for life and larger opportunity" (*Exemplary* 6).

14. The pursuit of such a balance is a hallmark of Chesnutt's recorded thought. In the well-known 1880 journal entry in which he resolves "I think I must write a book," he articulates the "high, holy purpose" of writing to help enact an end to the American caste system (*Journals* 139). Continues Chesnutt, his pursuit must be "[n]ot a fierce indiscriminate onslaught; not an appeal to force, for this is something that force can but slightly affect, but a moral revolution which must be brought about in a different manner" (140). In imagining what such a "different manner" might actually consist of, Chesnutt invokes the example of the abolitionists, who "appeal[ed] in trumpet tones to those principles of justice and humanity which were only lying dormant in the northern heart" (140). Though he by no means believed that the achievement of racial equality would be easy, Chesnutt consistently insists—often at the precise moments when he has seemed nearest to the "moral evil" of cynicism (136)—that one must believe in it as a possibility.

Chapter 4

1. For example, Dean McWilliams argues that "there are legitimate literary reasons" for the novel's dismissal by critics, but contends that "its neglect is unfortunate" nonetheless (180); Gary Scharnhorst, in arguing for the novel's significance, discounts its plot as trifling and episodic (271–72).

2. See Andrews, *Literary Career* 279–86 for a comprehensive bibliography of Chesnutt's publications as of 1980.

3. Similarly, Matthew Wilson contends that in *The Colonel's Dream* Chesnutt exposes "the connections between the lack of economic development and racism . . . in a self-consciously eccentric form that was designed to demonstrate that a significant portion of his audience was unwilling or unable to change" (*Whiteness* 150). Continues Wilson, "[h]is white audience was too imbued with racism to be open to change through fiction, and he increasingly came to see that his attempts at realism were received as provocations with no basis whatsoever in historical or social realities" (152). Chesnutt, however, privately cited his "faith in humanity" in predicting that what "for the colonel was a dream will in the hands of others or a succession of others more patient, become a reality" (*"To Be an Author"* 230). Though I concur with Wilson that Chesnutt lost faith in the audience he courted in his earlier fiction, it seems to me that Chesnutt retained faith in an unspecified population of "others" to locate more effective strategies for enacting a similar vision of enlightened social interaction to the colonel's.

4. Admittedly, *The Colonel's Dream* has its aesthetic blemishes. From a twentieth-century point of view, its narrator is prolix and exhibits occasional lapses of control so great as to seem self-satirizing: "[T]he colonel, undismayed by his temporary de-

feat, metaphorically girded up his loins, went home, and, still metaphorically, set out to put a spoke in Fetters's wheel" (227).

5. Lâle Demirtürk writes that *Savage Holiday*'s employment of white characters and absence of explicit interracial conflict represent "a strategy that enables [Wright] to make an effective political statement on the positionality of whiteness as an ideology in America that inevitably raises the issue of freedom for black people" (130). Hazel V. Carby writes that in *Seraph on the Suwanee* "Hurston repudiated theories of the uniqueness of black linguistic structures" and that the novel necessarily complicates the views of "critics who valorize Hurston for preserving and reproducing in her work cultural forms that they argue are essentially and uniquely black" (viii–ix).

6. Ernestine Williams Pickens suggests that Chesnutt's turn to white characters in his final novel represents an appeal to audience: he eventually "recognized that white readers were not interested in the black perspective on the South's problems" (90). While not disputing this account of white readers' self-involvement, I also find the focus on whites in *The Colonel's Dream* consistent with Chesnutt's career-long interests: in his oeuvre there is a consistent argument that the actions and attitudes of whites must, equally to those of blacks, be understood in any analysis of racism, and that racism's effects on both blacks and whites are documentable.

7. Demirtürk sums up recent developments in whiteness studies that sanction a reading of race even (or especially) in texts in which only white characters appear and/or in works written by white authors (131–32).

8. Pickens insightfully points out that Chesnutt uses all the tools at his disposal to produce a vivid account of the situation in the South: he "uses visual, tactile, auditory, and olfactory imagery to draw a portrait of poverty. . . . Not only does one see the poverty but one is saturated with it" (111).

9. French's childish traits are not idiosyncratic but strongly linked to his status as an arch capitalist. For example, he frequently expresses frustration at the slow pace of Clarendon laborers, approaching a tantrum when he cannot get what he wants when he wants it; furthermore, his and other capitalists' childish self-absorption—as when French's partner Kirby claims that the world should "cease to worry about the pains of poverty, and weep for the woes of wealth" (8), or when business dealings that influence many workers are referred to as a "game" (11, 18)—is accentuated throughout the novel.

10. For example, as McWilliams points out, the "victory" achieved by French and Company at the novel's outset allows them to "profit at the cost of the firm's employees and the general public," although only in passing does French contemplate this fact (168).

11. Chesnutt seems consistently interested in abandonment as a theme, particularly when it comes to his male protagonists: consider Tom Lowrey's failure to return or write to Mandy in *Mandy Oxendine* and John Warwick's callous abandonment of his mother in *The House Behind the Cedars*.

12. Laura Treadwell's refusal to abandon her family, even at the cost of her

engagement to Colonel French, puts his lack of fidelity into stark relief; her self-sacrifice is also coded feminine by Chesnutt, both here and in *The House Behind the Cedars.* Compare Laura's statement—"My duty holds me here! God would not forgive me if I abandoned it" (285)—to Rena Walden's in the earlier novel: "I shall never marry any man, and I'll not leave mother again. God is against it; I'll stay with my own people" (121).

13. French's reliance on a largely *aesthetic* sense that, he believes, helps him differentiate between right and wrong is exposed in the novel. Often he is more repulsed by aesthetic infractions—such as the huge tombstone raised by Fetters in honor of his parents, which Pickens points out is a marker of his "conspicuous consumption" (97)—than by material harms imposed upon people. Consider his discomfort at listening to Graciella's performance of a "coon song" (which, interestingly, is like most commodities in Clarendon imported from the North): "A plantation song of the olden time, as he remembered it, borne upon the evening air, when sung by the tired slaves at the end of their day of toil, would have been pleasing, with its simple melody, its plaintive minor strains, its notes of vague longing; but to the colonel's senses there was to-night no music in this hackneyed popular favorite. In a metropolitan music-hall, gaudily bedecked and brilliantly lighted, it would have been tolerable from the lips of a black-face comedian. But in this quiet place, upon this quiet night, and in the colonel's mood, it seemed like profanation" (49–50). The interpretation of this scene seems inescapable: the nostalgically minded colonel wants to revel in his dim memories of contented slaves, but Graciella's performance disrupts his enjoyment of these memories by exposing the underlying, commercialized cynicism of *any* such use of slaves' songs, then or now. He does not allow himself, however, consciously to acknowledge the reasons for his discomfiture, or to take note of the labor relations that are both exposed and obscured by their being rendered aesthetic products in his mind.

14. For example, Laura Treadwell wonders if the basis of French's attraction to her is "*merely* an abstraction" (188); French himself decides to abandon Clarendon and his reform movement only when he finally concludes that "[t]he best people . . . are an abstraction" (283).

15. I appreciate the contribution of an anonymous reviewer of a previous draft of this book in pointing out this apparent paradox. Would not a devoted capitalist like Chesnutt have limited his critique to Southern whites' attempts to restore a "feudal" economic arrangement between themselves and the black population? As I hope this chapter makes clear, I think that Chesnutt does not, in fact, so limit his argument in *The Colonel's Dream,* especially considering the degree to which the negative consequences of both Fetters's and French's actions are connected to their status as arch capitalists. The occasional disparity between Chesnutt's comments in his journals and letters and the attitude apparent in his novels has frequently been remarked upon, and Chesnutt's personal experiences may or may not be reflected in his novels; nor can his intent always be inferred with certainty. From my perspective, the novels are best read as something other than direct expressions of belief;

while a reader of his novels will find a fairly large degree of philosophical consistency, even more compelling is his attempt to struggle with contrary attitudes and assumptions that often put him in uncomfortable positions. Critics need not be overly influenced by Chesnutt's success as a capitalist in interpreting the commentary implied by his fiction, any more than his often inconsistent involvement with Civil Rights crusades of his day should dissuade them from appreciating the complexity and force of his antiracist fiction; on the latter point, for example, see Crisler, Leitz, and McElrath xxx–xxxi.

16. Once again, the stage has been set for French's current position in events that occurred when he was a young boy: "When he himself had been a child of five or six, his father had given him Peter as his own boy" (25), and now he finds himself buying Peter once again.

17. Chesnutt's account of the virtual enslavement of many Southern blacks even into the twentieth century is historically accurate. See William Cohen's account of the vagrancy statutes enacted by most Southern states during Reconstruction and inflicted with increasing frequency during the early 1900s, esp. 238–45.

18. This passage refers to an earlier one in which the narrator remarks upon a sign indicating "the office of a Justice of the Peace—a pleasing collection of words, to those who could divorce it from any technical significance—Justice, Peace—the seed and the flower of civilisation" (62). The nature of the commentary here is complex: the narrator wryly pokes fun at the distance between the words "justice" and "peace" as abstractions and their actual enactment in social circumstances, for example in law enforcement. Yet Chesnutt by no means valorizes these or other abstractions: his method is, in a realist vein, to fill in the social (or "technical") significance of such terms, recognizing that the analysis upon which his hopes for his novel rest must be historically specific, not abstract.

19. Susan L. Blake writes that the fate of the relatively minor character Henry Taylor is evidence that Chesnutt attacked the premise that "responsibility for their elevation can be left to black people themselves" (195). Taylor is an African American schoolteacher who loses his position due to both his powerlessness in the face of racism and (in Blake's words) "a negative kind of racial solidarity" that causes him to be castigated as a sellout by other members of Clarendon's black community (195). Taylor is also described, in the final chapter, as one who "is fully convinced that his people will never get very far along in the world without the good will of the white people" (293), and his fall from grace by no means repudiates a more radical position, which he does not share. Certainly, Chesnutt offers no facile analysis claiming African Americans' self-determination will be easy, but the relatively minor position that the Taylor narrative takes up in the novel suggests to me that Chesnutt is hinting at the difficulty and uncertainty of such a course, not disavowing it altogether.

20. In an essay locating *The Colonel's Dream* in the context of Booker T. Washington's economic proposals, Blake insightfully comments that "Chesnutt seems to

be trying to convince well-meaning white people to let Washington's program work at the same time he is persuading Washington and his followers that it won't work" (196)—which, although paradoxical, is from the standpoint of political strategy not a bad position to seek out.

Chapter 5

1. See, for example, chapter 7 of J. Noel Heermance's *Charles W. Chesnutt: America's First Great Black Novelist,* as well as Dickson D. Bruce, Jr.'s *Black American Writing from the Nadir: The Evolution of a Literary Tradition, 1877–1915* 185.

2. As Chesnutt acknowledged in "Post-Bellum—Pre-Harlem," "it is extremely doubtful whether a novel, however good, could succeed financially on its sales to colored readers alone" (*Essays and Speeches* 548).

3. The privileged vision afforded the insider/outsider may help explain why Chesnutt set *Paul Marchand, F.M.C.* in antebellum New Orleans. The cultural changes (especially in terms of racial intolerance) caused by the infusion of "Americans" into the city's Creole culture are referenced frequently in the novel; for this and other reasons, the setting is one that might seem both foreign and recognizable to a 1920s audience.

4. J. Hillis Miller, in a passage that inspired this part of my analysis, articulates what I take to be a similar phenomenon: "The authority that comes to me, that is, the obligation that I incur through the reading event, is not simply the authority of the text as a collection of words on the page and the meaning that they have for me when I read. What calls to me, makes demands on me, is something else, something that I would call 'other', something that this particular text gives me access to. That 'other' is the real source of authority that allows me to say, or obligates me to say, 'I must do so and so'" (*Hawthorne* 136). This "other" entity, which I am glossing as the historical contexts in which the novel was written, takes place, and is read, must not be seen as something "outside of" and enabling the text in any simple way; indeed, we have no access to it *other than* textually. Neither, however, can the text be detached from its context—both are dependent upon, and potentially deepen understandings of, each other in order to make their meanings count.

5. Hughes 28–29; Du Bois 22.

6. Rawls explains that he develops his theory of justice from social contract theory, as laid out especially by Locke, Rousseau, and Kant; his aim is to reconsider the nature of the "original contract" via the thought experiment he describes (11). In *American Literary Realism and the Failed Promise of Contract,* Brook Thomas connects the realist movement to late-nineteenth-century developments in contract theory, arguing that realist texts "evoke the promise of achieving a just social balance by experimenting with exchanges and negotiations among contracting parties" (8), although—more often than not—these texts represent the failure rather than the fulfillment of that promise. In light of these discussions, *Paul Marchand, F.M.C.* can

be seen as an experiment along the line of Rawls's, asking readers to re-envision the nature of the social contract. My point is that such an experiment, which may seem nonrealistic in that it relies on hypothetical rather than actual circumstances, works within the realist tradition as Thomas describes it.

7. The identity of the "quadroon" Beaurepas cousin is never directly stipulated in the text, but it is clearly Philippe Beaurepas, the most honorable of the cousins whom Marchand designates as the heir to the Beaurepas fortune, and whom Marchand would presumably never condemn for the accident of his racial heritage.

8. It is interesting, nonetheless, that Paul speaks of his commitment to Julie in terms of honor, not of love—highlighting, perhaps, the degree to which some abstractions become inhabited with meaning at the impoverishment of others.

9. Chesnutt's exploration of questions of identity in *Paul Marchand, F.M.C.* is similar to that of his short story "The Wife of His Youth," in which Mr. Ryder, formerly Sam Taylor, publicly considers his obligation to the woman he married in circumstances dramatically different to the ones that make up his life now. In that story, as in *Paul Marchand, F.M.C.,* Chesnutt concludes that integrity, or continuation, of identity is not a given but a choice—however, a worthy choice if forsaking that identity would allow one to abandon a responsibility to others.

10. In contrast, the novel is tinged from the outset by a subtle awareness of those who are deprived of such a choice as Paul faces, the slaves "whose arduous and unrequited toil, upon the broad, deep-soiled plantations of indigo, rice, cotton and sugar cane, furnished the wherewithal to maintain the wealth and luxury of the capital" (2). As Chesnutt suggests in the scene in which Paul threatens Zabet, to the extent a slave's "choice" exists it is the choice between "the slave gang, the whip, the pistol, or the sword" (95)—in other words, no choice at all. The bodily presence of slaves, barely mentioned after the novel's first chapter, suggests a point that is not explicitly developed in the novel but seems consistent with Chesnutt's analysis of discursive realities in the slaveholding age: the deprivation of choice inflicted upon the slaves enables meaning (which is hierarchical) to occur. If the meaning of at least one signifier—the slave's body—is not, by common consent, nonnegotiable, then slipperiness of signification becomes more than a source of cultural anxiety, it becomes a threat to the very world in which Paul and his peers believe themselves to live, which Chesnutt recognizes to be a discursive world. Consensus, in this case the consensus about what words like "slave" and "free" mean and who inhabits these respective roles, "contributes fundamentally to the reproduction of the social order," as Pierre Bourdieu points out in *Language and Symbolic Power* (166). An important implication of this insight is that Paul's rhetorical agency, the employment of which is a key theme of the novel, is afforded him at the expense of others who are defined by the lack of that very agency, very much as his material success is (although indirectly) a product of slaves' labor.

11. McWilliams and Wilson also make this connection. McWilliams focuses on Twain's and Chesnutt's respective constructions of narrative personae that, in many

ways, depart from the authors' actual perspectives (205–6). Wilson notes Chesnutt's reversal of the plot of Twain's novel, in which "[t]he man brought up white is totally unsuited to be a slave, while the man brought up black is completely incapable of being a master"—whereas Paul Marchand, brought up black, has the capacities of an ideal master and Philippe Beaurepas, brought up white, unlike his counterpart in Twain's novel is "decent and humane" (*Whiteness* 192).

12. Roxana's unverifiable claim that the father of her child is the late Col. Cecil Burleigh Essex (119) rather than Percy Driscoll is unpersuasive, especially considering the strong physical resemblance between Tom and Chambers.

13. Chesnutt also further complicates the question of eugenics by attributing the prisoner's violent tendencies at least as much to his white as to his black blood.

14. In McWilliams's reading of this scene, the "strange recognition . . . between the white man and the mulatto . . . saves them both": referring to the narrator's mention of "some hidden change in the mulatto's expression," he suggests that the prisoner, "perhaps out of returned sympathy, alerts Paul to the other rebel's approach" (189). While McWilliams's reading seems plausible, in my view the most important factor is not the immediate reward of the prisoner's "returned sympathy" but the *risk* Marchand undergoes in identifying with him.

15. McWilliams uses similar terms in describing the scene in which Paul threatens Zabet: "As we watch him force her confession, we see how completely he has become the white oppressor whom he had hated" (188).

16. As McWilliams notes, "Bethany College" is based on Berea College, which educated black and white students alongside each other until 1904, when the Kentucky legislature abolished integrated education; the law was later upheld by the U.S. Supreme Court (*The Quarry* 290 n. 1 to chapter 13). Chesnutt had identified Berea College as the alma mater of his white protagonist, Hugh Manson, in the novel manuscript *Evelyn's Husband* (c. 1903).

17. Underlying the theme of a motivated education is the debate, which was at a head just as Donald attended public school in the early 1900s, between Booker T. Washington and W. E. B. Du Bois, who respectively called for a pragmatic, vocational education for blacks—correspondent with an overall political approach of "patience and forbearance"—and an uncompromising, idealistic approach which sets out "to slay with the weapons of knowledge and reason" (*The Quarry* 66). While probably closer in philosophy to Du Bois than to Washington, Chesnutt seems to be attempting to articulate a third way, one that balances pragmatism with fearless idealism; in this, he is aligned with Mrs. Glover, who "was a follower of the crusader [Du Bois], but . . . dreamed of Donald as a Messiah of whom these smaller men were merely the forerunners" (66).

18. Chesnutt's viewpoint, however, seems more closely allied to that of Senator Brown, the lawyer and "leading colored citizen of Cleveland" (33) who challenges Seaton to raise Donald as a *black* boy, as an experiment not in science but in political courage: "I should like to see a white man, by God, who had the courage to bring

up a colored child!" (37). As Helen Chesnutt explains, *The Quarry* was inspired by a white man who, having adopted a child he now believed to be of mixed race, approached her father much as Seaton approaches Brown (286–87).

19. More specifically, McWilliams points out that works of scientific racism by Galton's intellectual heirs, Lothrop Stoddard and Madison Grant, were popular in the 1920s, and that Chesnutt identifies these particularly in the next-to-last draft of *The Quarry* (219).

20. As her own sister puts it, Mrs. Glover is "a good match for those crazy white people" (47). Chesnutt expands this analysis in suggesting an affinity between white supremacists and the Garveyites who preach racial "purity" and espouse hatred toward whites and light-skinned blacks, although leaders like Marcus Garvey (represented in the novel as "the President of the African Empire") are portrayed as cynical, whereas Mrs. Glover is firmly idealistic (165). Garvey's movement, in Chesnutt's analysis, is a moneymaking venture more than a political enterprise, and for this reason it crosses the line between productive and disreputable responses to the racial climate.

21. In her nearly Frankenstein-like eagerness to "make a good Negro of" Donald (51), Mrs. Glover can seem nearly as chilling as the eugenicists, though Chesnutt demarcates her efforts as moral in a way the eugenicists' are not.

22. Consistent with Chesnutt's analyses throughout his career, *The Quarry* suggests that most whites, as well as blacks, are harmed by racism, which is "an expensive luxury," as white merchants' loss of black patronage proves (57). His role model for whites' behavior seems to be not Donald but his roommate at Bethany College, Henry White, who regards African Americans as genuine equals and eventually dies in World War I, "fighting . . . to make the world safe for a democracy which had meant little to him" (103)—terms which, in traditional discourse, would usually be applied to a nonwhite soldier.

23. Donald's mother turns out to be one Teresina Milfiore, the descendant of "a noble but impoverished Sicilian family" (259) who, victimized by a botched tonsillectomy and her disadvantageous economic position, is left helpless upon her husband's (Marvin's) death; when she dies in childbirth, her son—Donald—is adopted out to the Seatons (261). Although Dr. Freeman claims that Milfiore's pedigree proves that Donald was born to "a lady of noble birth and lineage" (261), McWilliams points out that, according to eugenicist thought, her Sicilian heritage makes her "no less objectionable" than if she had been African American; thus Donald's parentage further refutes racialist assumptions (220).

24. The novel seems to reinforce this conclusion with the words of Senator Brown, who—upon hearing that Seaton has discovered Donald to be white, and wishes to tell Donald—rejoins, "[t]he boy was as white [when you gave him to the Glovers] as *you think he is* now. . . . There was one slip-up in a perfect system. There may well have been another" (262, 264; emphasis added).

25. McWilliams also notes the novel's vagueness on this point but suggests that Donald's implied position is close to that of Senator Brown, who says he sees "no

ultimate future for the Negro in the Western world except in his gradual absorption by the white race" (216).

26. This character is, as McWilliams points out, based on the anthropologist Franz Boas (*The Quarry* 291 n. 1 to chapter 15).

27. Bakhtin uses this term in arguing against a form of "abstract" stylistic analysis that "ignores the social life of discourse outside the artist's study, discourse in the open spaces of public squares, streets, cities and villages, of social groups, generations, and epochs" (259).

Works Cited

Ames, Russell. "Social Realism in Charles W. Chesnutt." McElrath, *Critical Essays* 147–54.

Ammons, Elizabeth. *Conflicting Stories: American Women Writers at the Turn into the Twentieth Century.* New York: Oxford UP, 1991.

———. "Expanding the Canon of American Realism." Pizer 435–52.

Andrews, William L. "Chesnutt's Patesville: The Presence and Influence of the Past in *The House Behind the Cedars.*" *CLA Journal* 15 (1972): 284–94.

———. Foreword. *Mandy Oxendine.* By Charles W. Chesnutt. Ed. Charles Hackenberry. Urbana: U of Illinois P, 1997. ix–x.

———. *The Literary Career of Charles W. Chesnutt.* Baton Rouge: Louisiana State UP, 1980.

———. "The Representation of Slavery and the Rise of Afro-American Literary Realism, 1865–1920." *Slavery and the Literary Imagination.* Ed. Deborah E. McDowell and Arnold Rampersad. Baltimore: Johns Hopkins UP, 1989. 62–80.

Baker, Houston A., Jr. *Modernism and the Harlem Renaissance.* Chicago: U of Chicago P, 1987.

———. "Theoretical Returns." Napier 421–42.

Bakhtin, Mikhail M. *The Dialogic Imagination: Four Essays.* Trans. Caryl Emerson and Michael Holquist. Ed. Holquist. Austin: U of Texas P, 1981.

Barthes, Roland. "Myth Today." *Mythologies.* Trans. Annette Lavers. New York: Hill and Wang, 1972. 109–59.

———. "The Reality Effect." *The Rustle of Language.* Trans. Richard Howard. New York: Hill and Wang, 1986. 141–48.

Bender, Bert. *The Descent of Love: Darwin and the Theory of Sexual Selection in American Fiction, 1871–1926.* Philadelphia: U of Pennsylvania P, 1996.

Blake, Susan L. "A Better Mousetrap: Washington's Program and *The Colonel's Dream.*" McElrath, *Critical Essays* 189–97.

Boeckmann, Cathy. *A Question of Character: Scientific Racism and the Genres of American Fiction, 1892–1912.* Tuscaloosa: U of Alabama P, 2000.

Borus, Daniel H. *Writing Realism: Howells, James, and Norris in the Mass Market.* Chapel Hill: U of North Carolina P, 1989.

Bourdieu, Pierre. *Language and Symbolic Power.* Ed. John B. Thompson. Trans. Gino Raymond and Matthew Adamson. Cambridge, MA: Harvard UP, 1991.

Brown, Sterling. *The Negro in American Fiction.* 1937. Reissue. Port Washington, NY: Kennikat Press, 1968.

Bruce, Dickson D., Jr. *Black American Writing from the Nadir: The Evolution of a Literary Tradition, 1877–1915.* Baton Rouge: Louisiana State UP, 1989.

Callahan, Cynthia A. "The Confounding Problem of Race: Passing and Adoption in Charles Chesnutt's *The Quarry.*" *MFS: Modern Fiction Studies* 48 (2002): 314–40.

Carby, Hazel V. Foreword. *Seraph on the Suwanee.* By Zora Neale Hurston. New York: HarperPerennial, 1991. vii–xviii.

Chesnutt, Charles W. *A Business Career.* Ed. Matthew Wilson and Marjan A. Van Schaik. Jackson: UP of Mississippi, 2005.

———. *Collected Stories.* Ed. William L. Andrews. New York: Mentor, 1992.

———. *The Colonel's Dream.* New York: Doubleday, Page, 1905.

———. *Essays and Speeches.* Ed. Joseph R. McElrath, Jr., Robert C. Leitz, III, and Jesse S. Crisler. Stanford: Stanford UP, 1999.

———. *Evelyn's Husband.* Ed. Matthew Wilson and Marjan A. Van Schaik. Jackson: UP of Mississippi, 2005.

———. *An Exemplary Citizen: Letters of Charles W. Chesnutt, 1906–1932.* Ed. Jesse S. Crisler, Robert C. Leitz, III, and Joseph R. McElrath, Jr. Stanford: Stanford UP, 2002.

———. *The House Behind the Cedars.* 1900. New York: Penguin, 1993.

———. *The Journals of Charles W. Chesnutt.* Ed. Richard H. Brodhead. Durham: Duke UP, 1993.

———. *Mandy Oxendine.* Ed. Charles Hackenberry. Urbana: U of Illinois P, 1997.

———. *The Marrow of Tradition.* 1901. Ann Arbor: U of Michigan P, 1969.

———. *Paul Marchand, F.M.C.* Ed. Matthew Wilson. Jackson: UP of Mississippi, 1998.

———. *The Quarry.* Ed. Dean McWilliams. Princeton: Princeton UP, 1999.

———. *The Rainbow Chasers.* Unpublished typescript. Charles Waddell Chesnutt Collection. Fisk University.

———. "Rena Walden." Unpublished typescript. Charles Waddell Chesnutt Collection. Fisk University.

———. *The Short Fiction of Charles W. Chesnutt.* Ed. Sylvia Lyons Render. Washington: Howard UP, 1974.

———. *Stories, Novels, and Essays.* Ed. Werner Sollors. New York: Library of America, 2002.

———. *"To Be an Author": Letters of Charles W. Chesnutt, 1889–1905.* Ed. Joseph R. McElrath, Jr., and Robert C. Leitz, III. Princeton: Princeton UP, 1997.

Chesnutt, Helen. *Charles Waddell Chesnutt: Pioneer of the Color Line.* Chapel Hill: U of North Carolina P, 1952.

Cohen, William. *At Freedom's Edge: Black Mobility and the Southern White Quest for Racial Control, 1861–1915.* Baton Rouge: Louisiana State UP, 1991.

Crisler, Jesse S., Robert C. Leitz, III, and Joseph R. McElrath, Jr. Introduction. *An Exemplary Citizen: Letters of Charles W. Chesnutt, 1906–1932.* Ed. Crisler, Leitz, and McElrath. Stanford: Stanford UP, 2002. xvii–xxxiv.

Delmar, P. Jay. "Coincidence in Charles W. Chesnutt's *The House Behind the Cedars.*" *American Literary Realism* 15 (1982): 97–103.

Demirtürk, Lâle. "Mapping the Terrain of Whiteness: Richard Wright's *Savage Holiday.*" *MELUS* 24 (1999): 129–40.

Douglass, Frederick. "The Meaning of July Fourth to the Negro." *Pre-Civil War Decade.* Ed. Philip S. Foner. New York: International Publishers, 1950. 181–204. Vol. 2 of *The Life and Writings of Frederick Douglass.* 5 volumes. 1950–75.

Dreiser, Theodore. *Sister Carrie.* 1900. New York: Penguin, 1994.

Du Bois, W. E. B. "Criteria of Negro Art." Napier 17–23.

Duncan, Charles. *The Absent Man: The Narrative Craft of Charles W. Chesnutt.* Athens: Ohio UP, 1998.

Elliott, Michael A. *The Culture Concept: Writing and Difference in the Age of Realism.* Minneapolis: U of Minnesota P, 2002.

Ellison, Ralph. "Notes." *Juneteenth: A Novel.* By Ellison. Ed. John F. Callahan. New York: Random House, 1999. 351–63.

Ferguson, SallyAnn H. "Chesnutt's Genuine Blacks and Future Americans." *Selected Writings.* By Charles W. Chesnutt. Ed. Ferguson. Boston: Houghton Mifflin, 2001. 428–39.

———. "Rena Walden: Chesnutt's Failed 'Future American.'" McElrath, *Critical Essays* 198–205.

Finseth, Ian. "How Shall the Truth Be Told? Language and Race in *The Marrow of Tradition.*" *American Literary Realism* 31.3 (Spring 1999): 1–20.

Fleming, Robert E. Rev. of *Paul Marchand, F.M.C.,* by Charles W. Chesnutt, ed. Matthew Wilson. *African American Review* 34 (2000): 363–64.

Foucault, Michel. *Discipline and Punish: The Birth of the Prison.* 1975. Trans. Alan Sheridan. New York: Vintage, 1995.

Frederic, Harold. *The Damnation of Theron Ware.* 1896. New York: Holt, Rinehart and Winston, 1960.

Garland, Hamlin. "Productive Conditions of American Literature." Pizer 151–58.

Gates, Henry Louis, Jr. *The Signifying Monkey: A Theory of Afro-American Literary Criticism.* New York: Oxford UP, 1988.

Geertz, Clifford. *The Interpretation of Cultures.* New York: Basic Books, 1973.

Gillman, Susan. "Micheaux's Chesnutt." *PMLA* 114 (1999): 1080–88.

Glover, Katherine. "News in the World of Books." Rev. of *The Marrow of Tradition,* by Charles W. Chesnutt. McElrath, *Critical Essays* 84–85.

Habegger, Alfred. *Gender, Fantasy, and Realism in American Literature.* New York: Columbia UP, 1982.

Hackenberry, Charles. Introduction. *Mandy Oxendine.* By Charles W. Chesnutt. Ed. Hackenberry. Urbana: U of Illinois P, 1997. xi–xxviii.

Hansberry, Lorraine. "An Author's Reflections: Willy Loman, Walter Younger, and He Who Must Live." *The Village Voice Reader.* Ed. Daniel Wolf and Edwin Fancher. Garden City, NY: Doubleday, 1962. 194–99.

Haraway, Donna J. *Simians, Cyborgs, and Women: The Reinvention of Nature.* London: Routledge, 1991.

Hardwig, Bill. "Who Owns the Whip?: Chesnutt, Tourgée, and Reconstruction Justice." *African American Review* 36 (2002): 5–20.

Harris, Trudier. "Chesnutt's Frank Fowler: A Failure of Purpose?" *CLA Journal* 22 (1979): 215–28.

Hattenhauer, Darryl. "Racial and Textual Miscegenation in Chesnutt's *The House Behind the Cedars.*" *Mississippi Quarterly* 47 (1993–94): 27–45.

Hawthorne, Nathaniel. *The House of the Seven Gables.* 1851. New York: Bantam, 1981.

Heermance, J. Noel. *Charles W. Chesnutt: America's First Great Black Novelist.* Hamden, CT: Archon, 1974.

Hemingway, Ernest. *The Sun Also Rises.* 1926. New York: Scribner, 2003.

Hossfeld, Leslie H. *Narrative, Political Unconscious and Racial Violence in Wilmington, North Carolina.* London: Routledge, 2005.

Howells, William Dean. "Mr. Charles W. Chesnutt's Stories." McElrath, *Critical Essays* 52–54.

———. "Palacio Valdéz, Realism, and Effectism." Pizer 91–98.

———. "A Psychological Counter-current in Recent Fiction." Rev. of *The Marrow of Tradition,* by Charles W. Chesnutt. McElrath, *Critical Essays* 82–83.

———. *The Rise of Silas Lapham.* 1885. Ed. Edwin H. Cady. Boston: Houghton Mifflin, 1957.

———. *The Shadow of a Dream* and *An Imperative Duty.* Ed. Edwin H. Cady. New Haven, CT: College and University Press, 1962.

Hughes, Langston. "The Negro Artist and the Racial Mountain." Napier 27–30.

Hurston, Zora Neale. *Seraph on the Suwanee.* 1948. New York: HarperPerennial, 1991.

Jameson, Fredric. *The Political Unconscious: Narrative as a Socially Symbolic Act.* Ithaca: Cornell UP, 1981.

———. "The Realist Floor-Plan." *On Signs.* Ed. Marshall Blonsky. Baltimore: Johns Hopkins UP, 1985. 373–83.

Johnson, James Weldon. *The Autobiography of an Ex-Colored Man.* 1912. New York: Dover, 1995.

Kaplan, Amy. *The Social Construction of American Realism.* Chicago: U of Chicago P, 1988.

Kearns, Katherine. *Nineteenth-Century Literary Realism: Through the Looking Glass.* New York: Cambridge UP, 1996.

Keller, Frances Richardson. *An American Crusade: The Life of Charles Waddell Chesnutt.* Provo, UT: Brigham Young UP, 1978.

Knadler, Stephen P. "Untragic Mulatto: Charles Chesnutt and the Discourse of Whiteness." *American Literary History* 8 (1996): 426–48.

Lubiano, Wahneema. "But Compared to What?: Reading, Realism, Representation, and Essentialism in *School Daze, Do the Right Thing,* and the Spike Lee Discourse." *Representing Blackness: Issues in Film and Video.* Ed. Valerie Smith. New Brunswick, NJ: Rutgers UP, 1997. 97–122.

Ludwig, Sämi. *Pragmatist Realism: The Cognitive Paradigm in American Realist Texts.* Madison: U of Wisconsin P, 2002.

McElrath, Joseph R., Jr., ed. *Critical Essays on Charles W. Chesnutt.* New York: G. K. Hall, 1999.

———. "W. D. Howells and Race: Charles W. Chesnutt's Disappointment of the Dean." McElrath, *Critical Essays* 242–60.

———. "Why Charles W. Chesnutt Is Not a Realist." *American Literary Realism* 32.2 (Winter 2000): 91–108.

McWilliams, Dean. *Charles W. Chesnutt and the Fictions of Race.* Athens: U of Georgia P, 2002.

Michaels, Walter Benn. *The Gold Standard and the Logic of Naturalism: American Literature at the Turn of the Century.* Berkeley: U of California P, 1987.

Miller, J. Hillis. "The Fiction of Realism: *Sketches by Boz, Oliver Twist,* and Cruikshank's Illustrations." *Dickens Centennial Essays.* Ed. Ada Nisbet and Blake Nevius. Berkeley: U of California P, 1971. 85–153.

———. *Hawthorne and History: Defacing It.* Cambridge, MA: Basil Blackwell, 1991.

Morgan, Stacy I. *Rethinking Social Realism: African American Art and Literature, 1930–1953.* Athens: U of Georgia P, 2004.

Morris, Pam. *Realism.* The New Critical Idiom. London: Routledge, 2003.

Morrison, Toni. *Playing in the Dark: Whiteness and the Literary Imagination.* New York: Vintage, 1993.

Napier, Winston, ed. *African American Literary Theory: A Reader.* New York: New York UP, 2000.

Pfeiffer, Kathleen. *Race Passing and American Individualism.* Amherst: U of Massachusetts P, 2003.

Pickens, Ernestine Williams. *Charles W. Chesnutt and the Progressive Movement.* New York: Pace UP, 1994.

Pizer, Donald, ed. *Documents of American Realism and Naturalism.* Carbondale: Southern Illinois UP, 1998.

Prather, H. Leon, Sr. "We Have Taken a City: A Centennial Essay." *Democracy Betrayed: The Wilmington Race Riot of 1898 and Its Legacy.* Ed. David S. Cecelski and Timothy B. Tyson. Chapel Hill: U of North Carolina P, 1998. 15–41.

Rampersad, Arnold. "White Like Me." Rev. of *Paul Marchand, F.M.C.*, by Charles W. Chesnutt, ed. Matthew Wilson. *New York Times* 25 Oct. 1998, late ed., sec. 7: 32.

Rawls, John. *A Theory of Justice.* Cambridge, MA: Belknap-Harvard UP, 1971.

Roe, Jae H. "Keeping an 'Old Wound' Alive: *The Marrow of Tradition* and the Legacy of Wilmington." *African American Review* 33 (1999): 231–43.

Rohrbach, Augusta. *Truth Stranger than Fiction: Race, Realism, and the U.S. Literary Marketplace.* New York: Palgrave, 2002.

Scharnhorst, Gary. " 'The Growth of a Dozen Tendrils': The Polyglot Satire of Chesnutt's *The Colonel's Dream.*" McElrath 271–80.

Sedlack, Robert P. "The Evolution of Charles Chesnutt's *The House Behind the Cedars.*" McElrath, *Critical Essays* 181–88.

Sheehy, John. "The Mirror and the Veil: The Passing Novel and the Quest for American Racial Identity." *African American Review* 33 (1999): 401–15.

Smith, Shawn Michelle. *American Archives: Gender, Race, and Class in Visual Culture.* Princeton: Princeton UP, 1999.

Sollors, Werner. *Neither Black nor White yet Both: Thematic Explorations of Interracial Literature.* New York: Oxford UP, 1997.

Steinbeck, John. *The Grapes of Wrath.* 1939. New York: Penguin, 1992.

Sundquist, Eric J. "Introduction: The Country of the Blue." *American Realism: New Essays.* Ed. Sundquist. Baltimore: Johns Hopkins UP, 1982. 3–24.

———. Preface. *American Realism: New Essays.* Ed. Sundquist. Baltimore: Johns Hopkins UP, 1982. vii–ix.

———. *To Wake the Nations: Race in the Making of American Literature.* Cambridge, MA: Belknap-Harvard UP, 1993.

Thomas, Brook. *American Literary Realism and the Failed Promise of Contract.* Berkeley: U of California P, 1997.

Tompkins, Jane. *Sensational Designs: The Cultural Work of American Fiction, 1790–1860.* New York: Oxford UP, 1985.

Tourgée, Albion W. *A Fool's Errand: A Novel of the South during Reconstruction.* 1879. New York: Harper and Row, 1966.

Trachtenberg, Alan. *The Incorporation of America: Culture and Society in the Gilded Age.* New York: Hill and Wang, 1982.

Twain, Mark. *The Tragedy of Pudd'nhead Wilson and the Comedy Those Extraordinary Twins.* 1894. Ed. Shelley Fisher Fishkin. New York: Oxford UP, 1996.

Warren, Kenneth W. *Black and White Strangers: Race and American Literary Realism.* Chicago: U of Chicago P, 1993.

———. "Troubled Black Humanity in *The Souls of Black Folk* and *The Autobiography of an Ex-Colored Man.*" *The Cambridge Companion to American Realism and Naturalism: Howells to London.* Ed. Donald Pizer. Cambridge: Cambridge UP, 1995. 263–77.

Watson, Reginald. "The Tragic Mulatto Image in Charles Chesnutt's *The House Behind the Cedars* and Nella Larsen's *Passing*." *CLA Journal* 42 (2002): 48–71.

Wideman, John Edgar. "Charles Chesnutt and the WPA Narratives: The Oral and Literate Roots of Afro-American Culture." *The Slave's Narrative*. Ed. Charles T. Davis and Henry Louis Gates, Jr. Oxford: Oxford UP, 1985. 59–78.

Wilson, Harriet. *Our Nig; or, Sketches from the Life of a Free Black*. 1859. Ed. Henry Louis Gates, Jr. New York: Vintage, 1983.

Wilson, Matthew. Introduction. *Paul Marchand, F.M.C.* By Charles W. Chesnutt. Ed. Wilson. Jackson: UP of Mississippi, 1998. vii–xxxv.

———. *Whiteness in the Novels of Charles W. Chesnutt*. Jackson: UP of Mississippi, 2004.

———. "Who Has the Right to Say? Charles W. Chesnutt, Whiteness, and the Public Sphere." *College Literature* 26.2 (Spring 1999): 18–35.

Wonham, Henry B. *Playing the Races: Ethnic Caricature and American Literary Realism*. New York: Oxford UP, 2004.

Wright, Richard. *Savage Holiday*. 1954. Jackson, MS: Banner, 1994.

Zinn, Howard. *A People's History of the United States, 1492–Present*. Rev. ed. New York: HarperPerennial, 1995.

Index